ANOINT MY HEAD

ANOINT MY HEAD

A MEMOIR

ANDY MACLEOD

OMNIBUS PRESS
London / New York / Paris / Sydney / Copenhagen / Berlin / Madrid / Tokyo

(A Division of Wise Music Limited)
14-15 Berners Street
London W1T 3LJ
England

Cover designed by Mecob Design

ISBN: 978-1-9172-7432-6

A catalogue record for this book is available from the British Library.
Typeset by Evolution Design & Digital Ltd (Kent)

Printed in the Czech Republic.
www.omnibuspress.com

For the birds...

Contents

Exclusive Song Giveaway

The Pointy Birds – 'Benefit Office'

Before we start the words, a few words.

Pointy Birds songs are not available anywhere in the world. You won't find them on Spotify, YouTube or Apple Music and they never made it on to vinyl or CD in the racks of Selectadisc or Tower Records. Their only existence is on a couple of fading cassette tapes, but now some of these rare creatures are daring to show their face. The first track to see the light of day is called 'Benefit Office'. If you enter the weblink below into your browser then these three minutes of perfect indie-pop pleasure can be all yours. Enjoy! (But please forgive the out-of-tune harmonica.)

https://andymacleod.ck.page/92e9f324e3

Prologue

Growing up in the UK during the seventies and eighties, bands were everywhere. The Beatles and The Stones had kicked things off the decade before, becoming the country's proud export to the world. There must have been something in the water because the UK was bloody good at producing great bands – year after year after year. Band after band after band, producing hit after hit after hit. Not sure why. Population density? A British tendency for introspection? The combination of shitty weather and high-quality electronics? Margaret Thatcher certainly helped provide something to kick against for inspiration. Maybe great art thrived in misery like the prettiest flower could bloom in manure. But whatever it was, bands were part of our heritage – we lived and breathed them, created sub-cultures around them. It was tribal – all-consuming. How could you not want to be part of the fun?

And this fun was encapsulated every Thursday night on BBC1 at 7.30 p.m. on *Top Of The Pops.* To get there one had to live through the agony of *Tomorrow's World* – boring, grey-faced men with thin lips and dry hair talking about dull inventions in the future, 'yadda yadda yadda', but who cared? I wanted to live in the present and *Top Of The Pops* was very much now. Even though I was tuning in to a party I wasn't invited to, on a beige carpet where I sat a few inches from the TV screen in our semi-detached house in the suburban commuter territory where we lived, that party looked a lot of fun. A vicarious thrill for my impressionable mind, another world where people seemed to have a good time all the time.

And it never let me down – from the disco and punk of the late seventies to the new romantics of Human League and Visage and Soft Cell and ABC of the early eighties. Was your world expanded by Wham or Duran Duran? Or Spandau Ballet? Boys dressing like girls and girls dressing like boys. Uber pop stars like Adam Ant and Bros. The silliness of Madness and The Cure videos and songs that stubbornly stayed at number one for weeks. The Smiths gatecrashing the party in 1983 with a singer who had a hearing aid and a guitarist with a beehive haircut. Post-punk going mainstream with the likes of The Jam, The Clash, Dexys Midnight Runners, The Stranglers, Tears For Fears, Talk Talk, Simple Minds and U2. Band after band after band. Year after year after year, producing hit after hit after hit. Even Kid Creole and his bleeding Coconuts sent chills of excitement through me. As if it were meant for me, videos and songs soundtracking the ups and downs of growing up. What was this world of lunacy? The spell was half-broken when the camera occasionally and accidentally panned back to reveal a half-empty studio, but who cared. What would it be like on that stage performing and receiving admiration, applause and adulation?

Increasingly, I was becoming aware of a disconnect between the ordinary world I existed in and this technicolour other world that was beamed into our sitting rooms on TV each night. And it wasn't just bands I loved, it was films, TV, comedy – this whole world of fun, of play, of laughter. Even from the age of five, I was enthralled by the dancers in leotards that would star-jump and leapfrog across the stage at the start of Saturday night entertainment shows like *Generation Game*. And the crazy anarchic live television shows like *Multi-Coloured Swap Shop, Saturday Superstore, It's A Knockout*. (Maybe after years ravaged by war, Europe needed a TV show hosted by a laughing policeman with teams competing to throw wet sponges at giant chickens?)

One night as I entered my teenage years something profound happened. I was allowed to stay up late to watch a new comedy show called *A Kick Up The Eighties.* It wasn't particularly funny except for this one sketch with a daft private investigator from Birmingham called Kevin Turvey. Who was this person that seemed to jump out of the TV screen? His real name was Rik Mayall, and he was soon to appear again in a show that would make his name, playing his namesake 'Rik' in a new BBC2 sitcom *The Young Ones.* It was anarchic punk rock comedy that featured a live band in each episode, and along with every other kid my age, I was riveted and learned every line. With the launch of a fourth TV channel, aptly named Channel 4, he appeared again in *The Comic Strip Presents Five Go Mad.* Once more, he was brilliant with an intensity which meant he owned every scene. He wasn't bothered by what anyone thought and was having great fun, not caring.

As the eighties progressed, I became more and more seduced by the world of comedy. One Saturday afternoon, at the age of 13, my mate Tim and I got the bus to Tunbridge Wells to go to the cinema, and with the clever tactic of chewing gum to make us look older we got into an AA film (14+). The film was called *Monty Python's Life of Brian* and I came out a changed person. I sat in open-mouthed awe throughout the whole film, fuelled by the excitement of watching an adult movie. I needed repeated viewings. I memorised every line, every scene. ('We're all individuals. I'm not!') And through the eighties, it kept coming – a series of films by US comic Steve Martin with the same zany anarchic silliness as Rik Mayall, the willingness to completely go for it and not care what people thought. *The Jerk* and *The Man With Two Brains* had me in stitches. Meanwhile, the funniest film of all time was being made, the most elegant expression of music meeting comedy, *This Is Spinal Tap.*

It wasn't just that these films and TV shows were funny; it was more profound than that. How had these people done it? How had they made that happen with their life? There didn't seem to be a school lesson or a university course which would teach you to be in a band or make funny films, but I knew for sure I wanted to do it. All these bands and comedians – Rik Mayall, Steve Martin, Michael Palin, Billy Connolly, John Cleese, Robert Smith, Jim Kerr – were prime examples of those who had just gone for it, not caring. No data input. No filing records. No emptying bins. Growing up didn't have to mean an office job or being a desk slave. If they could do it, then why couldn't I?

PLAY >

1. ULU

A phone call leads to a meeting and the start of a new relationship. Followed by some musings along Hampstead Road.

I first met our manager Ricky in 1992.

I had graduated from college the year before into a recession but was able to find work in an independent record shop called Selectadisc nestled in the heart of Soho. My job was to file away recordings – vinyl, cassettes and CDs – all day, every day, day after day. It was dull and relentless and would have broken my spirit but for one key fact: I knew it was only a matter of time before I became a rockstar.

One day the shop phone rang and Big Phil picked up.

'Oi, 'alf a job. It's some bloke called Ricky asking about your demo?'

I plonked my heavy pile of unfiled vinyl on the floor, trying to remember which one Ricky was. I had been handing out demo tapes for weeks and had lost track of who had what and why. Big Phil held the phone to his chest and arched an angry eyebrow.

'Not happy about these extracurricular calls during work hours, Horace.'

I snatched the receiver, mumbling something it was better Phil didn't hear. I'd have to make this quick. As interested as I was in whoever was on the phone, I also needed to keep my job. A small, excited voice was at the other end of the line.

'Is that Horace?'

'Speaking.'

The voice sniggered.

'Is that your real name? Love it. My name is Ricky. I'm the entertainments manager at London University.'

'Oh, right. Hello.' I lowered my voiced.

'Have I got you in trouble ringing at work?'

'Um, a little bit.'

'Don't worry, I'll make this brief. Someone passed me your demo, of The Pointy Birds?'

'Right.'

'I love it. Brilliant. Do you have management?'

'Um, no.'

'Well, I'm interested. I manage bands. Do you know Suede?'

'Yes.'

'Well, I used to manage them… but I moved on.'

'Wow… OK.'

There was a slight pause and then some commotion at the end of the phone line. Ricky had been distracted by something or someone; he released a hyena-like laugh and then returned to me.

'Sorry about that, Horace. Madness here! Where was I? Oh yes, would you like to meet?'

'Sure.'

'Can you do this evening? Say 6.30 p.m.?'

'Er… OK. Sure.'

'Great. Come to ULU. It's the big building on the corner of Malet Street. Ask for me at reception. Everybody knows me here.'

There was a click at the other end of the line and the small, excited voice disappeared. I put the phone down and returned to filing in a bit of a daze. At last, someone was interested. But who was this person? I could feel Big Phil glaring at me, but I didn't care. I would be out of here soon. This was the beginning of something. I could feel it.

1.2

I left work at 6 p.m. and made my way through the streets of Soho to ULU – the Union of London University near Goodge Street, or 'Yoo-Loo' as it was more commonly known. A rabbit warren of students colliding by day, at night it was better known for putting on great gigs featuring the best up-and-coming bands. Tonight there was a gig with some band from Oxford called Radiohead. What sort of uncreative tossers named their band Radiohead? Never heard of them. Probably rubbish.

I approached the receptionist, who looked like she had had a very long day. Annoyingly, I couldn't remember the name of the person I was meeting. Was it Roger?

'Hello, I'm here to see the Entertainments Manager, um, Robby?'

'You mean Ricky?'

'Ah yes, that's the kiddy.'

She gave me a tired, blank stare and then pressed a button on her switchboard.

'You seen Ricky?' she said into it, looking me dead in the face as someone replied via her earpiece. 'Is he? With Gordon?'

She gave a deep sigh and pressed another number. A pink bubble appeared from her mouth and then exploded.

'Gordon? Are you with Ricky?' A pause was followed by another sigh. 'Is he? Well, I just tried there.'

She shook her head like she had better things to do. I suspected this was not the first time today she had sought him out. A girl with frizzy red hair and dungarees rushed past carrying a walkie-talkie.

'Debs – you seen Ricky?'

'He's in the bar,' she said without stopping, uttering the words that suddenly made him real and me a bit nervous. The receptionist ushered me through the gates.

'Upstairs. He's the little round fellow with a big laugh. You can't miss him...'

I pushed my way upstream against a tide of students and followed the signs to the union bar through a maze of brightly lit corridors. The bar, in contrast, was a dark, noisy hubbub that reeked of body odour and the sour stench of bleach. Here, the less studious sprawled about on sofas with their hands down their pants, curled up asleep or playing drinking games. It reminded me of my own student days when success was measured by whether you could convince a friend or relative to do your laundry.

I looked around for someone resembling an entertainments manager. At the bar, a magician was surrounded by students. He was doing a mindreading trick. He had asked a student to think of a number followed by a series of sums so that the student arrived at another number. He then asked the student to think of a country starting with the corresponding letter of the alphabet. And then a mammal and then a colour. The magician paused for dramatic effect and then revealed the answer.

'You are thinking of a grey elephant.'

The student nodded, gobsmacked. The huddle of students reacted with impressed noises.

This had to be Ricky. His voice from the phone was instantly recognisable.

He looked through his adoring fans and clocked me staring at him.

'Horace?' he called over their heads.

I nodded.

'Be with you in a minute.'

Despite cheers and jeers and requests for explanation following his magic trick, Ricky declined and came over.

'Hello, I'm just entertaining the troops.' He giggled. 'Got to keep morale up in this place. So, Horace – if that *is* your real name – pleased to meet you. I'm Ricky.'

I shook his hand. He wasn't what I was expecting at all, not that I had really known what to expect, never having met an entertainment manager in real life before. Ricky was somewhat ageless. It was hard to tell if he was in his twenties, thirties or forties. His shirt was tucked tightly into trousers pulled up high around his waist, which seemed incongruous next to the scruffy students he was hanging out with. He wasn't exactly rock'n'roll, but then I suppose band managers didn't have to be. There was something of Noel Edmonds about him.

'Come on, let's go to my office where we can talk. Walk this way.'

He did a silly walk, waddling like a penguin, and then guffawed.

I laughed politely and followed him down a further maze of corridors as Ricky high-fived everyone we passed, introducing me like I was a special guest. It felt good after nine hours in the dark, filing vinyl.

'This is Horace. That's Gavin. Gavin works in the canteen, don't you, Gavin?'

Gavin acknowledged me with a tired smile and then went on his way. Everyone seemed to know Ricky or share a joke with him. Before I knew it, we were in his office and the atmosphere changed.

'Sit down,' he said. The sing-songiness in his voice to which I'd become accustomed in the brief moments I'd known him disappeared.

The office was a pretty standard dreary and beige. I sat down on a chair by his desk which was swamped by a mountain of paperwork and a big pile of CDs and cassettes that had toppled over. Although my job filing vinyl was bad, it wasn't as grim as having a desk job in an office. I shuddered. Thank god I was going to be a rockstar soon. Outside I could hear traffic and the laughter from students leaving or gig-goers arriving.

Ricky sat on the other side of the desk and gave me a brief but serious look. Then quick as a flash, his smile re-appeared, and his eyes twinkled. A phone was ringing somewhere under the pile of papers on his desk but he ignored it. He put his feet up on the desk.

'Soooooo, "The Pointy Birds". Love it. Love the name,' he said enthusiastically.

'Yes, it's from a poem in the film—'

'Yeah, I know,' Ricky interjected, the first person ever who didn't need to have it explained. 'Steve Martin's film *The Man With Two Brains*, it's my favourite poem of all time.'

He wasted no time in reciting it from memory.

I was impressed he knew it. I was about to speak, but Ricky wasn't finished. He launched into one of the scenes from the film, quoting the lines verbatim. I felt uncomfortable as an audience of one but Ricky was enjoying himself so much I smiled politely. His routine was interrupted by a knock. The girl who'd passed by reception with frizzy red hair popped her head around the door.

'Ah, there you are – Gordon is in reception looking *everywhere* for you.'

'I know.' Ricky winked at me. 'Did he ask for a long weight?' said Ricky to the girl.

'Yes, and he's not pleased.'

Ricky howled with laughter.

'Brilliant! Horace, you got to hear this. I got Gavin from the canteen, you know Gavin, to get Gordon to ask me for a long weight, right? So Gordon asked me for a long weight not knowing what one is and I said I'd be right back and left him there waiting. That was about an hour ago. So, he's definitely had a long wait. Classic.'

Ricky looked at me, wagging his tail. I had no idea what was going on.

'He's not happy,' said the red-haired girl.

This set Ricky off again.

'Honestly… too much,' he said, wiping his eyes.

'What should I tell him?' she asked impatiently.

'Tell him I need him to go to the hardware store on Goodge Street and get some tartan paint.'

She rolled her eyes as Ricky collapsed into laughter again. The door clicked shut and I looked to Ricky, forcing a laugh. It sounded more donkey than human. Once Ricky had recovered, the sober silence returned and I knew that this was it.

'Sorry about that, it's madness here. Anyway, where was I? Ah yes, here it is. Love the demo.'

Ricky rummaged around his desk and then held up a cassette tape and spun round in his chair like a CEO, and with his other hand shot me with an imaginary pistol. It felt weird to see the cassette with my handwriting on it. I had scribbled the song titles in biro, 'Benefit Office', 'Lift Me' and 'Blowing Your Brains Out' on the cover. It looked a bit amateur. How had it made its way to him? He read out the track-listing and then asked about the line-up.

'Well, there is currently four of us. We're between drummers…' I said.

'A bizarre gardening accident?'

'What?'

Ricky snorted.

'*Spinal Tap.* You seen it?'

'Ah yes, of course.'

'Funniest film of all time. No question.'

I nodded in agreement. Ricky smiled, resisting a rendition.

'Sorry, Horace, continue.'

'Yes, so there's, er, Marcus on bass. We met at college. We did a degree in politics…'

'D'you get a Desmond?'

'What?'

'A "Desmond"? As in a Desmond Tutu?'

'Ah, right. Yes, I did, actually.'

He clapped his hands.

'Knew it. Sorry, continue.'

'Right, yes… well, then there's my brother Dave on guitar and Josh on keyboards.'

'And who is sorting gigs for you? I would love to see it live…'

'This bloke Nadir has been helping us out. You might know him because I think he used to work with Suede too?'

'Ah yes, I know Nadir.'

Ricky held my gaze. I wanted to ask him more. Why wasn't Ricky with Suede anymore? Before I could ask, raised eyebrows replaced the goofy smile.

'So, tell me, Horace. How famous do you want to be? Really famous or just cover of *NME* famous?'

It was slightly disorientating how quickly he shifted gears between being silly and deadly serious. I had to think. This felt like a trick question. Also, I didn't know the answer myself. How famous did I want to be? Really famous? So famous that I wouldn't be able to walk down the street without being mobbed? Possibly. Iconic hairstyle? Wynona Rider's boyfriend? I was about to plump for the cover of the *NME*, but then he cut in.

'I mean, do you want to be really successful or are you happy to be just another "indie" band?'

He finger-quoted the word *indie* disdainfully.

'Yeah, well, I mean, it would be great to have the credibility of an *NME* cover of course, but I want our songs to be massive… have builders whistle our tunes…'

He liked this.

'Excellent. Love it. So, you would be happy with daytime Radio 1? Smash Hits covers?'

'Yeah,' I said unsurely.

'Kids TV?'

'Er, yep.'

'Puppet shows?'

'Eh?'

He started laughing. I felt confused and then realised the Spinal Tap reference. He stood up. He couldn't resist this time, acting out the puppet show scene, doing the voices perfectly.

'If I've told them once, I've told them a thousand times…'

He roared with laughter and then acted out more scenes from the film. His big laugh filled the room. My laugh felt small in comparison. It was hard to compete. He was having so much fun. He flopped back down in his chair, wiping his eyes.

'Too, too funny. THE funniest film of all time. Every line a classic.'

I nodded in agreement. I could feel the muscles in my face ache from my prolonged, forced grin. I was not sure where the conversation would go next. It seemed to have a life of its own. Eventually, Spinal Tap left the stage and Ricky got back to business.

'So, you really want it, Horace?'

'What?'

'Success.'

'Yeah… I mean… yes. Definitely.'

'A lot of indie bands think they do, but they don't really want what they think they want.'

I nodded like I knew this. He held my gaze. I could see a muscle twitch in his eye, the look of an officer interrogating a soldier, or the look one gives a dodgy hot dog seller.

He then posed what seemed like a series of existential questions:

What was our plan?

Were we talking to anyone else?

Which label did we want to sign with?

Who did we want to record with?

I wasn't really sure. It felt weird for someone to be taking us seriously. I felt like I was fluffing my lines. He continued.

'Well, it's the best demo I've heard for ages. I can get it to Saul, who runs Nude.'

'Wow, OK – that would be amazing.' This was the label who signed Suede and were now in talks with Sony.

'They will want to hear more stuff. Do you have more songs?'

'Yeah, loads,' I lied.

'Great. Do you remember The Blow Monkeys?'

'Yes,' I said, wondering where he would go next, 'I liked their single "Digging Your Scene".'

'Yeah, that one was all right, they're kind of a poor man's Bowie. Do you like Bowie?'

'Yeah, sure. Who doesn't?'

'All-time greatest.' Ricky started singing 'Space Oddity' in a perfect Bowie voice.

'Wow. You really sound like him,' I cut in, hoping he would stop.

'Among my party tricks. Anyway, I digress. I can get you some studio time through a friend who runs The Blow Monkeys' label if you'd like?'

'Right... wow, that would be amazing.'

Ricky smiled.

'OK, I'll sort it. Also, it'd be great to pop down to a rehearsal if that was possible? Meet the rest of the Birds?'

'Er, yeah, sure.'

'And when you're up and running with a drummer we can sort some shows out. Do you know Mike Greek? He's a Live Agent at Wasted Talent. He would love it.'

'Right, OK.'

'Actually, I know – you could support my band at our next gig and I can get Mike and some people along to see it?'

'Your band?'

He giggled. 'Don't take it too seriously these days. We're called The Passiondales.'

'Right... er... OK...'

We agreed to meet up again, said our goodbyes and I left ULU feeling a mixture of excitement and confusion.

1.3

Outside, it was a pleasant evening. The air still had some warmth in it, pubs overspilled with students and life seemed full of possibilities. I decided against the Tube and walked up Hampstead Road towards Camden, contemplating my thoughts with every step. The rush hour traffic had ground to a halt and I walked past the number 29 double-decker bus jam-packed with commuters, squashed together like sardines doing the nine-to-five, the same trip every day. Following the same footsteps home. Losers! That was not for me. I was headed for the big time. I was pleased there was a recession as it fobbed off the pressure from my parents of having to get a 'proper' job.

('There are no jobs, Mum!'

'This is Art, Dad! P.S. Can you lend me some money?')

The further I got from the reality of a normal job, or the normality of a real job, the more I realised a normal job was not for me. Being in a band was the only option. I had to go for it. There was no plan B. I knew what I wanted and was convinced I could do it, so it was just a case of doing it. I called this my Three-Hurdle Theory because I had decided in life there were three simple hurdles to jump:

1. *Work out what you want to do with your life.*
2. *Work out whether you can actually do it.*
3. *Do it.*

For most people, the first hurdle was the hardest and could take a lifetime working out. For me it was easy. Rockstar. I couldn't quite understand why other people didn't also want to be a rockstar. They probably did but then fell at the second hurdle which was working out the practicalities. Was it realistic? Did you have the talent, the inspiration, the perspiration? How about the ego, the hair, the *cojones*? Er, yes! Ego in spades, epic hair and bucketloads of *cojones*! So, then it was a case of jumping the final hurdle and doing it! It was a kind of twist on Roy Castle's 'dedication's what you need' meets the 'Just Do It!' Nike slogan.

As I approached Mornington Crescent, I saw a queue snaking its way outside The Camden Palace. A queue like that would soon be forming for us. This music venue was our mecca. It had five floors and was packed to the rafters every week. The band and I went every Tuesday to Feet First – a weekly indie music night that featured the top up-and-coming bands live on stage. Anyone who was anyone (who read the *NME* and liked indie music) went to Feet First – bands, music industry professionals and music lovers alike.

A familiar scene played out in my mind. We were headlining – it was our name on the Feet First flyer. The night would be sold out, ticket touts, guest list queues, family and friends in the balcony, press, labels, publishers, agents, famous peers. The gig would be a sea of people moshing and singing along.

'Hello, Camden Palace, I used to come here every Tuesday. Great to be up on the stage now. This one's called "Benefit Office". Let's rock!'

The place would go wild. And of course, there would be girls. Everywhere. SCREAMING! Yes, this dream was soon to be our reality and I was up for the challenge.

Life was good and we were on track. I'd play in the band during my twenties – record some classic albums and tour the world a few times – and then when I turned thirty, write, direct and star in my own BAFTA Award-winning sit-coms and Oscar-winning films, before writing bestselling novels in my forties. I might do a bit of oil painting and stand-up along the way too. That wasn't much to ask, was it? I knew what I wanted to do. I was convinced I had the talent to do all of these things. So, it was just a case of doing it – three simple hurdles. The only question was whether the band and I needed to find someone a bit more serious to manage our affairs as I wasn't certain we were going to get anywhere with a joker like Ricky. And I was on a tight schedule. I was kicking 23.

2. Selectadisc

A bit on Suede, some pondering on the future and a job description. Then a surprise visitor in the shop leads to exciting news.

Not long before Ricky got in touch, Suede had appeared on the front cover of *Melody Maker* with the headline 'Best New Band In Britain'. Selecting an unknown band for the cover was an audacious move from the editor, Steve Sutherland, but confidence was high they could carry it off. And carry it off they did. They were the love child of David Bowie and The Smiths, and the perfect two fingers from Britain to the US grunge scene swamping the music press and airwaves at the time. Their debut single 'The Drowners' sold out at record stores across the country. Including ours. The birth of Britpop was not for another year or so, but that cover was its conception.

And now the cover of the *Melody Maker* beckoned for us too. We were in the foothills; we had a map; Ricky was our trusty Sherpa. And we were headed for Everest. Events were conspiring; the stars were aligning. I was getting to know people who knew people who knew people who could make it happen. But Ricky? I couldn't work out if he was for real. And why had Suede got rid of him? And why was he working at the student union and still in a band? And how old exactly was he? It was impossible to tell. And that question he asked about how famous we wanted to be spun in my mind. Was it shrewd to find out the extent of our desire or a residual resentment due to the fact Suede were now adorning every front cover?

In any case, being on the cover of *NME* or *Melody Maker* was a summit to which we, The Pointy Birds, very much aspired. I had grown up fantasising about it. Although it felt slightly unsettling imagining what might lie beyond such a lofty peak.

2.2

Despite my dreams, the reality was that I was still filing other bands' music in a record shop. So, I returned to the gloom of work. Selectadisc was a big black mothership of a shop and felt a bit like entering the Star Trek's starship Enterprise with my three colleagues at the helm. Tracey the gaffer was a cross between Captain Kirk and Lieutenant Uhura, Dave known as Norwich (because he was a big Norwich City fan) was a bit like Scotty and Big Phil was definitely Spock, but with a horseshoe flat top haircut and a line in hardcore band T-shirts.

The worst day was Monday – not just because it was the start of another week, but because Monday meant new release day. New stock had to be out in shop racks double speed, otherwise sales would be lost to our main rival Sister Ray – a record shop further down on Berwick Street. So, the week started with quiet industry behind the counter as Captain Kirk, Scotty and Spock speedily processed boxes from Warners, EMI, Universal, Sony, Rough Trade and other smaller independent distribution companies. Their job was to open the boxes and check that the stock that had arrived from the distribution company corresponded to the delivery note and had been charged at the correct dealer price. Then to avoid theft, they would remove the CD from the case, or vinyl from the sleeve, and label it with a price and category. These empty sleeves would then be dumped on the counter for me to file away within the correct artist section or genre of music. Alternative, Acid Jazz, Metal, Soul, NU-Groove, Chillin', etc.

I also had to file away the stock that accumulated behind the counter. The CDs, vinyl and cassettes that had been removed from their respective covers and then put in a white master bag with date and quantity. This had to be filed away strictly alphabetically regardless of genre with any spare stock. So, when a customer brought an empty sleeve to the counter, one of my colleagues could then go to the relevant master bag and pull out the actual record to insert in the empty sleeve. Woe betides if they couldn't find that master bag. A sale was lost. The customer was not happy. And Horace got a mighty bollocking.

I didn't want to try and calculate how many records I filed each day but I guessed somewhere north of a thousand. It was never-ending. And the faster I filed, the more the records stacked up. Plus, the shop seemed to be getting busier each day and more popular with discerning new music lovers who loved their vinyl. My pace – which was slow – often frustrated my colleagues. But filing records from 9 a.m. till 6 p.m. was a marathon not a sprint, and there was bound to be the odd bit of human error. When Norwich found the reggae artist Horace Andy misfiled under 'H' for Horace rather than 'A' for Andy, my new name stuck. Horace. Or Half a Job Horace to give my full title.

The days were not just long; they felt longer. There was no lunch break and the four of us spent so much quality time in close proximity I could distinguish each of them by the smell of their farts. It felt like a prison sentence made worse by the golden Selectadisc rule: no one ever left Selectadisc. But I would. I would be out soon. My band and I now had a manager in Ricky who could make things happen. Selectadisc may have had my physical body, but they couldn't control my mind, and I had hour upon hour to think about the band and plot imminent world domination.

I had to admit there were some fringe benefits to having a mindless job. I had the headspace to make a mental list of improvements and adjustments to songs, new lyrics and rhyming couplets scribbled discreetly on scraps of paper when no one was looking, or failing that, on the back of my hand. Interview techniques were practised in the toilet, and although I was lugging around a massive pile of vinyl, each sleeve was a reminder of a dream fulfilled by an artist who had made a record, got it distributed and into the shop racks. What would it feel like to have our record unpacked from a box on a new release Monday? Our music on a CD and vinyl and in the shop racks under P for Pointy. Big enough to justify our own artist section! Some very illustrious neighbours would lean against The Pointy Birds:

The Pogues
The Pointer Sisters
The Pointy Birds
The Police
Iggy Pop

There were other perks to working in the shop. Making tea for everyone meant I regularly got a five-minute break while popping out to get my co-workers' lunch allowed some fresh air. Initially, I had found this a bit humiliating. I was a graduate reduced to gopher, but it was fun entering the hustle and bustle of Soho. It was a vibrant neighbourhood of market traders, media types, tourists and prostitutes all brushing shoulders with each other. Wandering the streets provided a type of inspiration – although we may not have made it yet, we hadn't failed. And the current situation was clearly temporary. The future was full of secret promises and my body tingled with excitement at the prospect of the commanding fame soon to be ours. Here, in an independent record store on Berwick Street, in the centre of Soho, in the centre of London, to me the music centre of the world, I was literally in the centre of things.

On a good day, lunch orders would be placed at several different cafes and by the time I returned to the shop a good hour would have passed, much to the fury of my colleagues who were not only hungry but had had to deal with the lunchtime rush.

Gaffer liked a jacket potato with chilli and cheese. In contrast, Big Phil rarely strayed off-piste from a chicken and sweetcorn filling which I would get from Cookies, the Polish cafe on the corner of Noel Street, which the owner, Cookie, would lather in his 'special creamy white sauce'. Norwich would mix it up with more complicated orders involving vegetarian options from the more upmarket Portafino run by Raj who added Asian spices to traditional Italian fare. My favourite came from Brunos, a Sicilian cafe on the corner of Wardour Street always packed with sharp-suited TV execs and dusty builders. Nothing beat their ham-cheese-tomato-onion toastie. Nothing. Lunch duty put me on friendly terms with the owners in each of these cafes to the point of first-name terms and being able to nod 'the usual'. We represented the real London. And they were serving a rockstar in waiting.

However, the main benefit of working in the shop was that I got to listen to music all day. Even though I wasn't allowed to choose what got played on the shop stereo, I was getting introduced to lots of seminal bands and albums I would not have chosen to listen to otherwise and I could feel my tastes changing and evolving. By the third listen, I found myself loving things I had initially hated. New albums from post-grunge bands from the US featured heavily – *Let Me Come Over* by Buffalo Tom, *Shame About Ray* by The Lemonheads and *Gish* by Smashing Pumpkins were mixed with classic artists from different eras and genres. Scott Walker, Aphex Twin, Joy Division, Husker Du, Sly & The Family Stone. I grew to love them all.

The only thing lacking was that apart from bands like Ride and Slowdive (known as 'shoe-gaze' by dint of the fact that they stared at their shoes while they played), there wasn't a vast amount of new British bands coming through. The ecstasy-fuelled ravings of Acid House and the 'Madchester' scene of the late eighties and early nineties had given us bands like The Stone Roses and Happy Mondays, but their indie-dance crossover sound was now on the wane. US grunge bands like Nirvana and Pearl Jam had taken over the airwaves – but that was about to change.

The shop stereo was very much Big Phil's domain. CDs were lined up, new releases were a priority and there was not really a music policy other than strictly no chart stuff. We were an independent record store. The only time my heart sank was when Big Phil would pluck a UK hardcore album from the shelves. This was a genre of music he had a particular passion for. And it had to be played LOUD. Filing vinyl was bad enough in a dark room but having hardcore guitars turned to eleven on the stereo was akin to having hot needles pushed into my brain. It was the aural equivalent of Dante's vision of hell – a gruesome orgy with the devil doing unspeakable things to people – a man's tongue being stretched and hammered on a lath while being buggered by a goat. Or something like that.

'Doesn't this challenge the notion that music should be pleasure, not pain?' I yelled one day above the maelstrom. It felt like my teeth were bleeding.

'That's the point, Horace,' said Big Phil, nodding and whistling happily away as if there were hidden melodies.

Not even on the third listen did Benediction grow in my affection.

Apart from Big Phil's masochistic tastes, the music policy at Selectadisc was mainly pleasure. It was certainly an improvement over my stint as a Christmas temp at Our Price in Brent Cross which had coincided with the death of Freddie Mercury. In a shameless attempt to shift as many units as possible, the command from central office was to play Queen's greatest hits all day every day. Not exactly 'Bohemian Rhapsody'. I liked Queen as much as the next person – you couldn't deny the genius of the bass line of 'Under Pressure' or the exhilaration of 'Don't Stop Me Now' – but there was only so many times you could hear 'Radio Ga-Ga' or 'I Wanna Break Free' on repeat without... well, wanting to break free.

2.3

Shortly after our first meet at ULU, I heard my name while I was filing vinyl behind the counter. I looked up, but no one was there.

'Psst, Horace.'

This time it was followed by the sound of sniggering. I knew that laugh. It was Ricky. His head appeared from behind the counter and giggled. He had been hiding.

'Only me,' he said in a perfect Harry Enfield impersonation.

I looked around nervously. The others didn't like me chatting when there was filing to be done.

He did an impression of someone going down an escalator as his body and then head slowly disappeared behind the other side of the counter. I heard him guffaw and then his head reappeared with a big grin on his face.

'Classic.'

I fixed a grin on mine and forced a laugh. I could feel Big Phil's eyes. Ricky and I stood in silence briefly. I didn't know what to say to him. He had a knack for making me lose words. It wasn't long before he broke the silence.

'Thought I'd pop in and say hello. So, this is where the magic happens?'

He smiled and his eyes twinkled as if he were about to reveal a secret. There was another pregnant pause before he spoke.

'Like your cardigan. Did your gran knit it?'

'What? No, I got it at Camden Market.'

I looked at my multi-coloured, chunky-knit cardigan. I had been getting a lot of stick over it from my colleagues. I wasn't sure if Ricky was joking too.

'It's a brave choice – quite Joseph and his Technicolour Dreamcoat.'

I didn't need fashion tips from a man who tucked his shirt into his pants. What was he doing here?

'I've decided to make a couple of purchases.'

He placed two record sleeves on the counter. One was a 7-inch single called 'Creep' by that new band from Oxford called Radiohead. The other was the new CD single by Suede called 'Metal Mickey'. I wasn't allowed to serve the customers and so Big Phil took the sleeves. Ricky looked up at him and stated the obvious.

'Tall.' Ricky giggled like a naughty school kid and then continued. 'What's the weather like up there?'

'What was that?' said Phil.

'Nothing.'

Ricky winked at me and I winced. Phil gave Ricky and then me a Paddington stare and went to put records in the sleeves.

'He's a barrel of laughs. Is he your boss?' said Ricky a bit too loudly.

'Kind of.'

'Don't worry, you'll be out of here soon.'

I smiled. He seemed to believe in me. The exchange felt illicit – like we were in a library rearranging the books. Phil returned with the records and the transaction was carried out in frosty silence.

'That's £3.99. Do you want a bag?'

'No, thanks. I'll wear them.' Ricky giggled, then changed his mind. 'Yes, a bag please.'

Phil handed the bag and receipt to Ricky and slammed the till shut. He went to serve another customer. Ricky lingered.

'Look, Ricky, I better get on,' I said.

But Ricky was about to change gear.

'I got you some studio time.'

'What?'

'This weekend, down in Catford. State of the Art studio – 16-track mixing desk, engineer. All paid for.'

'Seriously?'

Ricky smiled. 'Can you do it?'

'Wow, that would be amazing. But we haven't got a drummer.'

'Doesn't matter. They've got drum machines and can create any beats and loops you want.'

'Wow. Well, yes, would love to.'

'Cool. I'll ring you with details.'

Ricky trotted out of the shop, swinging his Selectadisc bag. He was a strange and annoying little fellow, but he represented a kind of freedom – a believer who wasn't wasting time. I felt my heart thump with excitement at the prospect of going into a recording studio. Big Phil reappeared.

'Who was that nob?'

I felt in two minds about telling him but I also wanted to remind him that I had a life outside of this hell-hole.

'That's Ricky. He's our new manager.'

Big Phil unleashed a loud scoff. 'Good luck with that then.'

'He used to manage Suede actually,' I said a bit too defensively.

'"Used to" being the operative words, Horace. You do realise no one ever leaves Selectadisc.'

I pulled a face to indicate that that rule would not apply to me. He pulled a face back at me to indicate that it would.

'I suggest you put your dream back in its pipe and continue with the filing, please. Those records aren't going to file themselves.' He motioned towards my pile of unfiled vinyl that somehow had tripled in size.

Big Phil left me to it and went downstairs to tell the others. I could hear them laughing at my expense. I felt a knot of anger in my stomach. *We'll see who's laughing when The Pointy Birds are on the cover of* NME *and have a video on* MTV. I wanted it even more now, just to prove to them that I could. And anyway, we now had two days' studio time courtesy of Ricky. Maybe he was our Sherpa, The Pointy Birds' Tenzing Norgay. I couldn't wait to get back to the flat to tell the others, followed by some quality air guitar and a hairbrush microphone in front of the mirror to celebrate.

I picked up my vinyl and returned to filing – the record on

the top of the pile was the debut album *Leisure* from a band called Blur. I laughed to myself – pretty boy no-hopers with a stupid name. Even though I was stuck filing records all day in a dark, smelly hole, things were looking up. The same definitely couldn't be said for Blur.

3. Town and Country Club

Marcus and I go to a gig and swap exciting visions of the future. We then sneak into the after-show where things get messy.

Blur were headed for the 'where are they now' files. That was a certainty. The past may have been theirs, but the future was ours. Their downfall was there for all to see at the *NME* Gimme Shelter charity benefit gig at The Town & Country Club in Kentish Town. Blur were headliners with Suede in support, plus two other bands on the bill. The running order was as follows:

BLUR
MEGA CITY FOUR
SUEDE
THREE AND HALF MINUTES

Until this moment, Suede's gigs had been sweaty affairs in tiny venues attended by chin-stroking music industry types. As I was to later find out, for the music industry, the actual music, whether good or bad, was a mere detail – bands were units to be shifted, like burgers. However, this gig was a chance for Suede to play on a bigger stage and on the same bill as Blur. The press had successfully concocted a rivalry between Blur and Suede, centred around the fact that both singers had dated ex-Suede guitarist Justine Frischmann. She had left Suede's lead singer Brett Anderson for Blur's lead singer Damon Albarn, but if this night was anything to go by, she was probably about to regret both leaving Suede and her new choice of boyfriend.

I went to the gig with The Pointy Bird's bassist Marcus to check out the competition. We had both studied Politics at the City of London Poly, but I had lured him away from a healthy interest in campaigning for the disadvantaged in society with the promise of the big time. Initially, he was a bit sceptical, but now things were happening – he had turned down the opportunity of studying for an MSc in Politics Research and got a job working the frozen foods counter at Sainsbury's to help pay the rent. It had also unleashed a latent desire within him to perform. He was a natural on stage, having acted in the past and narrowly missed being cast as Adrian Mole in the TV adaptation of the eponymous book series. He had also perfected the art of winking at the crowd and playing bass at the same time. His well-honed wink, combined with my inter-song banter, made us a potent force.

We got some drinks at the bar and surveyed the crowd. There was a palpable buzz in the air. Suede were due to come on stage.

Marcus nudged me. 'This will be us soon.'

'I know.'

'What's it going to be like?'

'What?'

'When we're famous. How big will we get?'

'Bigger than Everest.'

'Bring it on!'

Marcus started to dance to the music playing over the venue speakers. By chance, it was one of his favourite tracks, 'Buffalo Stance' by Neneh Cherry. Fuelled by the happy serendipity of the DJ's song choice and the excitement of the night ahead, he closed his eyes and sung along, lost in music. His signature dance move followed this. He raised his arms to the ceiling, euphorically taking it all in like the music was being transmitted through his body via his hands.

'Look, my hands are ears!'

I laughed; he was built for this – I had created a monster. As the song ended, the lights went down, and the crowd grew quiet with anticipation. Smoke machines, silhouettes of guitar technicians dashing across the stage making last-minute adjustments, the stage in darkness apart from tiny green lights on the amps suggesting the imminent arrival of the band. The tease of being kept waiting. This is what it was all about. This big music hall, empty and smelly by day, was about to be transformed and host a magical communion between artist and audience, an alchemy of junk to gold. What was happening backstage? What would it be like to walk out onto this stage to perform your songs, hear them sung back at you? The applause, the adulation, the affirmation. The three As. I couldn't wait to find out.

At last, Suede took the stage, and for the next thirty minutes, we witnessed a masterclass in how to blow the roof off a venue. They had got their deal with Nude Records on the strength of their demo, but their live shows backed it up, and they did not disappoint. But it wasn't just the music; it was their attitude. They didn't care if you liked them or not. And with their Oxfam chic, they had a look where grot met glamour, in contrast to the purposefully nondescript and rather grey grunge and shoe-gaze bands doing the rounds in the music press. Frontman Brett had obviously spent hours in front of the mirror with a hairbrush microphone (it took one to know one) and much of the set was spent swinging the mic above his head, avoiding serious injury to the rest of the band by inches. Or using it to spank his pert little bum. And in guitarist Bernard Butler they had the new Johnny Marr. His guitar playing was jam-packed full of ideas and played with a ferocious energy that gave an extra heft and excitement to their live set. They were the full package.

My only criticism was, where were the gags? Brett's inter-song banter left a lot to be desired. Perhaps this was why Justine left him. But as I watched them triumph in front of two thousand new fans, things were crystallising in my mind. No one else was combining music and comedy, and this was definitely a gap in the market. Also, if we were to take things up a level, we needed some glamour too. We needed sparkly shirts and floppy fringes. I knew this decision was not going to go down well with certain members of the band, but it was a fight worth having. Grunge was over. Our ponytails and cardigans needed to go.

Suede ended their set with the three-minute pop perfection of their new single 'Metal Mickey' which told the story of a girl working in a butcher's shop with rhyming couplets aplenty. Victorious, the band strutted off stage, leaving the amps and the crowds buzzing. Marcus and I needed to have a half-time team talk as the crowd got ready for Blur. We grabbed two pints and weaved our way through the crowd to a vantage point overlooking the gig. The audience was thinning out for Blur – you could sense a changing of the guard. It was strange, the psychology of the crowds. The excitement that had greeted Suede replaced with a collective feeling of apprehension and sympathy for Blur who were clearly on their way out. Or maybe I was just projecting? But Marcus felt the same.

'I wouldn't want to be following them,' said Marcus. 'I feel sorry for Blur.'

I nodded my head in agreement before a sly grin crept across my face. 'Nah, fuck 'em!'

We clinked glasses and surveyed the crowd. We didn't want to spoil the night with talk of our day jobs. We wanted to live in the now. Two hours earlier, Marcus had been wearing a brown Sainsbury's uniform, a clip-on tie and a name badge. As bad as my job was, at least I didn't have to surrender my dignity by dressing in a silly costume. I decided not to ask about the frozen peas. Marcus spoke.

'Ever feel like you were destined?'

I knew immediately what Marcus meant but decided to play dumb.

'What do you mean?'

'You know… do you think that we are destined to be famous?'

The answer was yes, yes and thrice yes. Of course we were destined to be famous. I was being pulled like a magnet; there was no choice. The stage was my home. The camera on me and mic in my hand would be pure oxygen. There was no need to drill into why I had this needy desire for fame – it was simple – I would be good at it, and it would be fun. It was time for my Three-Hurdles speech.

'In life, there are three hurdles you have to jump…'

Marcus had heard this sales pitch before, but I felt he needed to hear it again. Like an investor being reassured by a positive monthly report. Beer was spilling from my plastic pint, and my words were starting to slur and increase in volume, but the more I went on, the more Marcus nodded and the more he nodded, the more I went on until he was powerless to my advances. To my certainty about my certainty. The logic underpinning my Three-Hurdles Theory was impossible to deny. That if you wanted something enough, it was only a matter of time. And in that sense, it was destiny.

'So, you really think it's going to happen?'

'It's not a question of if, Marcus. It's when.'

I rested my case. Marcus was won over – his nodding could now be reserved for the music.

'We are so lucky,' he said. 'You know. Just to experience all this.'

I smiled in admiration at Marcus's wisdom. He was from the concrete jungle of Coventry, and in the words of Morrissey, his eyes had seen the glory of a disused railway line. Life could be hard, it could be terrible, but we were the lucky ones. Not just to be in a band but to be having a laugh. To be alive. This seemed enough for him. Why wasn't that enough for me?

The lights went down. It was time for Blur. Out bounced Damon the lead singer, pogoing like there was no tomorrow. He was really going for it, like Superman, (or Cher), trying to turn back time on the clock of destiny. His tactic to win over the crowd seemed to be to jump up and down as much as possible. It was ill-conceived, and the crowd weren't buying it. Making matters worse, it soon became apparent he and the rest of the band were very drunk. Sensing defeat, Damon doubled down during a tuneless dirge and climbed up onto the lighting rig, wobbling perilously 20 feet above the rest of the band. The death of their careers was one thing, but would there be an actual death? Miraculously, the talentless pretty boy made it down, but he probably wished he fell. By the end of the spectacle, the band and audience both knew that this was a slow, painful, embarrassing end to their careers as musicians.

Post-gig we snuck our way into the aftershow party and sat at the bar. This was our new world – free drinks and celeb mates. I nudged Marcus. Slumped in the corner of the bar was a hapless-looking Damon Albarn, all alone, Billy-no-mates. We laughed and shook our heads. What would become of him? Probably end up working in a shoe shop or something.

The rest of Blur were fairing little better. On the floor of the toilets in one of the urinals was their bassist, Alex James, clutching the porcelain in a puddle of piss. His lanky limbs and foppish hair soaked in urine. He didn't look so foppish now. He was hogging the entire toilet floor of the only free cubicle. Still, I was bursting, and he didn't seem concerned by the spray. Outside, as we paid for our kebab, we had to step over Blur's guitarist Graham Coxon. He had collapsed on the pavement, and someone had propped him up against the wall. He was slumped over and blocking the doorway. I offered him a vinegar-soaked chip out of pity, and it hung impotently in front of his nose. He sniffed it and then looked away like a sick puppy, so I scoffed it and moved on.

The streets of Kentish Town were empty. It was going to be a long wait for a taxi to take us to our flat in Golders Green. Marcus was dancing in the street with his hands raised to the sky.

'Look, my hands are ears. Woo hoo!'

He didn't look too steady on his feet. Most of his kebab had made it on to his frilly shirt. He looked pale and a bit green around the gills. There were no cabs in sight.

'Come on, let's start walking,' I said.

'Pointy Birds are so much better than Blur. They're rubbish.'

I smiled. He was a believer.

'It's really going to happen, isn't it?' he asked.

'It is.'

'When?'

'Soon.'

'What's it going to be like again?' Marcus hiccupped. 'Will we play on *Top Of The Pops*?'

'Yes.'

'And will we be on the cover of the *NME*?'

'Yes.'

'On the actual cover?'

'Yes.'

'And play Wembley?'

'Yes.'

'And groupies?'

I laughed. Marcus' voice petered out, and he made a strange gurgling sound. He stopped and looked at me with a pained expression on his face like terrible news was breaking. It was. His eyelids drooped, and he wiped his mouth. He was a tree about to be felled. The inevitable vomit was imminent. A few moments later, I was patting him on the back as he chundered into the bin. I looked up at the sky. It was rare to see stars in London, but they were out in all their glory tonight. This world of fame and success had been shrouded in secrecy for so many years, but stars were aligning, events were conspiring. I knew it was only a matter of time before we would get our chance to shine. Blur were in the gutter, and we were looking at the stars. The irony was not lost on me. I could feel a rhyming couplet coming on.

<< REWIND

The art of creation, the making of it, the being in control, the dream…

4. The Four Ds

1969–1987

An attempt to unravel a few things plus some childhood memories.

Someone had to be a rockstar, right, so why not me? After all, I had spent an unhealthy amount of time in front of the mirror, playing air guitar. Or bouncing around my bedroom with a hairbrush-turned-microphone. Imaginary gigs in front of imaginary crowds, moshing and singing along to my every word. I had also perfected the art of interviewing myself and was starting to give some good copy. Hours upon hours practising the finer art of being a lead singer when I should have been doing homework. Mum and Dad banging on the ceiling and asking what on earth I was doing.

'It's like a herd of elephants up there!'

But this was a battle they could never win. Didn't they realise I was putting in my ten thousand hours? Plus, being in a band was a vehicle to a new world. Life was out there to be lived, and I was going to live it. I had music I wanted to make, movies I had to direct, books I needed to write, paintings I needed to paint. I knew it was only a matter of time before everything clicked into place. I was an all-round entertainer bridging the gap between music and comedy – awards, blue plaque, statues and cultural immortality would follow. A band was a natural entry point to this sexy new world. Even if you weren't that good a musician, at least you could be a rockstar.

You just needed to know three chords on the guitar and you

could write a hit, rehearse it, get on stage and play it. Even if no one was at the gig, or if no one liked it – at least you were doing it, practising your craft, making your way. And then it was only a matter of time. OK, I couldn't hold a tune or sing a melody, but this wasn't necessary. Mariah Carey's ability to scale several octaves might have some in rapture, but the pure technical skill of that sort left me cold. Could Dylan sing? Could Lou Reed? Johnny Rotten? Robert Smith? Morrissey?

No. No. No. No. And no!

The best music sprang from attitude, and the best singers just went for it, communicating authenticity in their voice. True talent had the most essential ingredient of all – soul. My singing heroes were not shy to convey their truth. And neither was I.

Plus, I was willing to jump around a stage as no one had ever jumped around a stage. Iggy Pop? Not bad. Jagger? Yes, he could move. I mean, they were good, but if I could combine my pogoing abilities with some hilarious inter-song banter, I was surely on to a winner. Making people laugh and dance, maybe at the same time. Supercharged by the four essential ingredients for any aspiring rockstar: desire, determination, dedication and drive. The Four Ds.

Yes, I was willing to put everything into it – blood, sweat, tears and dignity. And maybe even some shame.

4.2

I had got a fatal taste for the stage at a young age. In 1978, at the age of eight, we moved from south London to a small town in south Oxfordshire called Watlington. The town and its surrounding countryside represented all sorts of opportunities for adventure, especially after the confines of life in London where our stomping ground was a small back garden and the back seats of Mum's car. Here, I could run free and my world seemed to burst into colour. There was so much to explore – farmyards, graveyards, streams and babbling brooks, football pitches and tennis courts, and best of all we could get around on our bicycles.

My new school was also very different. In London, I had attended Dulwich College Prep – an all-boys school – the teachers were thin-lipped and grey with bad coffee breath, and very strict. Plus there was a never-ending pile of homework. At Watlington Primary, by contrast, teachers were called by their first name, there was no uniform and, more pleasingly, there were girls. The headmaster put as much emphasis on visiting the local farm to watch piglets being born as the national curriculum. On my first day, I shocked my teacher. He pointed at a squiggle on the blackboard:

'Do you know what that is?'

'It's a comma.'

His eyes widened in surprise.

'And how about that?' He pointed at a full stop.

'That's a full stop.'

'We got a right clever clogs here, boys and girls. Well done, Andrew!'

I had been transported to easy street and loved it. Within a few months, I had bagged the lead at the school's production of a play called *Grandpa.* I had to wear a wig, smoke a fake pipe and do a silly walk. The drama teacher who was very pretty and didn't wear a bra (and who I was convinced I was going to marry) kept telling me that grandpa wouldn't be whispering the lines in a quiet, shy voice.

'Shout it! Yell it! GO FOR IT!'

So I did. And my new classmates laughed and applauded. It blew my tiny 9-year-old mind. A criminal shyness was inverted, a latent desire to perform had been unlocked and I wanted more. There was no onion to peel, no grist in the mill or grit in the oyster. My needy desire to perform had no more straightforward explanation than it was fun. If people were laughing then they were happy, so why not laugh and have a good time all the time? And I craved this sound of laughter like a hot dog craved mustard.

Within three years we had moved house again. Annoyingly, Dad had got another promotion and we found ourselves in a town called Crowborough, East Sussex. My new school was called Beacon – a huge comprehensive absorbing 2,500 kids from the surrounding area. But now drama lessons, school plays, impressions, mucking around – all these things took on far more importance and relevance to my future than O levels. And when a few of us got together to write and perform the Christmas review in an attempt to emulate our heroes Monty Python and the characters in *The Young Ones*, there was no turning back, although what we produced was perhaps more a *Carry On*-like film.

The euphoria I felt following the success of our lower sixth production of *Jack Bean and His Stalk*, and its sequel the following year, *Dicks Wittingly and his Pussies*, further fuelled my desire. I got laughs and the prettiest girl in the school smiled at me, and that was it: real-life was no longer an option. My drama teacher at Watlington (who I never did marry) had taught me something that I didn't realise I had learned:

WHO CARES WHAT OTHER PEOPLE THINK! A valuable life lesson that could bridge the gap of who I was and who I wanted to be.

5. City Poly

AUTUMN 1988

Enrol at college and move in with Marcus. Bond over rabbit jokes and watch a new band from Manchester play live at Student Union.

So, it was with some excitement I jumped off my train as it pulled in at Charing Cross, and walked up the platform concourse with a spring in my step, a plan in my head and a dream in my heart. I had scraped into the City of London Polytechnic to study for a degree in Politics and Government. Other people went to college to study and expand their minds, or didn't bother with further education and travelled the world. Other people climbed the career ladder and bowed to the money god. But none of that interested me. I was going to form a band.

Three years on a Politics course gave me the perfect time and opportunity to do just that – find some band members, learn my trade, grow my hair and then enjoy the inevitable world domination to follow. I was in precisely the right place: London, the city of wild ambition where a man could lose himself. Well, I wasn't going to lose myself, no siree, Bob, quite the opposite. And I had a Three-Hurdle Theory for success.

This, combined with the Four Ds of desire, determination, drive and dedication could lead to the three As, namely applause, adulation and affirmation, and ultimately to the promised land of the three Fs: fame, fortune and fun. And most fundamental of all was the mantra Who Cares What Other People Think. It could all be abbreviated into a formula which might double up as a neat tattoo:

WCWOPT x (3H+4D) = 3A+FFF

On my first day at college we assembled in the lecture hall to listen to Professor Flood, the head of the Politics degree course, tell us what he expected from us in the year ahead, and his words were music to my ears.

'You are not expected to attend college, but there are six hours of lectures a week. And these are optional.' I looked around the lecture hall, grinning like a Cheshire cat. Was he joking? I shook my head in disbelief. My fellow students nodded along as Prof Flood continued.

'You are not here to work for a degree. We are somewhat old-fashioned in that regard.' He chuckled enigmatically to himself. 'You are here to *read* for a degree. We expect you to be spending the lion share of your time reading around the subjects. We have libraries…'

I zoned out. I had heard enough. You have got to be kidding, I thought, I'm not spending three years in a library. No way. But still, much collective nodding and scratching of chins. I scanned the room for potential band members. It was slim pickings. I wanted to study English Literature and Drama up in Nottingham, where I thought there would be a good chance of finding like-minded musical arty types – the prospectus had boasted the highest concentration of pubs and the prettiest girls, so demand would be high. But my grades weren't good enough, and at the eleventh hour, I'd got on this degree course. I hadn't looked into what this course was about, but unbeknownst to me, this was one of the most militant colleges in the country. The campus was in Aldgate where the city met the start of the East End, a melting pot of cultures and ethnicities. A big chunk of the class were mature students with a quick serious look in their eyes. They were here not only to learn but to hold the fascist bully-boy Tory government to account for atrocities against the poor whether through protests, sit-ins, marches or appearances on Question Time. If that didn't work, there was always *direct action*, whatever that meant. They didn't look like they would have much interest in joining an indie band.

A few people had caught my eye, though. Chief in my crosshairs was someone about my age. He had a mop of blond hair and wore a leather jacket adorned with CND badges, but most importantly he was wearing a Wedding Present T-shirt. They were an indie band from Leeds that had just released a seminal album called *George Best*. He also had a copy of *NME* under his arm, which along with *Melody Maker* and *Sounds* was the must-have weekly newspaper for fans of new up-and-coming bands, or 'indie music' as it was otherwise known. Yes, he had definite potential. We acknowledged each other in the canteen queue; Marcus, he said his name was. There was something of Sylvester-the-cat about him. Little did the poor sod know what I had lined up for him.

I had been accepted on to the course late through a process called Clearing, which found degree places for students with low A level grades that no one wanted. It meant I had missed out on accommodation in the halls of residence so I had rented a room through Loot above a leather coat shop on Brick Lane, near the college campus. I paid a month's deposit in advance to a man who assured me other students would also be staying in one of the four bedrooms above the shop. The reality was somewhat different. My parents drove up more of my belongings for the big goodbye. I was 17 and leaving home, but when I rang the doorbell to my new dwellings, there was no answer. But I could hear voices. Eventually, the door opened, and an extended Bangladeshi family opened the door and wondered what I wanted. I explained that I had paid good money (well, my dad had) to rent a room in this house. Not only were they having none of it, but they also couldn't understand a word I was saying.

Eventually, the man who had shown me around a few weeks before and taken my deposit turned up and after much apologising to me and yelling at the others ushered me in. He showed me to my room to the dismay of his seventeen family members. He seemed to have sold their bedroom. Reluctantly, they carried out their mattresses. They didn't look pleased.

'Are you sure this is the right place?' asked my dad who was loitering behind me with a concerned look on his face.

'Yes,' I said proudly and with no doubt. This was London.

I waved goodbye and went to my new room, much to the bemusement of the Bangladeshi family. There wasn't anywhere to unpack my clothes or any furniture, just a mattress on the floor, but that didn't mean I couldn't put up my poster of The Cure's 'Boys Don't Cry'. I then sat on the mattress and strummed my guitar, soaking up my new London life. Something slid under the door, a Penthouse magazine. Someone was trying to make friends. I opened the door, and an older man smiled, revealing a lack of dentistry, and we exchanged pleasantries.

It wasn't long before the grimness of my situation became apparent – eighteen men (including me) living in cramped and squalid conditions with no running water or electricity. Plus, none of my new flatmates spoke English. And my Bengali was extremely limited. But maybe this was how everyone in London lived?

After a couple of weeks of no privacy and feeling guilty about stealing their bedroom, I realised I needed a shower. The smell I was emitting was limiting my ability to make new friends, so I paid a visit to student accommodation. It turned out two girls on my course also needed somewhere to live. And so did Marcus. Fate had thrown us together.

The student accommodation officer told us they had a four-bedroom house in Plaistow near the West Ham football ground if the four of us wanted to move in together. We looked at each other, nodded and the next thing we knew we had keys to what was to rapidly become known as the house that threw the biggest and best parties. It was also the house where I was to give Marcus a crash course in playing the bass guitar and teach him the finer points of becoming an aspiring rockstar.

5.2

Unbeknownst to us, our next three years at college were to coincide with a wave of exciting new alternative guitar bands breaking into the mainstream. The eighties had seen U2 and Simple Minds become stadium-filling globe-trotters. At the same time, The Cure, New Order, The Smiths and Echo & the Bunnymen became commercially successful while retaining a cult status. Still, the charts and radio had been taken over increasingly by the formulaic pop-dross of the hit-making machine that was Stock, Aitken and Waterman. It was time for a change – for something more authentic, and in late 1988 that change came predominantly through two indie labels. London-based Creation Records were incubating bands like House Of Love, My Bloody Valentine and Primal Scream, while Factory in Manchester would be at the centre of a new 'Madchester' scene influenced by the 1967 Summer of Love and Acid House. These bands combined alternative rock, psychedelic pop and dance culture. Little did we know, we were about to witness the leading proponent from this new movement at our first night out at the student union Friday night disco.

Marcus and I left our new house on Harcourt road and excitedly made our way to Plaistow Tube station sharing a can of Stella. The smell of beer mingled with the night air and the waft of too much aftershave. It was five stops on the District line to Aldgate East. We got out and spotted the student union entrance through a dodgy-looking door on Whitechapel road and climbed up five flights of stairs to a dark and dingy space at the top with a low ceiling and blacked-out windows. This was Fairholt. There was a low stage at one end, a dance floor in the middle and bar and cafeteria at the other. It wasn't exactly Oxbridge. There were no rolling lawns or punting on rivers, but it served cheap beer and salty chips, plus there were girls, and there was music. And it was happy hour.

We met another new friend Neil and over several rounds of Newcastle Brown Ale settled in for the night. Marcus was from Coventry, a big supporter of the Labour Party and controversially thought that cassettes were better than CDs. Neil dressed in black and worshipped at the altar of Depeche Mode and anything Mute Records. He was from Deal in Kent and his tipple was vodka. We exchanged funny stories and political views, presenting new and improved versions of ourselves, free from the constraints of old friends putting us in a box, by telling stale old stories of mistakes we had made and who we 'really' were. Of course, over time (and during the night) the mask might slip, and we would climb back into that box. But for now, we were new, we were free and several rounds awaited.

During our third round of drinks, Marcus looked around conspiratorially to check no one was listening and then beckoned Neil and me in closer as if to whisper a secret. Neil and I looked at each other and then did what he asked. Marcus glanced once more over his shoulder and satisfied no one could overhear said in a hushed voice.

'This rabbit hops into a butcher's, right…'

I felt the creep of a smile across my face. The small-talk was over. We were getting down to the business-end of the evening. Marcus was a pro in the joke-telling department and had regaled this one to his mates in The Dog and Trumpet back in Coventry. Marcus glanced around the room again like a spy worried that the walls had ears.

'And he hops up to the guy behind the counter, right, and he says, "Do you sell cabbages?"'

I spat my drink out and started laughing. Marcus seemed pleased by my reaction, but I had gone too soon.

'No, listen. There's more…'

Marcus continued. His rabbit had the same midland drawl as seventies puppet Hartley Hare.

'"We don't sell cabbages here," says the butcher. "This is a butcher's. You want to go to the greengrocers down the road there." "Oh right," says the rabbit and out he hops.'

Marcus paused for dramatic effect as Neil sipped his vodka. I got the impression Neil was not a joke man. Marcus stepped up the pace.

'Next day the rabbit is back in the butcher's, right.'

I nodded excitedly.

'"Oi, butcher! You sell cabbages?"'

Marcus was now doing the actions of a rabbit – with big ears and paws and a twitchy nose.

'"I told you yesterday, rabbit, we don't sell cabbages. There is a greengrocer down the road. Now hop it!"'

'"Sorry," said the rabbit. And off he hopped out of the shop.'

It was a master storyteller at work. Was there anything better than listening to a funny joke after three pints with new friends? I greedily slurped my beer.

'Third day he's back in the butcher's.'

I started laughing, knowing the punchline was imminent.

'"Do you sell cabbages?" asks the rabbit. "I told you yesterday, rabbit, and the day before that, we don't sell cabbages. Now if you come back here again, I'll nail your ears to the counter."'

We were on the final straight. Marcus checked once again; no one was listening in and beckoned us in closer. We leaned in, happy to be complicit. Our world had shrunk. It was just the three of us around the table under an umbrella of booze, and nowness shielded us from the outside world. The noisy din of the union bar no longer existed.

'The next day the rabbit is back in the butcher's. He hops up to the counter. "Excuse me, butcher, do you have a hammer?"' "No," says the butcher. "Do you sell cabbages?" the rabbit asks.'

There was a brief moment of silence like a tennis ball tossed in the air before being hit; or a car skidding on ice before a crash; or that brief moment after an orchestra finishes before applause kicks in, and then on the offbeat, I exploded with laughter. As I fell backwards off my seat, just like I was in the song 'Falling and Laughing' by Orange Juice, my world quite literally turned upside down. Neil nodded in appreciation that he had got the joke. Marcus stood up. His work was done.

'Who's for another?'

We raised empty glasses in the affirmative and moments later, he returned with two more bottles of Newcastle Brown Ale and a vodka and tonic for Neil. A few years previously on a family holiday to Lanzarote, I had met a guy from Liverpool who had told me a rabbit joke that I now claimed as my own. I needed a box of matches. As luck would have it, there was a box on the next table. I grabbed it and put it on our table.

'How do you get all the rabbits in the world to gather around this matchbox?'

Neil and Marcus looked at each other and then shrugged. I took a match out of the box and inserted the tip of it back into a corner of the matchbox, transforming the matchbox into a miniature walkie-talkie. The match sticking out was the aerial. I wiggled my eyebrows twice for comic effect and lifted it to my mouth.

'Calling all rabbits! Calling all rabbits!'

Marcus slapped his thigh and roared, even Neil liked this one. Our merriment was interrupted by the guitar intro to 'She Sells Sanctuary' by The Cult. It was time to pogo. With the fuel of alcohol, we took to the dance floor and expressed our new selves to indie classics old and new. 'This Charming Man' by The Smiths, 'Inbetween Days' by The Cure and a new track called 'Freakscene' by Dinosaur Jr (which was to become an indie anthem and forerunner for the imminent grunge scene). We were lost in the music, inside the songs, dancing and laughing, until the music was abruptly terminated. It was time for the live band.

5.3

All night I had been excited by the prospect of the band. On stage, a drum kit had been mic'd up, guitar amps were turned on ready for action and centre stage was the glorious microphone stand – the promise of it all. An empty stage soon to be brought to life with music and lights. I couldn't wait. A couple of puffs of dry ice wheezed out from a smoke machine, the lights went down, and the band strolled on. Four lads in colourful tie-dye T-shirts, fisherman's hats and denim flares picked up their instruments and started to run through their songs. The student audience gravitated to the bar, more interested in another round than in the night's entertainment. Still, the band didn't seem particularly bothered that they were playing to a half-empty room. They couldn't give a toss and were happy to play to their few dedicated fans who were in similar dress code and had travelled down from Manchester with the band.

I sat on the side of the stage and watched them play. Musically, the band was tight and kept my attention, but the singer's voice was a bit weak. He lacked imagination with his moves – confining things to a strange monkey-dance twirling the mic above his head when he wasn't singing. He was stiff like he had done an accident in his pants. And as for inter-song banter, there was none. I looked at the poster to make a mental note of the competition. They were called The Stone Roses. The singer would need to work on his routine if they were going to make it. That was for certain.

But contrary to my expectations, over the next year, The Stone Roses were to go from strength to strength. I read about their meteoric rise in the music press. I watched open-mouthed as they gate-crashed *Top Of The Pops* with fellow Mancunians Happy Mondays and launched a new musical movement. I bought their critically acclaimed debut album, now widely regarded as one of the greatest albums ever made, and played it to death. And I knew without any doubt if they could make it, then so could I.

6. Learning to be Rockstars

WINTER 1988–SUMMER 1989

Lure Marcus into the band and we start learning how to be rockstars. Eyes are opened at Glastonbury and Reading Festivals.

Our first year at City Poly continued. Days not attending college, which were the vast majority, we spent at our new home on Harcourt Road, West Ham, under a duvet in front of daytime telly eating toast, invariably with a hangover. These were fabulously productive times finding out who we were by doing nothing at all. We were so busy doing nothing that it was hard to find the time to squeeze in our optional six hours of lectures per week and they started to feel like a terrible injustice. Even the days we made it into college were spent at Fairholt Student Union lounging about in the bar playing drinking games rather than the lecture hall or the library.

Marcus, as I was to find out, loved a debate, so life alternated between eating toast, parties and arguments over things like fox hunting, private education and the dreaded poll tax. Our other housemates, the two Nickys, were less politically motivated and saw nothing wrong with chasing a fox in a silly costume or paying for school. Marcus battled on behalf of the proletariat, stressing aspiration and fairness and was minimally judgemental. Neither fox hunting nor private education, to his mind, seemed particularly fair. I realised by the depth and detail of the arguments that I hadn't given these issues enough thought to have an informed opinion. To compensate, I took on the role of the joker – I could sort this shit out later when I was famous and rich. I was on firmer ground discussing music or football. One bone of contention between Marcus and me was whether Gary Lineker was a decent centre forward. I agreed he didn't have a great touch, but you couldn't deny his goalscoring prowess. Marcus wouldn't have it, unswerving in his belief that Lineker was overrated. Yet as fun and intensive as these arguments were, I was getting distracted from why I was in London. I was here to become a rockstar.

After all, that's why I was here in the capital. I couldn't really play any instruments, I hadn't written any songs, but I had a vision and didn't care what people thought. All I had to do was put the pieces of the jigsaw together. Or buy the puzzle and rather than waste time assembling it, simply hammer the pieces together. The first piece was the name of the band. And one name rang in my ears: The Pointy Birds. It was the title of a poem in the Steve Martin film *The Man With Two Brains:*

The Pointy Birds, a pointy-pointy.
Anoint my head, a-nointy-nointy.

It ticked all the boxes: it was Shakespearean in its simplicity, Pythonian in its stupidity. As soon as Steve Martin uttered it in the hospital scene in the film, I knew it was the perfect band name, a glorious unity of music and comedy.

The second piece of the jigsaw was to lure Marcus into the band. He was the one. I bided my time and then one night as we sat on my bedroom floor listening to music, I turned the lights down low and poured him a tumbler of cherry brandy, a housewarming gift from our landlord.

'What do you really want to do with your life, Marcus?' I asked seductively.

Marcus talked about life's injustices and how he would like to help people. I stifled a yawn as he spoke. I needed to change the subject and move on to more pressing matters.

'Do you ever have the desire to perform?'

'I used to do a bit of acting actually,' he said bashfully.

'Really?

'Yeah, I got down to the last four to play Adrian Mole in the TV series.'

'Seriously?'

Marcus nodded modestly.

'Wow.' I was impressed. He had brushed with fame. Marcus continued misty-eyed about an acting tour of Russia when he was 12. It was my time to strike.

'So, you like treading the boards?'

'I love it, darling.'

I laughed.

Marcus was falling into my honey trap. 'Why? What do you want to do?'

'I'm forming a band.'

'Really?'

'Yeah, we're called The Pointy Birds.'

Marcus pulled an impressed face. I continued.

'I have this theory. It's called the Three-Hurdle Theory…'

Marcus listened as I cast my spell and weaved my web. I poured him another glass to the brim. Eventually, I got to the crux.

'Anyway, am looking for a bass player and wondered if you wanted to join the band?'

'Well, yeah, would love to, but I can't play the bass guitar.'

'Doesn't matter, I can teach you.'

'OK, I'm in!'

'You will have to grow your hair.'

'OK.'

'And dress up.'

'Sure thing.'

We clinked glasses and before I knew it, he'd purchased a red bass guitar and amp. Soon the rumbling sound of bass lines emanated from Marcus's bedroom. Marcus 'Fingers' Boyland was born.

6.2

The second piece of the jigsaw puzzle was in place. We had a name and now Marcus and I were partners in crime. We started to grow our hair out and consumed *NME* and *Melody Maker* religiously. These were our scriptures, our weekly catechism featuring our musical heroes and detailing access to their world. We listened to John Peel – the go-to radio show and stamp of approval for new bands – and we graduated from watching *Top Of The Pops* via *The Tube* to a new show called *Rapido* which featured live sessions and videos from all the best up-and-coming indie bands. We could read about bands, listen to them on the radio and watch them on TV, but best of all we could then go and see them live – The House Of Love at the Boston Arms, The Wedding Present at the Town and Country Club and many more. The more gigs I went to, the more I wanted it. Marcus and I had found much in common through this love of music. Our passion swelled as we enthusiastically swapped tapes of any new bands we discovered.

'You gotta hear this,' said Marcus one day knocking at my bedroom door. He handed me a cassette. He was a cassette man.

'They got this mad singer. Her voice is a bit weird at first, but by the third listen, it's amazing.'

The third listen. I looked at the cassette. It had a bright green cover and emblazoned in a garish pink font was the name of the band The Sugarcubes. The album was called *Life's Too Good.* I returned to my room, shut the door, popped the cassette in the tape machine and pressed play.

What was this shit? Utter dirge with a woman screaming out

of tune and a man talking over it with an out-of-time punk-jazz band? The singer's name was Bjork pronounced 'Bee-awk', but with a nod and a wink from Marcus, and backed up by the *NME*, it was essential to suppress one's first instinct to consign the tape to the bin. Their recommendations gave it gravitas. I had to take it seriously. I had to work to get the reward. As predicted, by the third listen, I was a Sugarcubes fan. Now instead of squealing and squawking and mayhem, I could hear all the hidden melodies and jazz rhythms and funny lyrics and the energy of a band – a group of weird and wonderful Icelanders who sung about car crashes and cigars. At least that's what I thought they were singing about, to be honest, I wasn't sure. But it didn't matter. They were different and original, and I was pleased with myself for liking them.

Listening to bands and going to gigs was more than just entertainment; it was an investment in learning the craft. These bands were teaching us, showing us how they did what they did. It brought to mind Professor Flood's advice that we were at university to *read* rather than *work* for a degree. We attended gigs to read about becoming rockstars. So we stopped attending lectures. There were more important things to do. And as we learned our instruments and the craft of songwriting, our hair started to grow. Pretty soon, my hair was covering my ears, and I had mastered the art of standing up and playing the guitar at the same time. But standing up, playing guitar *and* singing at the same time was trickier than it looked. More hair needed to be grown, more gigs attended and more cherry brandy drunk.

6.3

Gigs in London were exciting, but they were nothing compared to the spectacle of the 1989 Glastonbury Festival. We made the four-hour journey from Victoria by coach and arrived at a makeshift world in the Somerset countryside where music met comedy. Field upon field of bands of all shapes and sizes, old and new, playing every genre of music, along with a side order of performance artists, arts and crafts stalls, delicious food, magicians, fortune tellers, dogs running wild and women giving birth. It was all happening. (The only downside were the ubiquitous jugglers who seemed to turn up everywhere like wasps at a picnic, but you couldn't have everything.) The rolling valleys and hills had been covered in a stupendous multi-coloured quilt of tents as far as the eye could see and at the centre of it all was the Pyramid Stage, where the main acts played, with the headline slot on Saturday night reserved for the biggest band in the world. Headlining the Pyramid stage on a Saturday night was the pinnacle of pop music. That was our new goal, and The Pointy Birds would be back one day to plant our pointy flag on this summit.

In gloriously hot weather under powder-blue and flamingo-pink skies, with cow parsley scenting the air our shoulders relaxed, and woozy on pints of Somerset cider we spent three magical days and nights watching bands and comedians. High on sunshine and freedom and laughter and life. No sleep, no showers, no problem – curing the morning's hangover with a jacket potato and a pint of cider while watching the first band of the day. Any residual headache was carried away to the next valley by the hauntingly beautiful melodies of bands like The Waterboys and Galaxie 500.

On the Saturday, Marcus and I sat in the late-afternoon sun outside our tents surveying our kingdom. Our vantage looked down across a sea of tents towards the majesty of the Pyramid Stage and the gathering crowds. We had drunk just the right amount of the local scrumpy and everything with the world felt right. It was as if we had lived at Glastonbury Festival all our lives. I was trying to remember my former life in reality when Marcus spoke.

'Do you think we will ever play here?'

I looked at Marcus, shocked. 'Are you joking?'

'What?'

'Did you just ask me if The Pointy Birds will ever play Glastonbury?'

'Yeah, I mean, just imagine.'

'The answer is yes, yes and thrice yes. We will headline the Pyramid Stage.'

Marcus laughed.

'I'm serious.'

'So am I!'

Even though I was seeing double, I gave both Marcuses the sternest Paddington Bear stare I could muster. He deserved it for doubting the party line. The whites of my blood-shot eyes emphasised I wasn't joking. He swallowed like he had just received some life-changing news and gravely nodded, deliberating over whether to believe me, eventually calculating it would be better fun to be a believer. Our conversation was interrupted by the sound of a familiar baseline coming from the Pyramid Stage.

'Shit, that's The Pixies on stage!'

We ran down a grassy hill, leaping barefoot over tents like they were hurdles, to the bass-line of their opening track, 'Debaser'. Our hair in the air and the wind in our sails. Marcus misjudged his jump and crash-landed on a tent squashing a sleeping hippy (potentially fatally – we never found out). In the background was the sound of this excellently named four-piece from Boston, playing dark, catchy rock'n'roll pop tunes like a satanic Beach Boys. And as we tumbled through this beatnik campground that was Glastonbury, I knew that it didn't get better than this. We were learning to be rockstars. We were having fun and creating memories that could be cherished and embellished for years to come. Not that these memories needed to be embellished because the reality was perfect. We were the lucky ones, indeed.

*

We returned from Glastonbury knackered, exhilarated and very smelly. Our eyes had been opened by this crazy, colourful circus in the countryside that existed purely for everyone's pleasure and entertainment, knowing that we only needed to wait two months until we could do it all again at another festival. Shortly after we had booked tickets for Glastonbury, another advert appeared in *NME* for the 1989 Reading Festival. Up until then, Reading Festival featured tired rock dinosaurs like Alice Cooper and Def Leppard that were well past their sell-by date. However, new promoters Mean Fiddler had taken over, and their shift in booking policy from rock to indie not only had Marcus and me chomping at the bit to book tickets but thousands of other indie kids too. And it set the tone for festivals for years to come.

Reading was a much smaller affair than Glastonbury, and the focus was purely on the bands. And in 1989 it featured all our favourites in one place: New Order, The Pogues, Spacemen 3 and it was our chance to see The Sugarcubes, who did not disappoint. We were kids in a sweet shop, enjoying three more days of music and fun. The desire to be up on stage playing these festivals stoked like the fires we sat around at night.

7. Golders Green & Gong Show

AUTUMN 1989–SUMMER 1990

New decade. New flat. New guitarist.
Play 'Gong Show' prematurely. Find drummer and gain some unlikely fans.

We returned to college for year two, and the next jigsaw-piece clicked into place. Stu was a classically trained jazz guitarist and a doppelganger for John Travolta. He dressed in black polo necks, and his heroes were guitar virtuosos I had never heard of like Steve Vai, Pat Metheny and John Martin. He had a chronic fear of unnecessarily drawing attention to himself in public places, which didn't bode well for our live gigs, but Stu, Marcus and I had bonded and we recruited him as the next member of The Pointy Birds. It was a great signing. His guitar playing made us sound good. The only cause for concern was that he played a flying V guitar which made us look more Spinal Tap than indie, but we couldn't let perfect be the enemy of good.

The three of us had also decided to live together just like The Monkees, on their classic sixties TV show. We gave notice to our party house in Plaistow and found a three-bedroom flat above a hairdressing salon on Golders Green High Street. We didn't have a particular desire to live in Golders Green as it was considerably further from college (not that I planned to go much), but it was the closest we could afford near to Camden with our student grants. The flat was perfect for our needs and during the next three years my bedroom doubled up as the main living room and rehearsal space for the band. The front door was always open, quite literally, as the lock had broken. No one worried as there was little a burglar could steal.

Soon after moving in a new decade began. The nineties immediately felt different – more colourful, hopeful, full of promise. OK, there was a looming recession and a poisonous old witch called Margaret Thatcher clung to power in Number 10, but times were a-changing, and more than our hair was blowing in the wind. Love was in the air and the music scene. Even po-faced, indie-goth band Primal Scream had transformed into a dance act by releasing a groove anthem called 'Loaded' which asked the question: 'Just what is it that you want to do?'

Not only did this chime with the first of my three hurdles, but within seconds of seeing the video on *Rapido*, it caused me to leap from the sofa to press record. I somehow knew instantaneously that 'Loaded' would define the decade. And lead singer Bobby Gillespie proved my theory that you didn't have to be able to sing to make it – but I could hear the desire in his voice and he was another hairbrush mirror man if ever I saw one. 'Loaded' had followed closely on the heels of 'Fools Gold', a slice of psychedelic funk released by The Stone Roses, and now countless other indie bands were finding their rhythm to satisfy a new demand – indie kids wanted to dance.

7.2

It was time to get out there and show people what The Pointy Birds could do. So when I saw a poster on the wall of the student union, I knew our moment had come.

The City of London Polytechnic Rugby Club presents
GONG SHOW
Fairholt Student Union
Got a talent? Then enter the competition and win £100
Contact Ben or Dougy

I knew the rugby club might be a tough audience, but this was an opportunity. We had to enter. Force things to happen. I knocked on Marcus's bedroom door and excitedly told him we had entered the competition. He had one concern.

'But I can't play standing up yet.'

'That doesn't matter. We got a few days. And our hair is nearly the right length now.'

'True.' Marcus glanced in the mirror and shook his mane. 'OK, where do I sign?'

Stu was harder to convince.

'Are you joking? No way. We are shit.'

'Steady,' said Marcus.

'No, seriously, we are nowhere near ready to play in public, if ever.'

We decided to have a band meeting in the kitchen, ignoring the overflowing sink. Over a bottle of Jewish Sherry, a housewarming gift from our new landlord, Marcus and I explained the massive opportunity represented by playing the rugby club talent show. Stu didn't seem to see it that way and dug in his heels. I could see the whites of his John Travolta eyes and got the impression he might be scared. I refilled his glass to the rim and tried a different tact.

'What's the worst that could happen?'

'Utter humiliation.'

'Yeah, but just think, if you don't do this and you stay in and watch TV you won't have had an experience. That is why we're here. To experience stuff.'

Stu went quiet, processing this.

'The palace of wisdom is via the doors of experience,' I said.

We had been listening to The Doors, and I was developing a bit of a Jim Morrison obsession, so I was pleased to be able to drop one of his quotes into the conversation even though I wasn't sure I got the quote right. But Stu stubbornly clung to his one argument like wreckage in an ocean.

'Actually, the quote is "The road of excess leads to the palace of wisdom". It's William Blake. And we're shit.'

It was time to take the offer off the table. A classic sales tactic – make Stu realise what he would be missing.

'Fair enough, no worries. We'll do it as a duo, won't we, Marcus?'

Stu nodded sadly, letting this information settle. Marcus caught my eye. Was this madness? I winked to indicate I knew what I was doing. It was time to play the ace up my sleeve.

'Probably be lots of girls in the audience.'

I could tell this new nugget of information had penetrated. Stu was now calculating his options.

'OK, we do one song.'

We punched the air.

'Shall we play "Married To A Squirrel"?'

'No way. I'm not playing *that*.'

We agreed to work out the song choice later. Against all his better judgement, Stu knew he had no alternative but to do this gig. It would be a laugh. And as much as he feared public performance, I knew he was working to overcome his performance phobia. As Morrissey had sung, he 'suffered from a shyness that was criminally vulgar', but who cared what other people thought! Shyness was just a subverted ego knocking to be set free. Well, The Pointy Birds were here to help. We would provide the necessary psychotherapy, unleash his hitherto unseen ego and launch the next rock'n'roll guitar hero on to the world stage.

*

On the day of the show, we arrived at Fairholt early before doors opened. The contestants for the talent show were a motley assortment of wannabes – singers, magicians, comedians, jugglers, hypnotists – all delusional amateurs. Victory would be a formality. We just needed to get through the song with no mistakes and the £100 would be ours. There was one other band on the line-up which was a bit annoying. I didn't want them stealing our thunder, but on the bright side, we could borrow their drummer if we bought him a couple of pints. He didn't seem bothered about learning our song beforehand and waved away our concerns. This wasn't ideal, but it was better than nothing. He just needed to keep a steady 4/4 beat and we would do the rest.

Of slight concern was that members of the rugby club had been in the bar drinking since midday and to say they were getting rowdy was putting it mildly. Darker drinking rituals had started including chanting and the singing of 'Sweet Chariot'. Another song about a Zulu Warrior accompanied the consumption of various bodily fluids.

'Down in one you Zulu Warrior.
Down in one you Zulu Chief, Chief! Chief! Chief! Chief!'

It was strange, this desire to drink other people's bodily fluids. Downing a pint of someone else's urine was deemed entry-level child's play. As you climbed the pecking order, pints of vomit and other unspeakable things were happily consumed. Rugby players sure were a strange breed. Was it a symptom of cumulative head injuries? Or maybe they just liked the taste and wanted the affirmation of friends? I could relate to that – the Three As – affirmation, applause and admiration. Whatever the psychology of the room, the scene was making Stu very nervous. He was a distracted presence in the dressing room muttering about lambs to slaughter and lions' dens.

The union bar began to fill up with other students and at last, the talent competition could begin. A compère in a lame gold suit and silly wig revved the audience up with a few jokes. Not that they needed revving up. They were nearing peak rowdiness. We were due on stage about halfway through the evening and could use that energy. Perfect slot. Backstage, Stu was shaking like a leaf. I had to admit I felt a few nerves and the reception was quite hostile for the other contestants, but I was confident we could win them over.

Eventually, it was our turn. The Pointy Birds bounded onto the stage for their debut performance. It would become legendary; those lucky enough to be in attendance could brag about being there for the rest of their lives. Even I would recall this moment as pivotal when I wrote my memoir. I felt the heat of the spotlights and the energy of the audience. They were out there beyond the bright lights, assessing us, curious. We couldn't see them, but we could feel their presence. An unseen monster – sniffing us out of curiosity. We could not betray fear, this moment was crucial. If they sensed blood, we were for it.

I picked up my guitar and gave it a strum. No sound. Shit. Marcus pointed out that I hadn't plugged it in. A few sniggers from the unseen monster. The three of us stood in a row. We had decided to wear suits which suddenly felt ill-advised. Stu looked very nervous. He was giving the game away. I strummed my guitar again. It was horribly out of tune. Damn, how had that happened? Oh well, too late now. Our makeshift drummer sat behind the stool and looked at us for instructions.

'How fast is this song?' he asked.

'Can you do a kind of slow sexy groove?'

'No, mate. I only do punk rock.'

That was annoying. He could have mentioned that.

Without further ado, the drummer counted us in and started playing a beat that was far too fast for our chosen song. We did our best to keep up. We had decided to play 'Slide Inside' – a two-chord groove over which Stu laid a sleazy riff. I was particularly proud of the fact the two words rhymed. But as these two words slipped out of my mouth, I felt something whizz by my ears.

I wasn't sure what it was and continued trying to keep up with the drummer. He was playing far too fast, and the guitars sounded like cats being strangled. And not in a good way. Being out of tune or out of time with each other would have been one thing, but we each seemed to be playing different songs. I felt something whizz past me again. It was a plastic pint of beer. Or at least I hoped it was beer. Marcus was doing his best to keep to the rhythm but was having trouble multitasking – staring at the drummer, standing up and playing the right notes in the correct sequence. Stu had gone off-piste, and with his eyes closed was playing rather complicated Iranian guitar scales which, although impressive in their own right, had nothing to do with the song. The drummer continued with his eyes closed, oblivious to what we were playing.

I noticed two of my strings had broken. I decided to keep going, aware that it wouldn't make much difference. In any case, I didn't know how to re-string a guitar. Another pint whizzed past my ears. Shortly after that, a pint of warm lager hit Marcus and was followed by a big cheer. We kept playing. The rugby club had decided the four band members were the human equivalent of a coconut shy. Knock the coconut off its holder, win a prize. That wasn't our intention, but at least we were bringing merriment to proceedings, which might get us some points and a chance at that first prize. The crowd was really into the game and Marcus seemed to be the coconut in everyone's sights. He decided to do something about it, but having a stand-up argument on stage with the audience, although brave, was unlikely to be persuasive – quite the opposite. The drummer continued to play until a full pint hit him in the face, at which point he quite literally upped sticks and left the stage. Sensing defeat, and a potential visit to Accident and Emergency, we followed.

As we collected our thoughts (and guitars) backstage, I reflected on how quickly the audience decided we were rubbish. It took about ten seconds before pints started flying, and in total, we had barely lasted a minute on stage. Stu was distraught. There was no coming back from this, he said. I agreed there was work to be done, but it was a mere hiccup, a tiny bump in the road. As Yazz and the Plastic Population had sung in their chart-topper: 'The Only Way Was Up'. And although I was disappointed we hadn't won the competition, it had been sixty of the most exhilarating seconds of my life, and I wanted more.

7.3

Following this brief and possibly premature outing as a band, flying pints of warm beer and urine disturbed Stu's sleep. But soon, with some love and cajolement, he was ready to go again. He even saw the funny side. After all, as we kept telling Stu, what didn't kill you made you stronger. It was all part of life's rich tapestry, a purchase in the shop of experience. It would be our road of excess AND palace of wisdom.

We spent quality time jamming in my bedroom, and slowly, we improved. Tuning was still an issue, but at least we could now play standing up. We could also run through most songs from the beginning to the end without stopping. And on Stu's recommendation, we learned some cover versions to help us understand the structure and chord progressions behind 'well-written' songs. Although I was only really interested in playing songs I had written, this seemed a sensible move. I was determined to prove to Stu that The Pointy Birds could become a club worthy of his membership.

Two key developments helped me. Firstly, we found a drummer. And a good one. Paul may not have been much taller than his drum stool, but he made the drum kit sound like a musical instrument – he played the drums rather than just hit them. He also had Keith Moon facial expressions and drum roll to match. Marcus had snagged Paul at his new part-time job stacking shelves at Sainsbury's. Where Stu brought musicality, Paul tightened our testicles and gave us rhythm and a beat. Paul was also boundlessly validating. Everything we played was 'absolutely brilliant', suggesting that he might not have the most discerning critical faculties. Nonetheless, our new drummer provided a much-needed counterbalance to Stu's less positive take on things.

The second positive development was that, unbeknownst to us, we had picked up some fans. These fans were not who we had expected, or people we would have chosen, but we had to start somewhere and so we eagerly accepted the invitation to play a house party hosted by members of the rugby club. They had enjoyed our performance at the talent show so much they wanted to see us again. Stu was concerned that this was just a ruse.

'Are they not just going to throw glasses at us again?'

'No way. They're fans. And anyway, let's show them we can play.' Even though Stu's brow furrowed, he couldn't deny we were better now, especially with the addition of Paul. Plus, he knew he had to conquer his shyness.

We filled our set with cover versions and crowd-pleasers like Pink Floyd's 'Another Brick in The Wall' (Stu could play the Dave Gilmour solo), The Monkees' 'Stepping Stone', and 'Wild Thing' by The Troggs mixed with more discerning choices like The Velvet Underground's 'What Goes On' and The Pixies' 'Where is My Mind?'. Our versions were not that faithful to the originals, but in front of a sea of drunken faces at a quarter past midnight in a packed living room in north-west London just off the north circular, we took to the stage (not that there was a stage) and with the immortal line 'We don't need no education…' our rugby-playing fanbase kept hold of their pint glasses and broke into song.

Although our audience couldn't hear Stu's solo that he had practised so hard, or indeed much of anything we were playing, it didn't matter. There was a beat, and they knew the words to the songs, and that was all that mattered. Not a glass was lobbed. From the stage, we couldn't hear a thing either, and when Stu was caught eating a pork pie unaware we were mid-way through a song, the pork pie-eating guitar solo became incorporated into future sets. Our set ended with Paul falling through his drum kit following one too many drinks. That became a thing too. The reception from our fanbase was unambiguous and uproarious. They wanted more. 'Brick In The Wall' was a particular success and we performed it three times in a row. Our fans didn't want it to end, and neither did we. We could happily file our second gig in the huge success column, and we left the party not only as living legends but with a swollen fanbase, the size of which was enough to make up an entire rugby team.

8. The Major Years

SUMMER–AUTUMN 1990

Some important discoveries as a student of politics and then the discovery of some essential accessories in Camden as a student of rock'n'roll.

We settled happily into our life in Golders Green, and now with a successful gig in the bag and a proper line-up, I decided it was a good idea to show my face at City Poly. I needed to do the requisite amount of work to pass the end-of-year exams allowing me to avoid the boot. Getting thrown out would derail our nascent band and subsequent plans for world domination.

There was a pleasant novelty in attending lectures and seminars. I got to understand different political systems and the complexities of global conflicts. Things that on the surface seemed wrong had been made complicated by compromise (or compromised by complications). I was shocked to find out that there were quite a few skeletons in the UK's closet. And America was a complete basket case. Not the Disney world of wonder I had grown up thinking it was. Even democracy wasn't all that. The more I learned, the more I realised how little I knew.

Through osmosis, I started to learn about different political systems, although as soon as we drilled into any details on policy or constitutions, I zoned out. It didn't capture my imagination. I preferred the big picture and broad brush strokes. Pretty soon I found myself on sit-ins and marches not too aware of exactly what we were protesting but enjoying the atmosphere and the camaraderie of people power. Mind you, I still hated the jugglers, especially the smug ones. I also drew the line at calling the Metropolitan Police fascist pigs. Having spent my teenage years in leafy Sussex, there never seemed to be the need to refer to local constable Ken as a farmyard animal, even a right-wing one. But here in the capital, to lots of my fellow undergraduates, 'the met' were an enemy of the people.

I also learned all about beardy philosophers like Plato, Aristotle and Socrates. Well, I assumed they had beards – talking of hair, one nugget of information that captured my imagination was a technique to remember how the USSR picked Soviet leaders. They alternated between having hair and then no hair. It started with Vladimir Lenin in 1917, who was a baldy-coot. Joseph Stalin took over in 1924 with a full head of hair. Then along came Nikita Khrushchev in 1953, completely bald. His replacement was Leonid Brezhnev who ruled from 1964 for eighteen years with a thick black main. Next came the follicly challenged Yuri Andropov for two years from 1982 to 1984. His successor was Konstantin Chernenko, who for just one year ruled with a mop of blond hair until Mikhail Gorbachev shook things up in 1985 with glasnost, perestroika and his infamous bird-splattered chrome dome. This recital, along with various rabbit jokes, were to become the legacies of my education as a political scientist.

It was an exciting time to study politics and funny how this new decade seemed to precipitate the collapse of things – the Soviet Union, the Berlin Wall and soon the wicked witch of the west, Margaret Thatcher. In our third and final year, she was stabbed in the back, Julius Caesar style, with reference to a broken cricket bat by members of her party and replaced by someone called John Major. He had grown up in Brixton and had something to do with the circus. Major clearly wasn't going to last long as the Labour Party were miles ahead in the polls, and with their leader Neil Kinnock's rousing speeches capturing the public's hearts it was only a matter of time before he stood waving outside number 10.

But for now, these were the Major Years. And in the summer of 1990, I turned 21, so these were to be major years for me too. A new decade, a new prime minister and the start of being a proper adult. Not that I felt any different or more grown-up. The conventional route of careers and mortgages and responsibilities were not on my radar. My radar had more essential considerations like locating full-length mirrors to reflect on my air-guitar with a hairbrush microphone, arranging interviews with myself and attending feet first at Camden Palace on a Tuesday night.

8.2

Although Golders Green was our base, increasingly our stomping ground was Camden – just four stops southbound on the Northern line. My first impression of Camden had been one slight disappointment – random shops on a grimey high street. And not very nice ones – leather coat shops, tattoo parlours and Irish pubs, but if you wanted anything to do with music this was the place to be. Everyone looked like they were in a band or wanted to be in a band or liked going to see bands. It was fun aimlessly wandering around Camden Market, soaking up the atmosphere like we were in a big playground or film set, and although it was grotty and smelly, I wouldn't want to be anywhere else. The song 'Right Here Right Now' by electro-indie band Jesus Jones with the immortal line '*there is no other place I wanna be*' captured how I felt.

And it was a natural place to ponder and daydream about impending success. I knew that fame and fortune was imminent. No one here in this market knew me, but pretty soon people would be whispering and glancing at me, requesting an autograph. There would inevitably come a time when I would have to stop coming to Camden, and that would be a shame as I would miss the place, but it was worth the sacrifice. I could always try to hide my famous face behind sunglasses and a baseball cap if need be. Plus, there would be days when I wouldn't mind being recognised. This intoxicating seductive dream of fame always beckoning me with the promise of the big time. I couldn't see it, touch it, feel it – but it was ever-present in the background like the silent hum of electricity.

Around each corner were new opportunities for my rockstar fantasies. If I ran up an escalator on the Tube I didn't appear onto a busy street, but in front of my adoring masses on stage at Wembley. The donning of the guitar. The quick check with onstage monitor engineers and the rest of bandmates. Everyone ready to rock? We'd launch into that first song, the fan favourite that would send the place berserk – moshing, crowd-surfing, stage-jumping. Then, after the intro, the first line of the vocals to drive people into delirium. Oh! To spread love and joy through song, was there a more noble aim? OK, maybe helping refugees or being a nurse, but people needed a break from the woes of life too. That was the job of us artists and musicians.

But there was a vital piece of clothing I needed to complete the look. We couldn't expect others to take us seriously as rockstars unless we looked the part. That's when I saw it hanging up outside a stall at Camden Market calling my name – a leather jacket. As soon as I tried it on, I knew it was for me. It fit like Cinderella's slipper and I felt the power of transformation. I knew by the appreciative nods from the guy running the market stall that it was genuine admiration, not just a 'suits you, sir' to make the sale. The time was ripe for the next Jim Morrison – but with jokes rather than impenetrable poetry. And without the early exit at age 27.

I also bought a Dunlop Cry Baby Wah Pedal, the kind Jimi Hendrix used, and a harmonica. I didn't know how to play the harp or use the pedal, but that didn't matter. Meanwhile Marcus bought some glasses. Not that he needed them. But Marcus explained that these glasses were just frames. They didn't contain lenses. He was pleased as they gave him a studious look. I agreed it worked as a nice complement to my leathers. And then, at last, the day came, the arms race was over, both Marcus and I had hair long enough to tie back into a ponytail. There was no more excellent feeling than leaving our flat and strutting up Golders Green High Street towards the Tube in our new clobber with flowing locks. We quite simply rocked.

9. The White Horse

FEBRUARY 1991

A first live booking in a music venue is compromised by a force majeure.

It was time to play a proper gig on a proper stage in a proper venue playing our own songs. I rang The White Horse pub in South End Green, near Hampstead Heath, and told the music promoter we could bring a massive crowd. On the strength of this claim, rather than the sound of our non-existent demo tape, the promoter offered us a date. A bit surprisingly, we were given the headline slot. Little did we know headlining the first Monday in February was the graveyard of all graveyard slots.

The venue ran a 'pay to play' policy, a much-frowned-upon industry practice that moved the financial risk of the night from the promoter to the artist. The upshot was the music promoter might turn a blind eye to the standard of music if the band guaranteed a big audience. The artist had to buy a bunch of tickets from the venue and sold these on to their fans. Bands willing to buy tickets for a wet and windy Monday night in early February were like gold dust. The music promoter told me he would sell each ticket to us for £3, and we could sell on for whatever price we wanted and make a profit.

It sounded like a fair deal. I agreed to buy fifty, which covered his costs, and a few days later, a contract arrived in the post detailing all the vital information – including load-in and soundcheck times. We'd be on stage at 10.15 p.m. to play a thirty-minute set. The venue capacity was officially eighty, but the promoter had told me on the phone in a slightly hushed tone we could ignore that bit and could get 120 in. Not only were we now officially a proper band, but if we could sell all those tickets, we would also be in the money.

The venue itself was a dark and dingy room down some spiral stairs beneath the main pub. A rich history of bands had played and gone to bigger, brighter and better things. And it had that smell. That glorious smell of the night before and many nights before that. The ghosts of bands past. A concoction of blood, sweat, tears, piss, cigarettes, vomit, mould and bleach. I breathed it in deep. Was there any better smell than one of hopes and dreams? People could keep their fresh-cut grass or summer meadows or chicken stock. The grotty smell of irresponsibility was what it was all about. If that didn't stir your loins, then you were in the wrong business.

We lugged our amps and instruments into the cave and I made a beeline for the sound engineer. I had heard it was important to get them onside so they went that extra mile to give you a good sound. I remembered some advice about making the right first impression from when I went for an interview at the local Sainsbury's in Crowborough: look the manager firmly in the eye when you spoke to them. That interview had been a triumph and so I prepared to revive the first-impression stare.

The sound engineer was busy setting up mic stands and unravelling leads. He didn't seem in the best of moods. Nor did he have the rosiest of complexions – probably didn't see much daylight being locked away underground in dark venues. He could do with some fruit and fibre, and perhaps some skin moisturiser. I shook his hand and introduced myself with a wink.

'Hi, it's Andy, lead singer from The Pointy Birds. We are the headliners.'

It felt so great to say the word *headliners*. The sound engineer looked at his watch. He didn't seem that excited or impressed to have met me.

'Better late than never. Line-up?'

'What, in a row?'

'No, what is your line-up?'

'Oh, right, it's me, Marcus, Stu and Paul…'

'Don't forget Ringo,' yelled Marcus from the stage. We exchanged winks.

The engineer sighed impatiently.

'No, what is the line-up? How many vocals, what instruments?'

'Oh, right,' I giggled. 'Sorry, I'm new to this. Um, one vocal, two guitars, bass and drums.'

'Good, that makes my job easier. Last night I had a nine-piece string section with four-part vocal harmonies. Fucking nightmare.'

'Oh,' I said.

'What side of the stage is bass?'

I hadn't thought this through. 'Marcus, do you want to go on the left or the right of the stage?'

'Surely you know I'm left of centre.'

I laughed in admiration at his politically tinged gag and fired an imaginary pistol at him followed by a wink at the engineer. The wink was not returned. He obviously lacked a sense of humour. We started unpacking our gear and setting up. The engineer began by sound checking the drums. He placed microphones around the kit and then commanded Paul to hit a requisite piece of the drum kit to get the sound levels right in the speakers.

'Snare…'

Paul hit the snare drum on repeat, and the sound boomed out of the speakers like a particularly noisy neighbour hammering on the wall. Eventually, the engineer told him to stop, or rather yelled at him to stop several times before Paul heard his instructions over the sound of the snare.

Eventually, Paul was asked to play the full kit. It sounded huge. We all nodded along to the beat, waiting for our turn. Marcus was next. His bass rumbled ominously through the monitors, and then Stu played some guitar riffs. We were Concorde getting filled with petrol ready for take-off. At last, it was my turn. I plugged in my guitar and awaited my instructions.

'Rhythm guitar.'

I strummed some random chords and hearing them amplified through the speakers and monitors sent a thrill through me – the sound of a dream turning into reality. It also made me realise I was limited in what I could play. The engineer barked his next command.

'OK, vocals.'

I cleared my throat. 'Testing. One. Two. One. Two.'

'Can you sing something?'

'Gosh, OK, um… I suppose I could sing "Married To A Squirrel?"'

'No,' blurted Stu. 'You can't sing *that*. In public.'

A look of anguish swept across his face. 'Why not?'

'I thought we were doing covers?'

'No way, we got to play our own stuff.'

'Can you hurry up and sing something,' barked the engineer.

I ignored Stu, cleared my throat and started to sing the first verse of "Married To A Squirrel".'

'I had a Sunday roast, and I was feeling full.
I went for a walk. It's always the rule.
Kicking through the leaves and breathing fresh air
feeling the wind blowing through my hair…'

'OK, stop,' shouted the engineer.

I stopped, a bit relieved. Singing solo felt a bit like being naked. The engineer spoke:

'Is that how you are *actually* going to sing?'

'Um, no, probs a bit louder.'

'OK, can you give it some welly then?'

I looked at the rest of the band. From behind the drum kit, Paul gave me a double thumbs up. He was raring to go, grinning as ever from ear to ear. Marcus gave me an encouraging wink – he was raring to go too. I looked at Stu. He wasn't raring to go. He had sat down on his amp and was staring at the floor, shaking his head. I started to sing the second verse and could feel my confidence growing, helped by Marcus nodding and singing along.

'I looked up above and saw an oak tree,
And there was a squirrel just-a-staring at me.
What should I do and what should I say
Would this rodent make my blues go away?'

The engineer raised his hand, signalling me to stop again.

'Can we have the whole band, please?'

This was it – the chance to play through the song. Although no one was in the room other than the engineer, I suddenly felt very nervous. We needed to impress him. He knew people who knew people.

'Just keep going,' said Marcus. 'We'll join in.'

I started to strum as Paul kicked in on drums, and Marcus introduced his bass line and then right on cue, if a little reluctantly, the sound of Stu's Jimi Hendrix-esque guitar riff which sounded uncannily like a squirrel. The plane had taken off, and it felt magical. As we played, someone came down the spiral stairs. It was a man in his thirties or forties with thinning hair wearing skinny black jeans and Dr. Martens. He acknowledged the engineer and stood in the room watching us. He was carrying a tube of posters in one hand and holding some Blu-Tack in the other. Badges of CND and The Fall adorned his jacket – it had to be the music promoter. He was the personification of indie. I felt my heart quicken – our audience had doubled to two. I decided to put some extra welly into the vocals.

'I made the first move and asked the squirrel its name.
But it just ignored me, so I played the game.
I winked a few times and licked my lips.
And to my surprise, the squirrel wiggled its hips.
So I climbed up the tree to be polite
and pretty soon I was asked to stay the night.
Its fur was soft, and its teeth were bucked,
and this is the song about the squirrel I…'

'STOP,' shouted the sound engineer.

There was a long pause. Had he heard enough? Or did he share some of Stu's needless concerns about the lyrics? The promoter's poker face was giving nothing away, if anything, I detected a slight look of concern. Eventually, the engineer spoke.

'How is the level in the monitors?'

'Sounds amazing to me,' said Marcus. We all nodded.

'Please can I have some more vocals in my monitors?' said Paul. He was the only one who had done this before. This was a chance for the engineer to tweak the sound levels on stage through a series of onstage monitors. Each member of the band had their own monitor through which they could request an increase or decrease in volume of themselves or a different member of the group. Invariably, the drummer might require more bass, and the singer might need more vocals so they could hear themselves.

The engineer also had to get the levels sounding right 'front of house' so the audience could hear each band member equally. Adjusting these levels was a science in itself. The received wisdom was that the better the songs and musicianship of the band, the less work the engineer had to do. If the songs were well-written and arranged, the band could create these dynamics on stage through the performance and the engineer could keep everything level on the desk. However, for novice bands starting out, the tendency was for all band members to play continuously through every song like young kids chasing a football around, no positions, no passing, greedy for the ball. This was a nightmare for the engineer, creating feedback and a wall of noise. I feared we belonged to the latter group.

'OK, one last verse and then you're done.'

Stu sighed and started the squirrel riff. The drums kicked in, and Concorde took off again. It was the last verse, so I decided to go for it. It may have been an audience of two, but it was an influential audience of two.

'Pretty soon the love started to drain.
We couldn't even talk, and that was a pain.
It didn't like my friends. I didn't like its
And anyway, the squirrel didn't have a very nice personality…'

The promoter lifted a Roger Moore eyebrow. I couldn't tell if it was complimentary or not, but one of his feet were tapping, so that was a good sign. But halfway through the final verse, he went back up the spiral stairs, not staying to listen to the rest of the song. I felt a bit disappointed but consoled myself that he probably had important pre-show stuff to do like putting up posters. He could hear the full set later.

'ENOUGH!' was the amplified instruction from behind the desk.

I jumped down off the stage, feeling jubilant. The big time awaited. It was scary that my life was going to change so soon, but there was no choice. I was fronting an exciting new band. But Stu had other thoughts.

'Do we have to play that song?'

'Yes.'

'It's so embarrassing.'

He started rubbing his eyebrows.

It hurt me that he didn't think much of my song, but there was no way we were playing only covers. Stu went to the bar in a sulk with Marcus and Paul in tow. I went outside to get some fresh air, but to my surprise and slight horror, it was snowing. And it wasn't just snowing – it was a hard, swirling blizzard. A blanket of snow covered the streets. My heart sunk. It would adversely affect audience turnout. We had sold fifty tickets in advance, covering venue costs and were expecting another fifty on the door – our profit! The snow had even coated the chalkboard outside the venue advertising the gig. I brushed it off to reveal our name and the gig details:

TONIGHT LIVE MUSIC
The Pointy Birds
+ Bum Gravy
Doors 8 p.m. £5

But the cruel, indifferent snowflakes kept falling, once again obscuring our name. I looked up and down the deserted streets and cursed. People were more concerned about getting home. The more the snow fell, the more I realised we might be giving a lot of refunds. Maybe this gig wasn't going to be quite the money-spinner I'd hoped. I decided to go and find the others. They had congregated around a table in the pub by a log fire with a round of drinks. It looked like they were settling in for the night. Although I had promised myself not to drink, I could feel the siren call of alcohol beckoning me. It was fun to be among friends in a disaster situation. And the drinks looked so innocent and inviting. There was little else to do but drink and be merry and wait for our call. I ordered a pint and joined them as the snowflakes danced and swirled outside the bay window of the pub.

It wasn't long before news came in that the support band had cancelled following reports of closed roads. Trains and Tubes were not running. By 7.30 p.m. the doors to the venue downstairs had opened, but it was clear there would be no audience. London had officially ground to a halt. South End Green was a ghost town – only a fool would set out to see a gig. The final nail was when we saw someone ski past the venue. We had to face facts. It would be just us, the promoter and the engineer. At least it was a chance to impress the music promoter. He would know people. And playing to one person was the same as playing to thousands. Scratch that, it was much more difficult – especially if you were hammered. As I ordered another round at the bar, the thought occurred that we might be getting a little too drunk to play.

The music promoter appeared and got busy putting up some new posters for upcoming gigs. It was slightly rude he hadn't introduced himself, but he now came over to our table. In contrast to the high spirits of our table, he was stony-faced. Maybe he was facing financial ruin. I decided to ingratiate myself by keeping eye contact but was aware my vision was getting a bit blurred due to the drinks. He cut straight to the chase.

'You The Pointy Birds? I think you may as well go on now and then we can all get an early night.'

'What now? But we have advertised for a 10.15 start.'

The promoter gave me a stern look. 'I would pull the night, but as you have turned up, it's either you play now or not at all.'

There was a brief pause as we considered our options. The rest of the band looked like they had forgotten there was a gig to play. I decided we needed to keep in his good books. Annoyingly, I could feel my words slur.

'OK, we'll be down in five minutes.'

I left the others to finish their drinks. I needed to collect my thoughts. I climbed down the spiral stairs to the venue. Red lights basked the stage and no one was about. This gave me a few precious private moments with myself, the stage and my destiny. I breathed it in. It starts here, I thought. What a shame no one would be here to witness what we were about to do. I was a bit concerned the levels of alcohol in our bloodstream might adversely affect our timing, coordination and ability to remember chord sequences or to play while standing, but I put those fears to one side. We needed to focus and deliver a seminal gig. My moment alone was interrupted by the engineer. He was covered in snow and carrying a plastic bag. He sat down at the sound desk, pulled out a can of Diet Coke, snapped it open and then unwrapped a massive kebab.

I approached him gingerly, not sure whether to interrupt or inform him we had been told to get on stage, but I was distracted by the sight of his kebab. To my drunken eyes, it looked delicious as steam rose from the freshly baked pitta bread and thick slabs of hot salty meat covered in onions and sliced red cabbage. He had gone for the lot – plus chilli and garlic sauce. And pickles. This was a greedy pig after my own heart. I felt my mouth salivate and tummy rumble and realised I hadn't eaten.

'Are you staring at my kebab?'

'What?'

'I don't like people eyeing up my food, OK?'

God, he was a bit overprotective. He must have had a bad experience in the past. Still, it wouldn't hurt to give me a bite. Sharing is caring and all that. And it might soak up some of this booze. He gave me another stare, like a dog growling about to bite. I shook these thoughts away and remembered the task in hand.

'Sorry to interrupt your *meal*, but the promoter said we were to go on now.'

'Ready when you are, mate,' he said with his mouth full. 'Let's get this over with – you got thirty minutes max.'

He swished his food down with a glug of Coke, belched and then took another big mouthful. Unctuous juices dribbled down his chin. I was transfixed but decided to move on before I got bitten. I made a mental note to get one later and went to fetch the others.

I could hear shrieks and laughter up the spiral stairs and found the others outside having a drunken snowball fight. We needed to get sober. We needed to focus on the mission ahead, but as my bandmates clambered down the stairs covered in snow, I sensed that this might be easier said than done. The dark surroundings somehow made the alcohol levels more pronounced. My fears were not allayed by the sight of Stu carrying four more pints for himself to the stage. Paul was slurring his words and having trouble staying vertical. Marcus had a pre-vomit look. This gig was going to be interesting.

Although the alcohol might not be compatible with timing or tuning or musicality, I realised it would be perfect for the inter-song banter. I felt a surge of confidence. We could do this. A voice came through the loudspeakers barking orders for us to hurry the fuck up. We got on stage and assembled into position. The stage lights were turned up. We weren't completely ready, but it seemed like it was time to start. I looked over at the sound desk to get the thumbs up, but the engineer was ensconced in his doner. I went up to the mic and tapped it.

'Testing, testing.'

Feedback squealed, which briefly distracted him from his feast, and he adjusted the levels. The mic was now ready. The rest of the guys had donned their instruments. The music promoter had set up a table at the bottom of the spiral stairs with his cashbox and a door stamp. There was still no sign of any punters. He sat on a chair with his back to us. A bit rude. They were going to be a tough audience.

Marcus introduced the first song with his bassline, followed by a drum roll and immediately we fell into the seductive charm of blues jam 'Pube On My Lip'. It was a simple 12-bar progression. It allowed us to relax, introduce the band and show off a few musical skills. I let the music breathe before stepping up to the mic.

'Hi, we're The Pointy Birds. Great to be here in London Town. Let me introduce you to the band…'

I was surprised by how good we were sounding.

'Tonight on drums we have Paul, let's hear it for Paul….'

Paul went for his signature drum roll. It went on a bit longer than usual, and he dropped his sticks briefly, but in the scheme of things what did that matter? It was funny how alcohol could give you a big-picture view of life, quite a healthy perspective. Paul finished his drumroll. There wasn't much in the way of applause, but I carried on regardless. I would win our audience over.

'On the bass guitar, the one and only Marcus 'Fingers'…'

Marcus's fingers went for a bit of a stroll up the bass, but he seemed to get lost en-route and had trouble getting back. Stu started laughing. Eventually, Marcus's fingers returned from their walk. Paul dropped his drumsticks again.

Silence.

'And on lead guitar is blues jazzman extraordinaire Stuart.'

Stu broke into a solo. He had lost all inhibitions and decided to improvise. It sounded amazing. Maybe alcohol was a good idea? I decided it was time to sing. My every line was echoed by Stu in an American preacher man drawl begging for answers.

Me: 'Woke up this morning.'

Stu: 'Did you? Tell me more.'

Me: 'Yeah, and I fancied a dip.'

Stu: 'A dip?'

Me: 'Yeah, that's right. So I strolled to the mirror.'

Stu: 'You strolled to the mirror, you say?'

Me: 'Yeah, and I found a pube on my lip.'

We broke off with some guitar work to let this news digest with our audience. We soon returned for verse two.

Me: 'How did it get there?'

Stu: 'Yeah, how did the pube get there, man?'

Me: 'Oh, mother, please tell me so.'

Stu: 'Yeah, come on, Mum, spill the beans.'

Me: 'Was it when we went rolling around in the snow?'

The big reveal. And topical too, what with it snowing outside. I motioned to the weather outside and then it was time for another guitar solo.

'Take it away, Stu...'

I looked over at the desk. Annoyingly, the engineer was still engrossed in his kebab. How big was that kebab? The promoter still had his back to us. They were going to be a tough nut to crack.

'Pube On My Lip' came to an end and was greeted with a deathly silence. I would have to try a different tact. Warm them up with a bit of comedy.

'So, this bloke walks into a newsagent and says, "I'd like a packet of helicopter-flavoured crisps, please".'

I left the joke hanging for a bit. It was all in the timing,

'And the guy behind the counter says, "Sorry, sir, we only do plane".'

On cue, Paul came in with the comedy drum and then a smash of the cymbals.

Not a titter. But at least the engineer had finished his kebab. He scrunched up the paper wrapping, and we could hear the sound of it hitting the bin, followed by a belch. The promoter still had his back to us. He could at least turn around.

'Come on, let's get on with it,' snapped Marcus under his breathe.

The combination of alcohol and musical imperatives had got to him. Maybe he was a bit dehydrated or considering the deficit between the dream I had promised and the humiliating reality of our current situation. Meanwhile, Stu and Paul had downed another pint each. I was starting to feel a bit discouraged, but halfway through the song, a magical thing happened. Some snowy shoes appeared on the spiral stairs. It was Ben and Doug from the rugby club. They had trekked across London in a blizzard to see us. This was real dedication. Statistically, the audience had doubled.

It was time for 'The Bourbon Man', but my guitar was horribly out of tune. I still hadn't mastered the act of tuning up. It turned out it wasn't just about being in tune with yourself, you needed to be in tune with the other instruments too. During rehearsals, only Stu had the skills for this task, but he currently didn't seem to be in a fit state.

'Oh, fuck it, it'll be fine,' he said.

Impressing the music promoter was not on his list of priorities. Downing another pint was. I decided to abandon the guitar. Less was more, and I could dedicate myself to the performance.

'This one is for Ben and Dougy.'

At last, we got a cheer. The worm was turning. 'The Bourbon Man' told the story of a henpecked and emasculated man who 'pushes peas around his dinner plate' as he dreams of another life. The verse contained a sequence of sad minor chords as the melody described his humdrum world. Then the drums and bass kicked in for the chorus with Stu jumping up and down and screaming like Henry Rollins for silk sheets and a bourbon on the rocks. The song had a quiet-loud dynamic. It was a bit Pixies and a bit silly, but when Stu went to the mic and started screaming he, at last, grabbed our audience's attention.

We motored through the rest of the set. We were not in tune or in time or even playing the same song. Paul kept dropping his drumsticks, and Stu fell off the side of the stage. Twice. But Ben and Doug kept tapping their feet. And we had managed to get the attention of the promoter. We came off stage feeling pretty pleased with our work. It had been hairy, but we had got through it. What didn't kill you made you stronger.

It was time to pack up and figure out how we were going to get home. The promoter seemed a bit less stony-faced. Maybe we had earned some respect for at least turning up. He was putting up more posters. I decided to ask for some honest feedback and constructive criticism.

'What did you think?'

He wasn't in the business of mincing his words. 'Staggeringly unready.'

'How do you mean?'

'Well, I don't know where to start. All the basics. At least learn how to tune a guitar. You can buy a guitar tuner from Denmark Street. And then learn how to be in tune with each other. Also, learn how to restring a guitar. Maybe bring a spare guitar. Then think about writing some decent songs and how you are going to arrange them so they sound good on stage. "Bourbon Man" had potential. You need to think about the sequencing of the songs to bring a bit of drama to the set.'

I wasn't sure how to respond. I asked if there was anything else.

'Yes, the jokes were terrible, but they were probably the high point.'

I decided to take this on the chin.

'So, can we have another gig?'

'No.'

'Right. So, no positives?'

'I quite liked that squirrel one.'

Result! That was something.

'I don't suppose there is any money?' My words trailed off.

He laughed. 'I would say you are probably the worst band I have ever booked. But that in itself is quite an achievement, so maybe you have got something.'

So, we had got something. That was the quote. The promoter at The White Horse thought we had something. It was the thinnest of thins, but it was something to build on.

It was time to call it a night. The venue allowed us to leave our gear overnight to pick it up in a taxi the next day. Ours was a short walk back to Golders Green across the heath. The snow had stopped falling, and South End Green had turned into a scene from Narnia. Our feet crunched through the virgin snow under a twinkly night sky. So peaceful and magical. On balance, I would file this gig in the success column. An away draw maybe with everything considered. We had learned a few lessons. But now we had one thing on our mind and marched with a quiet determination to our destination glowing in the distance. Thank god it was still open. The windows had steamed up, and a bell rang happily as we pushed open the door. A large man greeted me with a big smile and asked what I wanted.

'A large doner kebab, please, with all the trimmings.'

10. Ninja Landlord

MARCH 1991

An explanation of the music meets comedy USP. A surprise new addition to the band solves a few issues and proves a hit with the audience.

The received wisdom was that being in a band was about making music, not comedy. But I didn't see why we couldn't offer both. After all, I had the mic, and there was a window for some light entertainment in between the songs. I even thought about turning the inter-song banter into the main event. It was feasible we could flip things and have inter-comedy music. No one was doing that. Maybe for a good reason. Kahlil Gibran had argued in his book *The Prophet* that 'passion and reason were the rudder and sails of our seafaring soul, and if either got broken we would toss and drift…' Well, to extend the water-based metaphor, if we were to combine music and comedy successfully, they needed to be in happy unison like two oars on a boat; otherwise, we would go around in circles.

And following The White Horse gig, I was aware that musically The Pointy Birds needed some work. I couldn't deny the words of the promoter had stung a bit. But at least we couldn't get worse. I had to remember the Three-Hurdle Theory – work out what you want to do; work out if you can do it; and then do it. We were negotiating the second hurdle. Having a grand vision for The Pointy Birds was not enough; we needed to fine-tune the details and the guitars. I bought a tuner and learned how to restring a guitar in double-quick time. We needed to learn the tricks of the trade and fast. It would be difficult to get any more gigs until we conquered how to play in tune.

Also, one thing gnawing away at me was that we needed all members of the band dedicated to the cause and Stu, for all his prodigious talent, wasn't taking the group that seriously. With his initial fear of the stage now gone, the gigs had become a chance for him to get pissed and have a jolly. That was all well and good, but I needed to pull the reins. It would be impossible to improve musically if the only talented member of the band was utterly drunk before going on stage.

But I knew now was not the time to ask Stu to take The Pointy Birds seriously. He would have died from laughter, like Monty Python's sketch about the funniest joke in the world used to kill people during the war. Instead, I determined the band should improve and prove to Stu we were worthy of his guitar-playing prowess. When we returned to The White Horse, we could blow that promoter's indie socks off. But for all my good intentions to get more professional, the next piece of the jigsaw took us in the opposite direction and tipped Stu over the edge.

10.2

Our flat in Golders Green was above a hairdressing salon run by a 20-something French dude called Vincent, who doubled up as the agent for the landlord. As we were soon to find out, he tripled, or maybe even quadrupled, up at other things too. He popped up to collect the rent each Wednesday evening, and as landlord agents went, we had fallen on our feet. Contrary to the usual rules and regulations for tenants to keep the noise down for fear of disturbing the neighbours, Vincent wanted us to turn our guitars up. He had an enthusiasm and love for our band that knew no bounds.

'I love hearing you English pig-dogs play rock'n'roll while I am cutting ze hair.'

Or

'I love Ze Pointy Birds. You are going to be so huge, man. Ze biggest band in ze world.'

We had found a fan, and it was nice to feel the love. But in return for not complaining about the noise we were making, he wanted to hang around the flat after work. There was another condition: Vincent had set his sights on joining the band. He fancied himself a bass guitarist.

'You guys teach me how to play ze bass guitar, and you can turn ze amps to fucking eleven...'

Although there was nothing wrong with a bit of healthy competition, I could feel Marcus bristling at the idea of someone moving in on his patch. Especially as within weeks Vincent had mastered some of the hardest Red Hot Chilli Peppers' slap baselines known to man. No mean feat. Something neither Marcus nor I could play. Within a few weeks, there was little we could teach him. He started showing us.

It was hard to know if Vincent was oblivious to the fact that The Pointy Birds already had a bass player, or if he was playing a sly game hoping to oust Marcus by stealth. Understandably, Marcus felt a bit threatened and called me to the kitchen for an emergency meeting.

'What are we going to do about him?'

'Who?'

'Vincent! He keeps eying up my bass guitar.'

I didn't say anything. It was a tricky biscuit of a situation. Clearly, there was no room at the inn for another bass player, no matter how much of a natural talent he seemed to be. However, if we kicked Vincent out, he might not let us rehearse.

'He has designs,' warned Marcus.

I nodded and decided Marcus needed some reassurance.

'There is only one bass player in The Pointy Birds and his name is Marcus "Fingers" Boyland.'

Marcus smiled a thank you, but there was concern in his eyes.

'I mean, who is he? And why is he here? And what's with all the swords? He's not planning to chop us up, is he?'

'Don't be stupid.' I laughed nervously.

'Maybe he's planning to chop me up and become the bass player?'

'Calm down, Marcus, that's ridiculous…'

I looked down the long hallway from the kitchen into my bedroom. I could see Vincent sitting on my floor playing Marcus's bass. Next to him was a big black bag full of very sharp swords.

*

In addition to being a hairdresser, landlord agent and gifted musician, Vincent was also a black belt in martial arts. He carried around a big bag of swords and other weapons and loved to show off various death-defying moves, often using us as guinea pigs. It was stressful to have lethal weapons flash past our noses when it was time for bed. But more concerning was the fact that he often combined his martial arts with smoking several spliffs. While we rehearsed, Vincent sat in the corner rolling and smoking, and once his eyes were rolling back in his sockets, the swords came out. To say this was a landlord agent that disregarded health and safety was an understatement.

It was clear Vincent wasn't going anywhere. He was popping up most evenings and would often stay the night, passing out on the red sofa in my bedroom in the small hours, the stubborn glow in the dark from yet another spliff while I pretended I was asleep. We had to tread carefully. The fact he was effectively our landlord meant we didn't want to upset him. Well, a stoned landlord with sharp knives to be more precise. But his ninja skills were to provide an opportunity when one night I asked him an innocent question.

'So, does it hurt when you break bricks with your fist?'

Vincent released an incredulous laugh like he had been insulted.

'No, it never hurts. I show you how to do it.'

It was a lesson I hadn't particularly signed up for but he wasn't taking no for an answer. He unloaded his bag onto the floor. It was full of slate tiles and bricks of varying size and thickness.

'Zis is not about strength. Zis is about technique and desire. And ze power of ze mind. You imagine your fist going through this brick and it will.'

I returned an incredulous laugh like the one he had given me.

He fixed me with a stern stoned stare. 'I am not bullshitting you. You will break zis brick. Focus.'

I nodded like a naughty school kid being told off.

'I show you.'

Vincent positioned a slate tile across two bricks, sat in the lotus position, closed his eyes and took a deep breath. Seconds later his fist came down, and the tile snapped in half.

'You see? Easy. I believe. In life, you want something you must go for it. You must believe, and you can do it.'

Hey, it was my Three-Hurdle Theory manifested physically. I was inspired to give it a go. It was no longer just about breaking a brick with my fist – it was about my career. If I could do this, then we were going on to superstardom.

Vincent set up another brick. 'I want you to hit ze brick here on ze sweet spot.' He pointed at ze sweet spot. I nodded. 'And remember, your fist is not hitting it. It is slicing through it like a knife through ze butter.'

I nodded again. Was I about to pay a visit to Accident and Emergency for a broken hand? It was my guitar-strumming hand too, but there was no wriggling out of this now. He was quite forceful. Or maybe it was the stoned glare and the French accent. Plus, he was our landlord. Plus, the knives, etc.

'Close your eyes. Now visualise your fist coming down in one clean movement and slicing through this brick. Remember like a knife through ze butter.'

I opened one eye. 'Should I make a noise or say something?'

'This is up to you. But total focus. You will not break ze brick if you do not imagine it, visualise it, see it and it will happen.'

I nodded and closed my eyes, now in the darkness, I saw the brick. I visualised my fist as a weapon. I lifted my arm and felt my heart pump. Vincent whispered in my ear. 'It's all about desire. If you want it enough, you can do it.'

The three hurdles.

I clenched my fist tight, and suddenly I knew I was going to break this brick with my bare hand. It was all in my mind. If I wanted it enough, I could do it.

My fist came down, and on connecting with the surface of the tile, it snapped in half like it was a piece of balsa wood. Vincent grabbed my shoulders and shook me, laughing loudly.

'See, I tell you, you English pig-dog…'

I looked at my fist. No cuts, no bruising, no pain. What a party trick. Up there with the rabbit joke and the Soviet Presidents hair/no hair thing. All I needed was belief, focus and desire. It *was* the three hurdles manifested physically! I suddenly had an idea.

'Hey, would you up for breaking some bricks while we play at a gig?'

'Yes, but I will break ze bricks wiz my head.'

'You can break them with your head too?'

'Sure. Why not?'

'OK, that would be great. But it's not dangerous?'

'No, anyone can break bricks with their head. It is all in ze mind.'

He tapped his head. Tapped in the head all right, I thought, but we had a new member of The Pointy Birds. The idea was a beautifully elegant solution. Vincent got to join the band and Marcus no longer felt threatened. We could still rehearse as loudly as we liked and could offer audiences something new. No other bands had sword-wielding, brick-breaking landlords.

A month later, we made our return to the stage at City Poly. A year on from being bottled off the stage, we powered through our set playing songs from start to finish, without stopping. Our hair had grown, and with my leather jacket and Marcus's spectacles, we were looking the part too. We kept in tune and peppered our set with a mixture of our songs and cover versions saving the best until last.

'I'd like to welcome onto stage a special guest. From France, please give a big hand for Vincent…'

We had not rehearsed with Vincent so didn't quite know what to expect. He had just said he would do some crazy shit while we played. To his credit, Vincent had kept it a secret from the band too. In full masked black ninja outfit, he bowed and then kneeled in front of the assembled bricks we had been careful not to knock over. He piqued the curiosity of some audience members. As Paul counted us in, we hit the first chord, and I sang the opening line:

'Wild thing…'

Vincent's head smashed through the bricks producing shock and awe among our audience. But he wasn't finished there. As we played the song, he produced swords and nunchucks and made some elaborate martial arts moves so that the wild thing we were singing about had to be him. I could tell from the audience's open mouths we were on to something. The gig was our biggest success yet. The only thing that put my nose slightly out of joint was that after the gig people talked about Vincent more than the music, but still, Vincent was the landlord that kept on giving, and I would be filing this gig in the success column.

'Zis is just the beginning. You have not seen anything yet.'

I laughed nervously. What else did he have planned? At our next show, Vincent was to crank it up a whole other level.

10.3

Stu called me for a meeting in the kitchen. I thought it was to discuss the fact no one had done the washing up for over a year. The putrid smell that hung in the air was infiltrating our hair and clothes. Something somewhere had died. We also had various infestations. We should tell the landlord, although Vincent was probably responsible for most of the clutter. But Stu had something else he wanted to say.

'All right, boy, yeah, just thought I'd tell you I've decided I'm going to move out.'

The words hung in the air like the pong that surrounded us. I wasn't expecting this news. My mouth went dry.

'Really?'

I didn't know what to say. I felt annoyed, betrayed, hurt – we were meant to be The Monkees.

'OK, why?'

'Been offered a room in Bromley By Bow and finals are coming up and…'

Wow, this was real.

'…yeah, so I need to focus. A bit of peace.'

'Right…' I didn't know what to say.

'It's been fun with the band and all that…'

God, a double blow. He was quitting the band as well.

'Sure, cool, no worries.' I tried to put on a brave face but felt my bottom lip quiver. 'I thought you wanted to talk about doing the dishes.' I released a small, sad laugh – it sounded like a full stop. We looked at the leaning tower of pizza boxes.

'Yeah, what is that smell?' said Stu attempting to change the subject.

We stood in silence for too long. It felt like the end of something.

'So, when you leaving?'

'At the weekend. I can pay a month's notice.'

We left it at that, exchanged sheepish smiles and went to our bedrooms. The news had rocked me. Stu made us sound good and covered the cracks of our amateur efforts. He would be missed. I was gutted, but after the initial shock, I realised it was maybe for the best. As good as Stu was, he didn't read the *NME* and hated most indie bands. I told Marcus. He was more philosophical but he also had news.

'Yeah, maybe we need to put the Pointys on hold for a couple of months?'

I answered his question with a question. 'Why?'

Marcus started to talk about eggs and baskets. I wasn't sure what he was talking about but soon got the gist that he was having a wobble. He had had fun but now needed to focus over the next few months on getting his degree. He mentioned the eggs and baskets again. I tried to explain that the band was another basket but he was really anxious about breaking eggs. The finals were approaching and I had noticed that Marcus had been avoiding me, taking his course work a bit more seriously and even going to lectures. This was worrying. To lose one member would be a misfortune, to lose two would be carelessness. He continued to talk about eggs and baskets. Realising that the line-up of me, Paul the drummer and Vincent would not be cutting it, I switched strategies. It was time to give him a quick dose of the Three-Hurdle Speech.

Marcus gave me one of his guarded, suspicious looks that he reserved for when I was trying to lure him further. But he was too weak to resist. Plus, I had him trapped in the kitchen. There was no escape. I made it sound so doable.

Do you live to work or work to live?

What is going to happen if you stay in studying?

If we don't go out tonight, we might miss the best night of our lives.

Although in practice our nights out typically entailed rabbit jokes, six pints and doner kebabs, it was the principle. But we came to an agreement I needed to give Marcus space so he could focus on revision. We would pick up the band after the inconvenience of the finals. For the next couple of months, Marcus got his head down and avoided me and my distractions like the plague. Meanwhile, I had a cunning plan. OK, Stu had left the band but with every door that closed a new one opened. It was time to put in a call to Duffy Moon.

11. Duffy Moon

APRIL 1991

Return home to Sussex on a secret mission. Reflect on the importance of fun. Demo some new songs and recruit the final two members.

My brother Dave and his friend Josh were two years below me at school, but in the mid-eighties had formed a band called (You Can do it) Duffy Moon, or Duffy Moon for short. The name came from the 1976 made-for-TV kids film *The Amazing Cosmic Awareness of Duffy Moon.* The film was a cheesy American import and starred omnipresent seventies child actor Ike Eisenmann as a sixth-grade boy with a pet raven. Tired of being short and picked on, Duffy buys a magic book which enables him to 'think big'. All he needed to do was puff out his cheeks while an inner voice urged 'You Can Do It, Duffy Moon' on repeat until he could make strange, mystical things happen. The film left an impression on my 7-year-old mind – the idea that if you wanted something enough, you could get it resonated with me, and maybe even subconsciously inspired my Three-Hurdle Theory.

Duffy Moon rehearsed in a shed in Josh's garden. Egg cartons covered the walls for soundproofing, and in this damp and cramped space Josh and Dave, plus their two other bandmates, made a fantastic noise. From the name alone I was a fan, but on seeing Duffy Moon playing their first gig in the back garden at a house party in a little village called Rotherfield in East Sussex, I became a superfan. Under a silvery moon, the band stormed through their set, an eclectic mix of cover versions – 'Orgone

Accumulator' by Hawkwind, 'Psycho Killer' by Talking Heads and 'Can Your Pussy Do The Dog' by The Cramps – combined with a few of their own numbers like 'Georgina Profound' and a song that The Pointy Birds were to pilfer later called 'Rocket Child'.

They particularly stole my affection with their attempts to emulate the great JJ Burnell of The Stranglers and throw the occasional leg kick while playing their guitars. It was a lofty ambition and accomplishing it was no mean feat, especially as JJ Burnell somehow managed to get his leg up as high as his ears. It also tallied into the main prerequisite for being in a band – the ability to have fun. A group enjoying itself on stage was contagious, and there was no better expression of a band having fun than the attempted JJ Burnell leg kick.

But it didn't end there. Duffy Moon also incorporated comedy drum rolls and could recreate the WAH WAH WAAAAAAH of a joke falling flat via the tremolo on their guitars. It was the very spirit I wanted to capture in The Pointy Birds. Madness were past masters at looking like they were having fun. Kid Creole and The Coconuts were at a continual party. Being indie and po-faced was not for me. It was the mid-eighties, and I was young, dumb and wanting fun. Eventually, an elderly neighbour appeared in her dressing gown, having rung the police and wrestled the drumsticks from the drummer. A more rock'n'roll ending to a gig there could not be. Whether intentional or not, Duffy Moon had inspired this member of the audience to pick up a guitar and form a band.

Now, all these years later, if I could draft in Dave and Josh, one half of Duffy Moon, I had the final two pieces of the jigsaw. The good news was that Dave and Josh were currently musically homeless. Dave was at Leicester University and had formed indie duo Wet Bus; Josh meanwhile was down at Cardiff University with his new incarnation, The Bombay Mix Fiends. Neither band were gigging or functioning in any meaningful way, and this represented an opportunity for me. Recruiting them, however, would take guile and patience. The main hurdle to overcome was that musically speaking, Marcus and I were like two toddlers learning to walk while Dave and Josh could already do scissor kicks.

Josh was the eleventh child in a musical household and had grown up surrounded by instruments. He had been weaned on Steely Dan in his nappy and would flare his nostrils excitedly at the mention of a diminished nineth chord (whatever that was). Our basic three-chord efforts were a bit beneath him, but he also knew that three chords were the basis for some of the greatest songs ever written.

Another issue was a geographical one – with Dave studying in Leicester and Josh in Cardiff, we would have to wait another year for Dave to graduate and two years for Josh as he had taken a gap year. Although I was in a massive hurry, these two pieces of the jigsaw were worth the wait. Their tastes were an eclectic and sophisticated mix of old and new – Happy Mondays, The Triffids, Rod Stewart – and this would bring another angle to our music. I would have to be patient. And in the meantime, Marcus and I could continue to hone our craft and learn our trade, while Dave and Josh could travel down to London for important gigs. With this cunning plan in mind, I went down to Crowborough in East Sussex to see my parents knowing both Dave and Josh would also both be returning for the Easter holidays.

11.2

Crowborough was a commuter town at the top of a hill surrounded by the Ashdown Forest and a profusion of pretty yellow gorse flowers from which it derived its name, from the old English Golden Hill. It was Winnie the Pooh country and the brief home of Arthur Conan Doyle, and home to some very pleasant views too. We even lived on Pleasant View Road, although our view wasn't all that. My bedroom looked at the back gardens and sheds of semi-detached houses that looked the same as ours. Although conveniently situated – roughly equidistant between London and Brighton – there wasn't a great deal to do in the town itself, especially once we hit our teenage years. Crowborough was a slightly spooky and claustrophobic suburban world of empty streets, supermarkets, car parks and rugby clubs. Popular pastimes included strolling the streets, attempting to get served in pubs, boy-racing in cars or inter-town fighting. In recent times no one famous had come from Crowborough, although there was a rumour that the actor David Jason lived nearby. I never saw him.

But it was always nice to get back home to visit Mum and Dad, catch up with Dave, eat some greens and see some greenery. Mum did my washing and Dad made the joke about how he could give my hair a quick trim with the garden shears. The exciting news from Dave was that we could borrow Josh's Tascam four-track Portastudio for a few days. The Tascam was an analogue tape machine for recording demos. The results were not broadcast quality as the sound was too compressed, especially if you 'bounced' more than one instrument onto a single track. Still, with a bit of practice, you could end up with a decent blueprint of how a song might sound once recorded in a proper studio. It took trial and error, and the Tascam was all about the fun of discovery.

I also loved the innocent charm of the four-track recordings themselves – the hiss and crackle, the sound of new ideas being harvested, of happy accidents and bum notes. It was a chance to capture a song at its freshest like a young flower in bloom. Often songs could lose their identity by being over-played and over-thought so by the time a band was in a proper studio to record, everyone was sick of the song. Melodies and lyrics unnecessarily altered, extra flourishes added to guitar parts that didn't need them. Of course, songs usually developed and improved through this process, but sometimes a song was nailed first go on the Tascam, and there were diminishing returns to subsequent recordings.

The Tascam was also my chance to impress the future members of The Pointy Birds. I had three songs to record. The first was a reworking of my two-chord dirty groove 'Slide Inside' renamed 'Liquorice' with a new vocal that emulated Bob Dylan's 'Subterranean Homesick Blues'. I began putting the pieces of the song together, and it started to take shape. The drums and bass bounced along, giving it a lazy, happy vibe that suited the stream-of-conscious lyrics with my voice accidentally distorting in places. I added tambourine and backing vocals and then put the guitar riff through an effects pedal which added a new texture. But the thing that lifted the song was the Casio keyboard. I stumbled upon a simple little three-note riff that worked.

DA DA-DA DAAA

DA DA-DA DA

It was simple but effective and would become the hook of the song. Blissfully immersed in the creative process, I bounced tracks left, right and centre and finally I sat back to play the track from start to finish. All the parts seemed to complement each other. It was a cohesive piece with the sum greater than its parts — the recording had an aqua sound like it had taken place underwater. I hadn't planned this effect, but it gave it quite a unique sound. I was particularly proud of how the guitar riff and keyboard interweaved, almost talking to each other. It wasn't quite the two guitars duelling in Neil Young's nine-minute masterpiece 'Down By The River', but still, they were chatting. And, OK, maybe they were saying the same thing on repeat, but still, it worked.

I had created something from nothing and what I had created wasn't half bad. It was a serious song. And the cherry on the top was the Casio keyboard riff that turned it into a hit. Who would have thought three simple notes on a keyboard could create such pleasure for me, and hopefully a wider audience too. Little was I to know that this keyboard riff was soon to create a rift within the band.

11.3

At the end of several happy days recording, Josh came around to pick up the Tascam and hear our efforts. I had recorded three songs – 'Liquorice', 'Poster On The Wall' and 'Had Enough'. Dave had also produced a bunch of new songs full of intelligent chord sequences, key changes and sublime melodies with cheeky guitar riffs that danced throughout. These recordings were early versions of three future Pointy Bird classics – 'Nostradamus Blues', 'Benefit Office' and 'Lift Me'.

Josh sat on the edge of the bed, picked up a guitar and strummed absent-mindedly, immediately making it sound musical. How on earth did he do that? He then addressed the elephant in the room.

'Let's have a listen to what you both done then.'

A smile crept across his face. I was pleased with my efforts but afraid to new ears they would be laughed at, especially by people who could play their instruments. I had not forgotten their reaction to my previous attempt a few months earlier – a song about a hippy with purple flares. And my ditty about a tomcat had reduced them both to tears of laughter. But I felt confident about these new recordings. Josh donned the headphones, I pressed play and heard the faint intro of the Casio-drumbeat startup. I studied Josh's face as the bass kicked in followed by the guitars and then that glorious keyboard riff with the vocal rap. But his mocking smile had been replaced by a look of concentration. He seemed to be taking it seriously. I noticed his foot tap. There was the odd laugh, but it was more appreciative like he had acknowledged the idea or was enjoying a rhyming couplet. Eventually, he moved the headphones.

'Not bad. I'm impressed.' There was silence in the room, but I felt my heart soar. Josh continued with the praise. 'It has a good structure.'

Higher and higher, my heart soared. I nodded in agreement that yes, it did have a good structure. Because it did.

'And I like the line "Potatoes, potatoes, and you say tomatoes".'

Yes, that was a great line.

'So, what's happening with The Pointy Birds then?'

It was it my time to strike.

'Yeah, going really well. Been doing the circuit and all that shit.'

I feigned a not-bothered look. Josh and Dave were interested.

'Yeah, actually, we're going to do The Shelley Arms.'

Josh arced an impressed Roger Moore eyebrow. 'Really?'

Playing The Shelly Arms was a rite of passage and a badge of honour for aspiring bands in the area. I could tell my audience was impressed. And envious. I upped the ante.

'The only problem is that our guitarist Stu just left the band.'

Dave and Josh leaned in.

'Yeah, it's left us in a jam. We'll be fine without him, obviously, but I just wish there were a couple of guitarists who could fill in. Give the local crowd our full effect, you know?'

I left the question hanging and hit the ball back over the net.

'Anyway, how's it's going with Bombay Mix Fiends?'

Josh explained that nothing was happening with The Bombay Mix Fiends. Likewise for Dave with Wet Bus. It was time to pop the question.

'I know! How about you both fill for the Shelley gig?'

They both looked at each other and then nodded a 'why not?'. It would be a one-off gig with a rehearsal in London to learn the songs. One step at a time, 'slowly, slowly, catchy monkey'. I knew they would love Marcus and drummer Paul, and our brick-breaking ninja landlord fit the Duffy Moon mould. This signing was a masterstroke as it kept Marcus onside and significantly improved our musicianship. This was our time to shine. Lots of people would be returning to Crowborough after the finals, so the timing of the gig in July was perfect. It would be a homecoming.

It had taken three years, but I had done it, I had formed a band. And although the rest of the band didn't realise it yet, I was going to take them on a journey to world domination. On the train back to Charring Cross, I reflected with satisfaction on my progress so far. It was a glorious late afternoon in May, summer was on its way and the sun streamed in through the grease-smeared windows as the Kentish countryside whizzed by. Rabbits sunbaked in the fields munching on dandelions, and all felt right with the world. A train screeched past in the opposite direction, carriages full of sweaty commuters coming home from their nine-to-five drag to domestic drudgery. I was heading in the opposite direction, swimming against the tide towards the big time. I put my dirty shoes up on the empty seat in front of me and stretched.

12. DA-DADA-DAA

JUNE 1991

The formality of the finals is over. Full band rehearsal ahead of The Shelley Arms gig takes our music to a new level but raises the question of whether the band should be a democracy or dictatorship.

For a couple of months, Marcus got his head down and avoided me and my distractions like the plague to focus on the finals. I decided I had come this far and so I may as well get a degree too, so I borrowed Marcus's notes and deadline-surfed to albums by Cocteau Twins and Talk Talk. I used the old elastic-band-wrapped-tightly-around-my-finger-until-it-went-blue trick and pretended I had sliced my finger badly to buy me a couple of extra days. I then roped in Mum with her secretarial skills to type up my half-baked thesis on Gorbachev and human rights which I made up as I went along. But at last, the finals were out of the way and it was time to get back to business.

Josh and Dave arrived at our flat in Golders Green, loaded with guitars and keyboards for the all-important pre-gig rehearsal. The added bonus of inviting them aboard the good ship Pointy Bird was that in addition to being able to play their instruments competently they came with a bunch of songs too – well-crafted compositions with middle eighths, changes of tempo and even sneaky key changes – songs I was planning to steal, or at least permanently borrow as Pointy Birds songs. We would add at least two of them to the set for The Shelley Arms. With Stu no longer in the band, we dropped 'Bourbon Man'.

'Married To A Squirrel' was axed too for being too silly. 'Pube On My Lip' stayed for now as it worked as an opening loosener, although its days were numbered.

We brewed some tea and opened a packet of chocolate Hobnob biscuits. I knew something special was about to happen. Outside, it was one of those days when the weather hadn't turned up. The sky was the colour of milk and all was silent and still. It was as if everything was waiting with bated breath in expectation for the arrival of something. Downstairs, Vincent was snipping hair. Upstairs, in our flat, there was about to be a meeting of minds, a chemical reaction, a rumble in the jungle, or at least a rumble in a flat in Golders Green. People milling about on the high street below were totally unaware they were about to hear the next big thing.

Paul started playing a drum beat with Josh and Dave joining in on guitars making stuff up as they went along. Marcus and I exchanged looks. It sounded great, but it was intimidating. We were limited in what we could play. The idea of jamming and making it up as we went along, let alone playing in the right key or being in tune, was beyond us. It was promotion to the big league – time to remove the stabilisers, take off our nappies, ditch the armbands and dive into the deep end. Trouble was we didn't know how to 'jam' off-piste. Marcus dipped his toe in the water and started playing the bass line to 'Liquorice'. The antenna of those around him picked up this new direction of travel and started riffing and inventing all sorts of new ideas that sounded effortless. Pretty soon we were all playing in happy unison.

Once we had limbered up, the hard work began of actually learning some songs. Another packet of chocolate Hobnobs was unwrapped. First off was one of Dave's songs that I had added some lyrics to and titled 'Nostradamus Blues', a swampy blues pop song. Dave showed everyone how to play it and quickly the song came together. I had bought a harmonica, and although I couldn't play it, I felt the song needed it. In a perfect world, the song would suit a brass section, but my harmonica would be the next best thing. I just needed to blow two notes to emulate two stabs from a trumpet and emphasise the hook in the song. The song told the uplifting story of a depressed clown lost in a desert choosing to look on the bright side of life and avoid the quicksand of depression. It was a catchy number and pleasantly reminiscent of 'The Only One I Know' by The Charlatans. And that had been a massive indie hit.

Next up was one of my efforts called 'Poster On The Wall' – a breezy summer anthem, unapologetically upbeat incorporating the jazz ninth chord to dizzying effect and a gravity-defying middle eighth. It told the simple story of a poster on the wall. The poster in question featured French actress Beatrice Dalle in a sexy pose from the film *Betty Blue*. It adorned student bedroom walls across the country, including mine. But in the song, our lovestruck protagonist has a revelation that although she is pretty hot, she can't compete with his new love which is real. It didn't get much deeper than that. The genius of the song was a catchy guitar riff that in the studio would be recorded as a whistle. It was a whistling song. And everyone liked a whistling song.

We rehearsed more songs, brewed more cups of tea and devoured more Hobnobs. It was fun, working hard towards a goal with focused minds. 'Rocket Child' by Josh had been a Duffy Moon fan favourite, a quirky verse with a jazzy beat gave way to a big rock chorus. It was a future number one if ever I heard one. Next was a song called 'Over and Out' written by Josh's brother's band Two Short Words, it was reminiscent of REM and interweaved two beautiful guitar riffs with a lilting vocal melody. Although it was a cover version, it was little known and brought a sophistication to our set. The last song to learn was my new song 'Liquorice'. The band seemed a bit tired but we needed to get this done. I felt a bit awkward – an amateur telling professionals what to play – but I knew it was good. I showed Josh the Casio keyboard riff.

'Yeah, it's quite simple. It's just these three notes.'

I played the first part of the riff.

DA DA-DA DAAA

And then I played the second part of the riff.

DA DA-DA DA.

'Doesn't need anything else. You need to do that on repeat throughout the whole song.'

Josh played the three notes and then did a little flourish around the riff. The rest of the band made impressed noises. I needed to nip this in the bud.

'Yeah, that was good, but just the three notes, OK?'

'Are you sure?' said Josh. 'Might get a bit tedious.'

'Yeah, the repetition works – trust me.'

Josh gave me a he-wasn't-convinced look.

'Anyway, let's give it a run-through,' I said, moving things on.

Paul counted us in, the band started and 'Liquorice' came to life, but it sounded so much bigger and better than I could have imagined. The rhythm section kicked things off with a simple groove, on cue Dave brought in the guitar riff followed by Josh with the keyboard riff. It worked, and over the top, I began my rap. It sounded like The Beatles' 'I am The Walrus' for the nineties.

We were flying. I was inside the song, lost in music – what more fabulous place to be? But then halfway through I noticed the keyboard riff started to morph and change. I didn't mind as Josh was finding his way around the song. But the more he improvised, the more it lost its identity until my riff had disappeared altogether.

I needed to be diplomatic. Josh's musical ability took The Pointy Birds to a whole new level, but he needed to respect boundaries when it came to how to play my songs. The simplicity and repetition of the keyboard riff emulated 'West End Girls' by The Pet Shop Boys. And that had gone to number one. The song landed back on the tarmac – amps buzzed with feedback and the band exchanged appreciative nods. But I felt like someone had ruined a scenic journey by farting in the car.

'Wow, those keyboards sounded amazing,' said Paul with more enthusiasm than usual.

'Josh, loved the tinkling on the keys there,' said Marcus. 'Like Ray Manzarek from The Doors.'

I threw some daggers at Marcus. What was he saying? Josh didn't need to be encouraged.

'Yeah, really added something,' echoed Paul.

Dave nodded in agreement.

'I know,' said Josh lobbing a told-you-so face at me

What were they all saying? There was an awkward silence as I remained muted in my enthusiasm.

'Yeah, it sounded great,' I said, not wanting to be too dictatorial. 'But can you keep to the riff, please? Less is more.'

'OK, you da boss.'

'OK, everyone, from the top.'

Paul counted us in, and the plane took off again. This time Josh did as told, but annoyingly it felt like something was missing. The song felt a bit empty, not helped by Josh looking bored. Did that riff still work? I knew the repetition of that riff worked on the demo but why did it feel a bit empty when playing live? I decided to park the thought and revisit it later. By the end of the rehearsal, we had our set. We were a grown-up band playing original material, the only exception would be 'Over and Out' and 'Wild Thing', as that was a good party piece finale for Vincent. There was no doubt, we were ready to rock.

13. The Shelley Arms

JULY 1991

News breaks that a local indie rockstar might attend our homecoming gig. Gig has a surprise ending for both audience and band.

Ahead of our gig at The Shelley Arms massive news broke: Simon Gallup, the bass player of The Cure, had moved to Crowborough. It had to be a joke, right? Rockstars didn't move to Crowborough, but soon more details emerged. Maybe it was true. Plus, The Cure were originally from Crawley, another small suburban town a forty-five-minute drive away. Then, Josh blew my mind with news that his mate Ben had befriended Simon Gallup and they were now drinking buddies. And there was now a chance that Simon Gallup (according to Ben who had told Josh) would be coming to our gig at The Shelley Arms.

It was further evidence of the stars aligning. If we could impress Simon Gallup, then surely we would be offered the support slot on The Cure's next world tour. And what if he brought singer Robert Smith to the gig with him? I imagined being invited back to Simon Gallup's house. Robert Smith would be in the kitchen making a snack. A cheese and ham toastie maybe. Then we'd sit back in wingback chairs by a log fire and drink wine. There was no doubt Robert Smith and I would hit it off as besties.

During the sixth form, while doing my A levels, I had developed a mild obsession with the holy indie trinity of The Smiths from Manchester, Liverpool's Echo & The Bunnymen and Crawley's

The Cure. It was hard to choose between them. Who could compete with the sophistication of The Smiths – the wit of Morrissey's lyrics and the inventive guitar playing and songwriting genius of Johnny Marr? Echo & The Bunnymen were a more rock'n'roll proposition. In the studied cool of lead singer Ian McCulloch and his slightly awkward wingman and guitar hero Will Sergeant, they inspired a similar devotion and amusing hairstyles among a significant slither of the male gig-going population.

But The Cure were closer to my heart. They were small-town suburban boys, and so their achievement seemed obtainable to me. I had initially found them a bit weird, but then with the help of a Sociology A level teacher, I realised that the real world was weird too. What was normal? The Cure articulated this. Robert Smith had bed hair, panda eyes and smudged lipstick. He might not have got a corporate job in the city but who wanted a corporate job in the city?

And musically, The Cure were the masters of contrast. Throwaway chart-topping singles like 'Love Cats', 'Let's Go to Bed' and 'Caterpillar' sat happily alongside the dark, claustrophobic gloom rock of albums like 'Faith', 'Pornography' and 'Disintegration'. They were simultaneously pop and alternative, dark and light, silly and solemn. They were critically acclaimed and commercially successful, and in their collaboration with film director Tim Pope, I saw that they took their art seriously but not themselves. Whether locked in a cupboard or dressed as cats in a video to sell the band, they achieved a perfect blend of music and comedy. Just as in politics, self-deprecating humour resonated with the public.

13.2

The Shelley Arms was situated in a little village called Nutley about five miles away from Crowborough. Not a lot happened in Nutley. The locals celebrated a windmill and a World War Two bomber that had crash-landed nearby, but over the years the pub had built up a reputation for live music hosting classic gigs from local Crowborough legends such as The Dead Bits and Hot Diggedy Dogs. But the pub's main claim-to-fame was that The Cutting Crew, from Cuckfield in West Sussex, had played before having a global smash hit with 'I Just Died In Your Arms Tonight'. And now The Pointy Birds were joining this pantheon of East Sussex greats.

The morning of the gig, a college friend Jeff the Chef picked us up from our flat in Golders Green and drove us down in the back of his transit van. We slid around with the amps arriving two hours later, a little bit giddy and car sick. We clambered out the back and stretched our limbs to the welcome sound of bird song. The air was warm and carried with it the honeyed scents of the surrounding countryside, the perfume of golden gorse and wild summer flowers combined with the earthier smells of a local farm. I could also detect salty notes from the sea not twenty miles away in Brighton. It was both invigorating and soporific, which made me feel pleasantly woozy and at home. In contrast to the streets of London which smelled of piss.

A cat wandered sleepily across the road. It was so peaceful, disturbed only by the sound of our footsteps on gravel wheeling our amps and instruments into the pub. A chalkboard advertised the evening's entertainment that made it all real:

TONIGHT LIVE MUSIC
THE POINTY BIRDS
9 p.m.

I felt my stomach tighten. Would tonight be a success or failure? I breathed in deep to gulp down some more country air and then entered the pub. It ticked all the boxes of an English country pub – the low oak beams, a roaring log fire, real ale on tap and the tobacco-filled air hiding some more of the unpleasant whiffs in the thirty-year-old carpet. Ah! The glorious bouquet of dreams, hope, fear, desire, regret. This needed to be distilled and made into a perfume – *eau de pub*. I would wear it.

These pubs were the lifeblood of the music industry – giving new young bands a chance to cut their teeth in the live arena. These were the music halls of our time, but they were soon to be under threat from the emerging gastro pub and the triple-fried chip cooked in goose fat. And delicious as these potato wedges were, small music venues needed to be championed and celebrated and given protected status because once they were gone, they were gone.

A slightly distracted landlord with whiskery sideburns and eyes like fried eggs pointed us in the direction of the stage. He looked a bit knackered after thirty years of pulling pints. He was probably propped up by a buxom landlady wife with superb organisational and people skills who kept the boat afloat. A partnership dynamic was replicated across the land. I didn't believe in broad brushstrokes and lazy generalisations about nationalities, but if anything defined Englishness, it was this quaint country pub. That, and The Antiques Roadshow.

A few elderly people dotted around the pub watched in silent curiosity, inscrutable like the local cows, as we carried in our guitars and amps through the pub towards the makeshift stage. At the bar, a few locals sat nursing pints of Harvey's Real Ale from the local brewery down the road in Lewes. There was the obligatory workman in paint-splattered white overalls trying to catch my eye. I would have to get used to this feeling of being stared at when I was famous. He was possibly a bit starstruck. Or maybe just desperate for some conversation at the end of another long and monotonous day painting walls? I acknowledged him with a nod. He took that as a cue to strike up a conversation by stating the obvious.

'You the band then?'

I nodded that we were.

'What you called then?'

'The Pointy Birds.'

'The what?'

'The Pointy Birds'

He laughed.

'You hear that, Alf? They called The Pointy Birds…'

Alf looked up at this strange fellow and turned up the volume on his earpiece. 'What?'

'POINTY BIRDS'

Alf stared for a while non-plussed and then returned to his pint, shaking his head and reduced the volume on his hearing aid. The painter returned his attention to me, wagging his tail with a big goofy grin. I would need to make this chat quick, I had things to do.

'So, what are you, a covers band?'

'No,' I said, slightly insulted at the suggestion. 'We play our own stuff.'

He was impressed.

'You write your songs? Originals. Wow. You hear that, Alf?' Alf ignored him. 'So, what do you sound like?'

I scratched my chin. It was a tricky question but represented a chance to sell ourselves to a potential new fan. This elevator pitch was an artform in itself and something we needed to master. The biggest turn-off when trying to lure in a new fan was to be vague.

'We're kind of undefinable…' I said.

He nodded his head unsurely. I decided to expand.

'We're sort of guitar-based indie…'

'Indian?'

'No, indie – independent… I mean, we don't like to be pigeon-holed.' I realised I wasn't exactly selling it. 'I don't know. It's hard to summarise the un-summarisable.'

The painter nodded but looked a bit confused. I needed to give him something more concrete.

'I'd say a bit like The Smiths maybe?'

I could hear the sound of Josh's scoffing. 'That's a bit of a wild claim.'

Marcus interjected. 'I'd say there's a bit of a dance influence. And a bit of The Doors. A dancey Doors maybe?'

That was not a bad stab at a marketing effort on Marcus's part.

'Yeah, maybe a dancey Doors meets The Cure?' added Paul.

Both of the painter's eyebrows were now aloft and interested. 'Well, The Cure are local boys. From Crawley. And one of them drinks here sometimes.'

'Yeah, apparently Simon might be coming tonight,' I said full of faked nonchalance but wanting to scream it from the rooftops. 'Anyway, stick around and catch you laters, yeah?' I winked at him and strolled over to the stage. I was born for this.

*

Around 7 p.m. the pub started to fill up. Familiar faces from school drifted in, friends who had been away to university or gone travelling, and those who had stayed in Crowborough. The evening doubled up as a reunion, but it was hard to socialise. I felt restless. There was too much to think about – would the guitars go out of tune? Would the strings break? Would we perform the songs well? Would Simon Gallup turn up? Seeds of doubt started to grow as the pub got busier. This wasn't just any old gig. It was a homecoming – the night when three years of hard work came together. If this went wrong, it would be a mass humiliation in front of everyone I knew.

My fears were not allayed when Josh asked me to remind him what the chords were for all the songs. I took the chance to remind him about the keyboard riff in 'Liquorice'.

'Remember, keep it simple. Just the three notes on repeat.'

He wafted my concerns away. 'It'll be fine,' he said.

Vincent cornered me to ask about fire regulations but I pointed him in the direction of the landlord without asking why.

He wandered off carrying a bag of swords and bricks. I left him to it and went to the bar and ordered a pint of lager and a double whiskey.

By 9 p.m. the pub was packed, and this was the hottest ticket in town. Well, the only gig in the village. The landlord gave me the five-minute nod. I gathered the band to the side of the stage for a final team talk and gave out copies of the set-list. We were keeping it short and sweet, leaving the crowd wanting more:

'Pube On My Lip'
'Liquorice'
'Poster On The Wall'
'Nostradamus Blues'
'Over And Out'
'Rocket Child'
'Wild Thing + Vincent'

We took to the stage and I looked out at a sea of faces. The place was heaving – standing room only. People were standing on tables to get a view and even watching through windows from outside. I surveyed the room one last time for Simon Gallup. It wouldn't be hard to spot him with his whole Cure hairdo, but maybe he was lurking in the shadows incognito with a baseball cap and shades. Whatever, it was time to put on a show.

'Hello, Shelley Arms. We are The Pointy Birds, and this first song is called "Pube On My Lip".'

As the dulcet sound of Marcus's bass got the audience in the mood, and I introduced each member to whoops and applause, I knew this gig was going to go well. We pressed down on the accelerator and hurtled through the rest of the set fast and loose playing the songs at double speed like we were a punk band. A combination of nerves, adrenaline, alcohol and the fact we had only had one rehearsal created an exciting wall of noise. We were flying without a license, driving without breaks, riding a runaway horse without a saddle. Although the songs had lost their shape and identity, it sounded musical and in tune. As each song finished, we were met with a roar of appreciation from our home crowd.

The only annoying thing was when we came to 'Liquorice', Josh didn't so much go off-piste with the keyboard riff, he never went on-piste. My three-note riff never made an appearance in the song, once. The song was unrecognisable from my original demo. I glared at Josh throughout and made a mental note to have stern words. And then during the penultimate song 'Rocket Child', our friend Johnny Foulkes's pint glass shattered as I hit the high note during the chorus. Astonished faces greeted this, but it was all part of the new folklore we were writing to rival the local windmill, the World War Two Bomber, The Cutting Crew and Winnie the Pooh. The Pointy Birds weren't just creating music but sorcery and magic. If Simon Gallup was out there, we surely had the support slot in the bag.

It was time for the finale. Vincent appeared dressed as a masked black ninja brandishing a sword. A lot of the locals hadn't seen a masked ninja before. There were a few gasps. His appearance sobered up the room. He bowed to the audience and then spoke.

'In life, there comes a day when you realise no one gives a shit about you, and we are all alone in zis fucking world.'

This wasn't exactly in the party spirit.

'But tonight, we go on a journey…'

We started to play 'Wild Thing', and he began his routine with swords and nunchucks. The ceiling was low and they swung a bit close for comfort. I was starting to question the wisdom of having him join the band, especially in such a confined space. As we played, he jumped off the stage and climbed into the audience and beckoned them all to follow him outside. We carried on playing as our audience turned to each other perplexed, and then out of curiosity, decided to follow him outside. Were we meant to keep playing? I kicked myself for not scrutinising what he was planning to do. He had just said 'some crazy shit'.

We carried on playing, but the pub was emptying. Only our painter at the bar showed any loyalty. Realising the gig had now permanently moved outside we stopped playing, dropped tools and decided to join the throng.

Outside in the beer garden, Vincent had removed his mask and settled into the lotus position with his eyes closed, waiting for calm. In front of him were a stack of bricks. There was a lot of excited chatter. Ninja warriors didn't turn up often in Nutley. What was he going to do? We were as curious as anyone. People were taking photos and gossiping loudly. Who was this strange person?

He waited until everyone was quiet and then produced a box of matches and set the bricks alight. It was an arresting image that brought to mind that monk in Vietnam who set fire to himself in protest. Vincent composed himself with a few deep breaths. I had to admit he was good at building suspense. People were transfixed with their cameras at the ready. I faked a shrug like this kind of shit happened every day up in London. Vincent uttered something, and his head came crashing down through the flames and demolished the bricks. The crowd whooped and hollered. Suddenly, he was upon his feet.

'For my final trick I will fly through ze air over the band… please give a round of applause for Ze Pointy Birds.'

Taking our cue from Vincent we crouched in line, but as he did a running jump and somersaulted through the air over us Bruce Lee style to massive applause from the crowd, I thought to myself, he's hogged the limelight with his antics for the last time. Although his party trick had gone down well, once again he had upstaged us. Leading the audience on a conga out to the beer garden while we were still playing was a no-no. Vincent would have to go.

But for entertainment value, we had delivered. The gig

could be filed as an unqualified triumph. There was no doubt that The Pointy Birds were on the up, and I was on cloud nine. The essential jigsaw pieces were in place. We travelled back to London, satisfied. Back at the flat I checked the answerphone for messages. Annoyingly, no one from The Cure had got in touch.

PAUSE |

A slight detour.

14. Destudentisation

AUTUMN 1991

Reality bites as post-college life begins but inspired by trip to Edinburgh fringe, we embark on a complementary career move.

Flush with success from The Shelley Arms, Dave and I travelled up to Edinburgh to hang out at The Fringe Festival. It had a special place in our hearts. As kids, we drove the four-hundred miles up to Edinburgh each year for our summer holidays to spend two weeks seeing two sets of grandparents (and spend quality time dressing up their dogs). Our visit always coincided with the festival and the main event of the Royal Edinburgh Military Tattoo. If it was your misfortune to have tickets, an evening performance could feel like it went on for a lifetime. Watching kilted soldiers parading military hardware to the sound of bagpipes for hours on end induced eye-watering levels of boredom that caused physical pain. If this is what the royal family had to endure, they could keep their crown jewels – they deserved them.

But something else was going on in the city. As kids, our grandad had told us about this underground movement called The Fringe. It was all very hush-hush. Not something you spoke about openly in public. The Fringe was not officially part of the festival but an 'alternative' festival that took place in the pubs and clubs featuring comedians, theatre, exhibitions, performance art – no kilts, no machine guns, no bagpipes. And then one year, when we were old enough to get the bus into the centre of town by ourselves, Grandad handed us a copy of The Fringe programme, a guide to all the different events that were happening. He gave us some pocket money and with a twinkle in his eye encouraged us to choose a show. He was too old to go himself, but he was curious and wanted us to report back. He could live The Fringe vicariously through us. We flicked through the pages to see hundreds of different performances taking place, spoiled for choice. Every year The Fringe grew, and so did our love for it. The shows were not always fully formed, and the comedians not necessarily funny, but still I loved the ambition and endeavour.

And now in the summer of 1991, we were back again, in the centre of Edinburgh at a cafe on The Royal Mile soaking up the atmosphere. The Edinburgh Fringe had grown up, swallowed the festival and become the main attraction. It was now the Glastonbury for comedy, and these were my people. We caught up with Scottish pals, David Rome and Johnny Foulkes, and watched Crowborough's most excellent The Hot Diggedy Dogs busking at Arthur's Seat. We went out at night to watch nearly famous comedians and heckle unfunny ones. We hung out starstruck with Sean Hughes for about three minutes at an after-show party. I had seen him do his stand-up comedy routine at our student union canteen to three people, and now here he was: the king of comedy with a Perrier Award for Best Newcomer. I returned to London inspired, knowing it was only a matter of time before I would return to scoop the same award for myself.

14.2

As the summer of 1991 drifted into autumn, the release of two significant records in September would have a big influence on us and the decade ahead. *Screamadelica* by Primal Scream was the album that lived up to the hype and promise of their earlier singles. The band had scaled back the guitars and embraced beats and bleeps completing their transformation from indie goths to dance-rock pioneers. Meanwhile, a three-piece from Seattle had picked up their guitars and turned them up to eleven. 'Smells Like Teen Spirit' by Nirvana was the first single from their new album *Nevermind.* It was an instant hit that stole from The Pixies, REM and The Beatles and overnight reminded people why guitars were great, especially when played loud. It was the start of grunge and US alternative rock bands were soon to dominate the airwaves, as well as the hearts and minds of indie kids for the next couple of years. With that came an increase in the sales of woolly hats, checked shirts and cardigans. I needed to re-think my Jim Morrison sixties beatnik look. Maybe the cowboy boots and leathers had to go.

With summer over there was one rather large issue that I hadn't entirely foreseen: the seven-letter word REALITY. Our three years at college was over, and that meant no more student grant. Looming was the spectre of that terrible four-lettered word, WORK. Or its evil three-lettered little sister, JOB. That the rent and various bills needed paying represented something of a challenge. It was an outrage. I was a musician and entertainer in waiting and so shouldn't have to be troubled by things like paying the rent. I needed to work out how I could give the band the full-time attention it required and pay the rent at the same time.

My dad called this period post-college 'de-studentisation'. He said it would take about two years before you would need to buckle down and get a proper job and start to climb those two dreaded six-letter words. CAREER and LADDER. The thought of having to climb up this thing gave me vertigo. Luckily, two things came to my rescue. Firstly I had graduated into the mother of all recessions and so getting a job was tough for anyone. I had a second-class honours degree in politics and a fat lot of good that was going to do me. There weren't any jobs advertised for prime minister. And secondly, there was a beautiful four-letter word that provided a perfect solution, DOLE.

All I needed to do was pop along to the Department of Housing and Social Security, or DHSS, and fill out some forms. Then hey presto, I got the rent paid courtesy of housing benefit and some spending money to boot from income support. I could even supplement this with a bit of cash in hand busking on the underground, which doubled up as a kind of work experience. With the odd withdrawal from the bank of Mum and Dad, I was almost able to live the life to which I had become accustomed as a student. I could then continue to focus on the next stage of our bid for world domination – to record a demo, find a manager and then sign a record deal. Any downtime I would put to writing a sitcom and my first novel.

I could morally justify being on the dole by the return on investment from The Pointy Birds' future turnover in record sales, ticket sales and merchandise not just for the band, but for the economy as a whole. And I wasn't even factoring in the significant boost for the country standing internationally. The dole was a relatively small investment for a country to make – sure, not all aspiring artists guaranteed a return, but overall the treasury would be quids in. The DHSS was effectively an indie label offering a development deal with major backing. That's how I saw it anyway. And George Michael had articulated these sentiments rather poetically in 1983 with their UK number eight smash hit 'Wham Rap' by rhyming the words jerk and work, and giving a wham and a bam but not a damn, because the benefits gang were going to pay.

Marcus had a different take on things to George and me. He had a moral objection, a work-ethic issue. Taking money from the state was a no-no if you could work, he said. That was fair dos but I had chord progressions and middle eights to think about and lyrics to write, not to mention sitcoms and novels. I needed quality time with myself. The debut album wasn't going to write itself.

But the good news was that following his wobble, Marcus

was back on board. We had both graduated with a 'Desmond', graduate rhyming slang for a 2:2 (as in Desmond Tutu). Initially, Marcus's nose was a bit out of joint that we had got the same grade when he had put in some hard yards revising, but we consoled ourselves that he was probably nearer a 2:1 and I had perhaps just scraped a 2:2. Now that the band was fully formed and things were moving in the right direction, Marcus had deferred studying for an MSc in Politics Research and joined drummer Paul at Sainsbury's with a full-time job in the frozen veg aisle. It was a sacrifice for rock'n'roll I wasn't sure I could make, but he hadn't grown his hair and learned the bass for nothing, and he loved playing live. Improving the fortunes of the poor and society's inequalities could wait.

The exciting news was that Marcus's mum, who was becoming a big fan of the band, had managed to reel in a couple of gigs up in the midlands. The first was the 'Biko Bar', part of Coventry University student union supporting ska band The Bonediggers featuring Roddy Radiation of The Specials fame. Granby Halls followed this in Leicester which we were surprised to find out was a two-thousand-capacity arena. I thought it was a bit premature in our career but assumed it was part of a festival. The news we were the only act was cause for some concern as was the fact no tickets had been sold. The promoters decided to seal off some of the arena, but this didn't reduce the size of the tumbleweeds when only about twelve people turned up. Still, it was a gig and we were professionals. And although the sound through my guitar amp was a bit muddy as soon as the drumbeat started so did our audience.

We returned to London with a few more hairs on our chest and Dave and Josh returned to college. We agreed to only draft them in for essential shows. Josh needed a bit of convincing. Musically, we were still beneath him and I saw he was frustrated that I was pulling the reins and preventing him from expressing himself on 'Liquorice'. I knew deep down he loved every second of the Shelley gig though. I also needed to have the conversation with Vincent but there was no need. He quit the job at the hairdressers and the last I saw of him was at a party. He was sitting on a window ledge – a big drop below him. One minute he was there and the next he was gone. Had he jumped? We looked out of the window but there was no sign of him. He had vanished like Rent-a-ghost.

In the meantime, through a friend of drummer Paul we accepted the offer of a monthly residency at the Railway Tavern in West Hampstead supporting a band called Paint. These shows represented a chance for Marcus and me to perfect our stagecraft but were not worth the expense for Josh and Dave to travel down from university each month. As a result, we roped in a friend of Paul's called Eamonn who was a session guitarist, and over the next few months he raised our standards and helped tighten things up.

The band moved along steadily, and we started to improve as a live act. We also got offered a last-minute cancellation at The Camden Falcon, one of the most prestigious venues on the toilet circuit playing with a band called Mad Cow Disease on a Monday night in November. The venue was unusually quiet but we were getting closer to the source. The venue was very much a stepping stone to the big time. We had also managed to get on the flyer advertising all the bands playing that month. They had names I didn't recognise like Verve, PJ Harvey and The Divine Comedy, but at least in the future they could boast they were on a flyer with The Pointy Birds before they were famous.

Without the distraction of college and with most of our friends moving on to climb career ladders, I suddenly had a lot of spare time. I spent this quality time in the park on long walks, thinking about lyrics or interviewing myself about my ideas, but it was tricky to escape a feeling of unease about the future. Success and the big time still felt a long way away, and there were only so many hours I could strum guitar each day. I had hit a wall with my novel and sitcom too.

My attempts to supplement the dole money were proving tricky. Initially, I had tried busking songs by The Cure on the Underground. But after a few days, I realised that even though the escalators provided a never-ending audience, the lack of daylight and pollution was too much like hard work. Plus, the decent pitches were fought over and singing for hours on end in a dirty, smelly, polluted Underground was not as glamorous as I'd hoped. There had to be other ways to make a living that didn't give you throat cancer.

Luckily, I bagged a cash-in-hand job in a video shop on Golders Green high street two nights a week. The only annoying thing was having to pause the films to serve the customers, but I could watch two movies per shift. Could there be a better job? But then tragic news came in – the shop was closing and I was back to square one. I needed to bring in some extra bacon and I had a plan. Inspired by my trip to the Edinburgh festival, it was time to bite the bullet and launch my career in stand-up comedy.

15. Silent Comedians

WINTER 1991

Lure old school friend into partnering stand-up routine and tread comedy boards for the first time.

For a stand-up comedy routine, all I needed to do was tell some of my funny stories. The mystery of who had defecated on the wicker basket during a school skiing trip always got big laughs up the pub. The time my drinks got spiked with horse laxatives on my eighteenth birthday had the potential to have them rolling in the aisles. I also had no end of tales about the family dog – our beloved golden retriever, Max. Most of these stories involved poo – stepping in it, sitting in it, accidentally eating it – but there was always a market for toilet humour. Plus, dogs were funny. It was a brilliant combo.

Ideally, the aim was to become the new Billy Connolly. With a guitar, I'd embellish my act with funny songs. Then I'd throw in a bit of slapstick or visual humour in the vein of Jacques Tati and Steve Martin. The trouble was every time I tried to write my stories down they lost some of their punch. The words were flat on the page. Another worry was that I would be telling these stories to a room full of strangers and maybe the humour relied on knowing the people involved. I stared at a blank page, frustrated. It was trickier than it looked.

A solution presented itself through the arrival of an old school friend Pete, who turned up late one night on our doorstep carrying a large suitcase like Paddington Bear. He had just graduated and like me was finding the adjustment to reality a challenge. I hadn't seen much of him since school where he had been the tennis champ and boasted having the highest IQ in the year. He also had an impressive party trick having memorised the Oxford English Dictionary and could recite the definition of any word within its pages. But in the intervening three years, he had spent his time questioning the nature of existence and was now suffering from anxiety, confusion and a fear of the future.

I showed him in and he plonked himself down on the red sofa in my bedroom. I sat down opposite him resigned to the fact his visit might be long-term.

'Thing is Macleod, I've got nowhere to go. There is no one I want to see from college and don't think they fancy seeing me. So thought I'd come see what happening in your world.'

'Right.' I could smell booze and fags. He had come here via the pub.

'And I just spent summer back home with my folks. Ended up locked in my bedroom like being a teenager again. Can't go back there either.'

Pete ferreted about in the ashtray assembling a rollie out of old fag ends.

'My old man's desperate for me to do an MA in business studies. That's his answer. Get rid of all the philosophical bollocks. He's offered to pay for it so it would mean I can avoid the real world for a bit longer, but an MA? What's the point?'

I nodded in agreement. It did seem like a colossal waste of time and money. Pete continued.

'And the thought of getting a job, well, it's not an option. Look at me. Would you employ me? I'm unemployable. Got any booze?'

'Not really. There might be some Jewish Sherry in that bottle.'

Pete held the bottle to the light. A cigarette end floated on top of the sherry like a dead body. He took a swig.

'Do you still see any of the old crew?' I asked.

'Not really. Julian gets his toes removed for science on a regular basis. They cut off a toe and then pop it back on again. £500 a toe. Think he makes quite a good living out of it. Been considering it myself. They're talking about doing his fingers next. Reckons he'll get a couple of grand for his nob…'

I laughed.

'So, the band is going well, is it? These some of your lyrics?'

Pete picked up one of my notebooks and flicked through the pages full of half-finished lyrics and ideas for sitcoms. I cringed, suddenly embarrassed by Pete looking at my scribblings.

'They're not finished… just ideas.'

'"*Love, love, it's hit me like a boxing glove. I used to be a cynic but now I need a clinic.*"'

Pete threw the notepad dismissively back on the floor.

'Very good, Macleod. Gold star. So, you want to be a pop star?'

'Well…'

'Sorry, or should I say a songwriter?'

'Well, yes, I suppose…'

'London is the place for wild ambition. You're lucky. You know what you want to do. Have fun giving it a go…'

'What about you? What do you want to do?'

'That is the big unanswered question, Macleod. Every time I think about what I want, I get a big fat blank zero. If I can entice Vicky into marrying me, then I can live off her family trust fund and write maybe…'

'So, you want to be a writer?'

'Dunno, not sure what I can bring to the party. It's all been said before and far more eloquently than I could. Miller, Orwell, how can I compete with these brilliant minds, and why add to the morass?'

These words pricked. I hoped I wasn't adding to the morass.

Pete finished making his cigarette. He lit it and dry-retched.

15.2

For the next few months, the red sofa in my bedroom became Pete's refuge. I didn't mind too much as Pete was interesting and entertaining company and we bonded over our shared desire to avoid getting a nine-to-five. Days turned into weeks sat in my room chatting and swapping ideas, drinking into the small hours, drilling into the nitty-gritty of things. Although my aspiration to become a pop star was to his mind highly vacuous, at least it was a rejection of working in an office as a grey slave to the money god. The mention of work or a job produced a physical reaction in Pete like he was about to vomit. Pete was more interested in trying to unravel the human condition and referenced Jung and Kierkegaard and Nietzsche in a never-ending loop of philosophical questions – did the self exist? What was morality? What was the truth in a post-post-modern world? For Pete, our late-night conversations were a genuine attempt to try and understand and interpret the world around him, as well as helping to quash his growing feelings of alienation and paranoia.

But for me, it was all potential material for a comedy routine. And the more desperate Pete was about his situation, the funnier I found it. The more he dry-retched, the more I saw a funny prop. The obvious cure for his ills was joining me in stand-up comedy. Pete met my suggestion with a look of horror. The last thing he wanted to do was get up on stage in front of a load of strangers in an attempt to make them laugh, especially with his chronic agoraphobia. But I knew deep down Pete wanted to be famous too. Who didn't crave the three As of applause, admiration and affirmation? Plus, he had a talent which I could use. Pete was a brilliant writer with a funny turn of phrase, and as I explained, his best route to a seductive new world as a bestselling author and philosopher was to join me on stage.

'Come on, Pete, if we think we're funny we can do this.'

'But I don't think we're funny.'

'What's the worst that can happen?'

'People laughing at me.'

'Exactly, that's what we want. It's a win-win.'

This had stumped him. He dry-retched.

'And even if they don't laugh, who cares!'

My logic was simple: we had everything to gain and nothing to lose. Except, Pete argued, things like dignity and confidence, which were particularly fragile in his case. For a long time he stubbornly resisted my advances. He had an alternative masterplan: in the absence of a beautiful trust fund girl who could pay the bills while he worked out the meaning of life in the south of France, his plan was to go and live on a commune. And he wanted me to join him. There was no way I was going to waste my time doing that. You couldn't become famous on a commune, except if it became a murderous cult.

I needed to get Pete excited about the steeplechase of fame. Just three hurdles to jump fuelled by the Four Ds of determination, drive, dedication and desire.

'But I don't have any of those Ds,' said Pete. 'Plus, shouldn't it just be one D, because they are effectively the same thing?'

Pete was being pedantic. And his eyes weren't on the prize. We were funny and there was a gap in the market for funny comedians. Comedy could be a vehicle to a new exciting world. His heroes were American comedians like Lenny Bruce and Bill Hicks – weren't they the real poets speaking truth to power, holding a mirror up to society to reveal its absurdities? Plus, we could earn good money. This piqued his interest and like Marcus and Stu before him, I lured him into my web, making the impossible dream seem possible, spinning it like it was candyfloss.

To seal the deal, I reused the classic sales tactic of taking this once-in-a-lifetime offer off the table. I told Pete that with or without him I was going to book a stand-up comedy slot. I saw the whites of his eyes as he calculated a cost-benefit analysis. Gone were the unanswerable questions about the self and morality, now he had one tangible problem: was he actually about to agree to this madness? And who was madder – the first lemming jumping off the cliff or the lemming who followed him?

In the end, the chance I might pull it off was too much of a risk – Pete would never forgive himself if I turned this seductive vision of swanning around the globe making people laugh into a reality. Plus, he had no other options other than graduate study in toe removal which seemed like hard and painful work. Eventually, he agreed on the condition that if the comedy didn't work, we would go live on a commune. I humoured him knowing that in the unlikely event that the stand-up didn't work, I always had the band.

15.3

Our metamorphosis into comedians created some tension with Marcus. He was not so enamoured by the arrival, and the distraction, of Pete. We crossed paths in the morning as Marcus tried to make breakfast while Pete and I giggled like fools having been up all night plotting and drinking. Later Marcus returned from a monotonous ten-hour shift in the frozen veg aisle to find us just getting up. I needed to reassure him this situation was only temporary and the comedy would ultimately benefit The Pointy Birds. Plus, it was only a few months until Dave and Josh would be free. But there was concern in his eyes like I was having an affair, and with each passing week it felt like we were drifting apart – Marcus a diminishing dot on the beach of sanity. As we passed in the corridor, I avoided eye contact. His looks of disappointment and sad sighs were made more profound by his brown Sainsbury's uniform, name badge and clip-on tie – his sacrifice for rock'n'roll.

The only issue was we didn't have any comedy material. We

worked on one routine called 'The Body Cocktail' which was like a fake cookery show where we ate parts of our body in times of austerity. The routine had potential but it lost some of its pizzazz when we attempted to write it down. Plus, our styles were quite different. My silly storytelling involving funny characters and impressions was hard to fit with Pete's cynical rants. We knew all comedy was all about non-embellishment. If we could tap into the truth then we would find humour, or tragedy. And that applied to any comedian, whether Bill Hicks or Billy Connolly.

Slowly, we created a world that was a piss-take of the one that existed outside our window, with a mantra that had three main tenants:

Philosophy is War
Art is Sex
Comedy is Truth

But it was still hard to shape into a rehearsed routine. There was only one solution: it would be better to be spontaneous. We should just do it and see what happens. And the perfect way to dip our toes in the water was at the new comedians' open mic night in Old Street. I had been a few times and never thought much of the competition. Next stop the Edinburgh festival and scooping the Perrier award. Pete looked at me with horror like he had seen a ghost. Was I completely nuts? OK, he had agreed to do it, but doing it without rehearsed material was crazy. Maybe he had agreed not quite believing it would actually happen. But when I returned from shopping with a new purple denim jacket and jeans combo, he knew I was serious. The new outfit went with the hair and boots and was the perfect rockstar-comedian look.

*

The Comedy Cafe on Rivington Street near Old Street Tube ran an open mic comedy night every Wednesday. Each comedian had five minutes to make the audience laugh without being booed off. We arrived before doors and signed up. Out of twelve new comedians, we were last to go on. Everything depended on my ability to bluff our way through the set. It would be a long hard fall if this goes wrong, Pete kept telling me. The room was busy and the audience had suffered eleven terrible comedians but were in good spirits. They were now drunk and wanted to laugh. Backstage, Pete's eleventh-hour pleas about the insanity of what we were about to do fell on deaf ears. I repeated the mantra: if we think we're funny, we can do this. Comedy is Truth. We took to the stage.

Pete was shaking like a leaf. His long greasy fringe covered his face. A pint of lager in trembling hand, a fag in the other. He was the perfect counterpoint to me, who was loving the limelight. It was a bit weird to not have the safety blanket of the band, and the inter-song banter. We had piqued the crowd's curiosity as we took the stage but then my mind went blank. The cat had caught my tongue.

I wasn't sure what to say. Or how to say it. Like in the scene in *Life Of Brian* when the crowd waits eagerly to hear what Brian has to say, but he has nothing. I noticed the lead singer of the pop band King in the audience. They had had that big hit with 'Love and Pride' in the eighties. The catchy chorus rotated in my head:

'That's what my heart yearns for now. Love and pride.'

I had watched him on *Top Of The Pops* and now he was here watching me. Freaky. I lifted my finger, about to speak just like Brian. I held it there for a while and then decided against. I really did have this audience in the palm of my hand but the trouble was I didn't have any snacks to feed the horse. Pete stood by my side shaking. It was at this point the compère re-entered the stage.

'Sorry, lads, that's enough.'

'What?' I protested, relieved but sensing an opportunity.

The compère wasn't having it. 'This night is for new comedians that have a routine worked out...'

He had seen through us but the audience hadn't. The crowd booed the compere and wanted more of us. I bowed, waved and left the stage. Pete followed. We went to the bar and got a drink calibrating what had happened as people came up to us and slapped our backs.

'That was really funny.'

'Shame the compère chucked you off.'

There was no doubt we had hit comedy gold – silent comedy. No one else was doing it. We would go on stage, say nothing and the Perrier Award would be ours. It had helped turn Brian into the new messiah so there was no reason why it couldn't work for us too.

16. The Chuckle Club

FEBRUARY 1992

First proper booking as comedians does not go as expected and some harsh lessons are learned.

We needed another booking so I scanned the listings of *Time Out* and rang a comedy venue called The Chuckle Club hosted by the larger-than-life comedy promoter, Eugene Cheese. Eugene answered the phone and I told him we were a new comedy duo just off the back of winning the new comedian's night at Comedy Cafe.

'Well, you're in luck because I had a cancellation this Friday. Opening slot.'

'Great.'

'What are you called?'

I hadn't thought.

'Andy and Pete.'

'OK, see you there at 7.30, doors will be 7.45.'

We had our second gig in the bag. This comedy lark was easy.

The Chuckle Club was a regular Friday night fixture on the comedy circuit situated above a pub near Russell Square Tube. An old school friend Tim had just returned from backpacking around China and fancied coming along for a laugh. We arrived at the allotted time and entered a busy pub. Pete scanned the room nervously and dry-retched – he was having second thoughts. A bell rang, followed by an announcement.

'The comedy starts in fifteen minutes – please make your way upstairs.'

The crowd started to snake its way upstairs. Pete made some protestations but they fell on deaf ears. We followed the queue and introduced ourselves to the cashier at the top.

'Hi, we're the comedians for tonight, Andy and Pete.'

It felt great to say these words out loud. She eyed us up and down and waved us through. I could tell she was impressed by my purple clobber.

'Eugene is through there. You can't miss him.'

The venue was a large and slightly sterile room with big bay windows, high ceilings, a stage in the corner and rows of stack chairs. It was already busy, mainly rotund businessmen with loud laughs and trophy wives. It was the end of a long week; they'd paid good money to hear some jokes and have a laugh, a brief anaesthetic to their bills and broken hearts. Tim made a beeline to the bar; even he looked anxious – if we went down, he went down too.

As the room filled, and the chatter and clatter increased, I was feeling less sure about the task in hand. At the Comedy Cafe we had gone on much later, and the audience had had a few drinks, plus they were much younger. This Chuckle Club crowd were much older, currently sober and we were going on first. I needed to remember what the drama teacher had said all those years ago, who cares what people think! This mantra had served me well so far, but I could feel my confidence seeping like air from a tyre and like all punctures it wasn't happening at a convenient time.

Tim returned from the bar with three pints of lager and a big grin fixed on his face, betrayed by the concern in his eyes.

'Here you go, guys. I can't believe you're going to do this.'

'It's fucking nuts,' replied Pete.

We shuffled over to a quieter spot in the corner away from the crowd and sipped our beers in silence. Pete stared ahead, not blinking like a man condemned to execution. Tim kept shaking his head and tutting and laughing incredulously to himself, punctuating the silence with the same question on repeat.

'You not seriously going through with this, are you?'

I avoided eye contact, pretending I hadn't heard his question. My mouth had become too dry to answer. Tim needed to stop with the questions. It was making Pete very fidgety. The promoter Eugene appeared.

'Ah, gentlemen, I assume you are Andy and Pete?'

We nodded.

'I can always tell a couple of comedians when I see them. Nice to meet you. We won't be long now. Give this lot a chance to get watered and comfortable, and we'll get cracking.' He looked at his watch. 'You should be on in about twenty, yes? Got any other gigs tonight?'

I shook my head. The power of speech had left me. He scanned the room, nodding and smiling and acknowledging people as they filed past and then whispered conspiratorially.

'Could have sold it out twice over tonight. We'll be turning people away…'

I lifted my eyebrows in an attempt to feign enthusiasm. It didn't correspond to how I felt inside.

'…and a few television bods in tonight too.'

He lingered for a bit longer and then left us to it – Pete dry-retched.

As people started to settle in their seats, the doors, proudly adorned with a 'sold out' sign, were squashed shut. It was showtime. Tim appeared with another three beers. Pete grabbed one and drained it. I could hear him muttering to Tim.

'I need to talk to father. He was right. If I transfer my degree to something vocational, maybe an MBA… Macleod has led me up the garden path for too long…'

As the lights dimmed, a new clarity formed in Pete's mind: what we were about to do was lunacy, and he needed to leave immediately. He looked for the exit, but he was on the wrong side of a very packed room. Too late! The lights went up to reveal a larger-than-life MC Eugene Cheese on stage.

'Good evening, ladies and gentlebums! Welcome to the Chuckle Club!'

The audience roared like a lion, and my grip tightened around my pint glass as Eugene Cheese produced a banjo and broke into song. The crowd knew the words and sang along.

'Tickle my teeth tickle my teeth.
Scratch my chin scratch my chin.
Slap my thighs slap my thighs
Wiggle my bum wiggle my bum
Welcome to The Chuckle Club.'

The words and laughter became muted as if I was underwater – my body's pathetic attempt to escape the madness of the current situation. Now was not the time to question the logic. We were about to board a high-speed plane, and I was a blind pilot without a license. We had no parachute, and the plane was aflame.

The song ended. Eugene continued.

'Yes, we've got an incredible line-up for you tonight, ladies and gentle-buttocks. '

The crowd giggled.

'Headlining we have the Perrier Award winner, Doug Anthony All-Stars with a sneak preview of their forthcoming Edinburgh show…'

The crowd whooped and hollered.

'We have *Time Out*'s best new comedian.'

More whoops and hollering.

'And a special mystery guest.'

The crowd make a big 'OOO' sound.

'Now, in all the years I been slapping my thighs and tickling your teeth, I think this might be the best Chuckle line-up ever. I've got all the best ingredients I just need you to give it a stir and season with your laughter, and we'll all enjoy feeding on the feast of comedy that I have for you tonight.'

A man in a pinstripe and braces stood up and shouted out, 'SAY SOMETHING FUNNYYYYYYYY!'

The lion roared.

'All in good time, sir, all in good time. Now, you might be wondering why I'm dressed as a bumblebee?'

''Coz you got a little prick?' said the heckler in pinstripes still standing.

The lion roared again.

'Now bear with me, bear with me, I'll explain. You see, earlier this week I had a wee accident!'

'What, you pissed yourself?'

More sniggering

'Good one! No, no, not that kind of accident. It was quite nasty, actually.'

In unison, the crowd sigh in sympathy.

'Yes, I slipped in the shower, and I hurt my bottom.'

A few sniggers ripple through the crowd.

'That's funny? I just said bottom?'

More sniggers.

'Bottom?'

A big laugh.

'But yes, ladies and gentlebums, I hurt my bottom. Ladies and gentlemen, I slipped in the shower and damaged my coccyx…'

Eugene started another song wiggling his colossal bulk to the routine he had practised:

'It ain't a laugh to fall out of the bath.
And land on your bum it didn't make me hum,
I need some lotion to rub it in slow motion.
Caress, massage in the tiger balm,
Anything to relieve the harm.
Is not a ruse I got big bruise…'

The audience clapped along until the song ended to rapturous applause. The room was alive and kicking. Eugene threw in some topical satire on Kinnock and Major, seasoned with a few references to people in the audience.

'Nice to see Bob Gladville commissioner at ITV – let's hear it for Bob.'

The crowd cheered.

'And, Bob, if you are wondering, yes, I am available to host next year's BAFTAs.'

He was a pro and in the space of five minutes had created a warm and happy atmosphere. He ended once again with the Chuckle Club sing-song.

'Tickle my teeth tickle my teeth…'

It was nearly time.

'Now, first up tonight, two young lads who earlier this week won the newcomers night at the Comedy Cafe so, now I'm going to put my neck on the line here.'

A hush descended in the room.

'Here at the Chuckle Club, we pride ourselves on our ability to pan for gold and showcase tomorrow's stars today. Now I only just met them, but I like to think I have a nose for comedy and I got a feeling we're in for a surprise…'

It was hard to hear what he was saying from the loud thumping in my chest.

'I'm looking forward to seeing what they can do as much as you…'

THUMP THUMP THUMP.

'Please tickle your teeth…'

THUMP THUMP THUMP.

'And welcome on to the stage…'

THUMP THUMP THUMP.

'Tonight's hors d'oeuvre …'

THUMP THUMP THUMP.

'Andy and Pete…!'

The bubble popped. The lion roared. The moment was upon us. I looked at Pete, and for the first time in the months we had spent together, our eyes properly locked together. I could see the 11-year-old I had first met at school flash before my eyes, holding a tennis trophy aloft. Those same pale blue eyes, just visible in the now bloated and weary face – the only remnant of that Golden Boy now frightened and desperate to flee.

If we think we're funny, we can do this.

We weaved our way through the crowd. The stage was only a foot high from the ground and less than a foot from the front row. A hush descended as we took our positions. Pete was visibly shaking; head bowed with a long and greasy fringe covering his face, unlit cigarette in one hand, empty pint in the other. At the Comedy Cafe, I thought we were an amusing sight, but in this brightly lit pub in front of a group of tired city workers, Pete was a sobering vision.

The room was now as quiet as a library. Muted laughter and gaiety floated up through the floorboards from the pub below. All eyes were upon me, waiting for me to say something funny. They all wanted to laugh. A pregnant woman in the front row was smiling sweetly, holding hands with her partner – maybe this was their last night out before they started a family. It was suddenly all too real. I tried to smile, but frustratingly my facial muscles were on strike, and I produced a grimace instead as if about to impart some trapped wind. She returned a half-smile and then averted her gaze. I tried to swallow, but my mouth was parched. I stupidly hadn't brought a drink with me on to the stage. The room was at a complete standstill. The only sound was of the barman drying glasses, but eventually he stopped, sensing the squeak of the towel on glass was a distraction. I could see Tim at the bar with his head in his hands. I could feel the vibrations through the floorboards from Pete's shaking body.

The silence continued. I looked down at the floorboards of the stage and examined all the nooks and grains, the intricate details of the wood. I wondered, was that oak or pine or Peruvian mahogany? Funny how little I knew of real-life things and how much there was to learn. I re-entered the bubble – even the noise from the pub below seemed to have stopped, just the steady beat of my heart thumping loudly in my ears.

THUMP THUMP THUMP.

I looked up and noticed some of the audience members were looking at Pete in a concerned fashion; others were confused. Was this the act, or was it chronic stage fright? How long should we give them? Some had bowed their heads and didn't want to look; some were still with us – they had faith in Eugene. One man had a grin from ear to ear as if he'd seen this all before and this was just a prelude to something hilarious. He gave me a wink and a little bit of hope.

OK, this had been going on long enough, it was time to break the ice. I took a step forward. The board creaked, people visibly rose in their seats, Pete slightly turned his head, the woman in the front row looked up.

Please, say something funny.

Slowly, I lifted the microphone to my mouth. It was my moment, the whole room was with me, willing me on. It didn't need to be much, anything to puncture this silence. But still, nothing came. My mind was blank, the tyre completely flat. If we could hold out a bit longer then maybe this silence would start to become funny, rather than strange and uncomfortable. It was our only hope. I waited with the microphone in my hand, but the silence only grew louder, the atmosphere thicker, the air thinner. Maybe if I adopted a funny posture, it would draw the audience into our world, but my limbs felt heavy – a kind of paralysis was setting in. Most of the audience were now not only silent but had become very still like each member dared not move. They were holding their breaths. We had in the space of one minute managed to turn the euphoric atmosphere in The Chuckle Club to that of a funeral.

At the bar, Tim was ruminating on the long-term future of our friendship, The towering figure of Eugene was silhouetted at the window, but still the silence; still the beating heart; still the flat tyre; still the bubble. I knew our silent comedian's experiment wasn't working and a feeling of resignation slowly started to come over me like warm honey bringing with it a perverse calm.

I reflected on my life. Maybe I wasn't cut out to be an entertainer. What was holding me back? Was I just a small fish in a small pond? A bit delusional? A dreamboat in a leather coat? Maybe I did need to make some changes. A steady girlfriend would be nice; a job with prospects perhaps. And Pete was doing my head in with his never-ending questions about morality and the self, unanswerable theories spinning round and round like boomerangs. Marcus was right – 'Bloody existential bollocks.' Dad was right – I needed two years in the real world. A bit of de-studentification.

I tried to lift the microphone once more, but it was too heavy. I was about to admit defeat when I remembered our mantra. The Truth! Great comedy was the truth, tell it like it is, like it really is. I could feel a seed of inspiration growing. I lifted the microphone confidently, looked up at the audience and delivered the truth.

'My girlfriend just left me.'

There followed a brief moment of further silence as the words hung in the air. Not the kind of moment that Mozart might experience as his last note faded before his audience exploded into rhapsody. It was more the kind of a car skidding on black ice before a head-on collision. And then a solitary voice from the back row, a perfectly timed hand grenade of a heckle, filled with venom and sarcasm from the man in the pin-striped suit and braces.

'Yeah, and I wonder why, mate.'

The room exploded in laughter, the bubble burst, the lion roared. It was a tennis professional demolishing a flimsy serve. Fatally, I had no comeback. We were about to be eaten alive.

Come on, think, the truth, hit them with it.

But alas I couldn't remember what the truth was as torrents of abuse start getting hurled our way.

'What, she didn't like the quiet type?'

'Couldn't get a word in edgeways?'

As I grappled unsuccessfully for a retort, the chorus from John Lennon song 'Gimme Some Truth' spun aimlessly in my head. My humiliation was complete. There was only one thing for it: embrace the heckle, they can't hurt me. I closed my eyes, bowed my head and flinging my arm either side adopted a crucifix pose. It provoked more merriment – maybe this was my truth.

It was at this point that an inaudible murmur started up over the PA. Initially, it sounded as if someone was moaning in pain, but pretty soon words were decipherable over the cacophony of abuse being hurled in our direction. Pete had decided to speak. It was monotone as if he was reading from a list, but he was definitely speaking.

'In times of recession we all need to eat, but food can be expensive, so we have come up with a solution that is not only affordable but healthy and damn tasty too.'

From my cross, I opened one eye and tilted my head sideways. I couldn't believe my ears, the one routine we had practised. I tried to warn him.

'We call it The Body Cocktail.'

Too late, but it had brought some calm from the audience as they quietened down to hear what Pete was trying to say. Pete was still staring at the floor, and the microphone kept feeding back, but Pete continued undeterred.

'The body cocktail is our way of saving money while keeping you fed through the long winter months.'

I bowed my head. The crucifixion was complete. Each word a nail.

Slowly, Pete raised a finger. 'First take your index finger and insert it up a nostril, any nostril will do.'

Pete inserted his finger up his nose and continued, adding a nasal quality to the monotone.

'Think of it like a pig hunting for truffles. In this case, we are hunting for nose candy, and there is plenty. Come on, everyone, have a go yourselves, either nostril will do.'

There was a collective intake of disgust from the audience as Pete continued to walk the fine line between comedy and tragedy. The pregnant woman in the front row squeezed her partner's hand and yelped as Pete extracted something long and stringy from his nose and brandished it at the audience.

'Here's one I made earlier,' he said.

Was Pete about to send her into labour? He inserted his other index finger up the other nostril. I decided to keep my counsel and my crucifix pose, although my arms were aching. There was confidence in Pete's voice now; he even embellished it with a fake celebrity chef accent.

'People think eating le bogey is disgusting, but we all secretly do it – let's not be hypocrites.'

There were increased levels of disgust from the audience, but he soldiered on. I had to give him some respect for at least trying.

'We believe nose candy is a nutritious substitute, take what the body naturally produces. Now roll it up into a little ball like so. Now we need a little bit of sweat or binding agent from the genitalia.'

As Pete put a hand down his pants, Eugene started to make his way through the commotion in the audience. Pete was warming to the theme as he turned full cookery show host.

'Don't be afraid to taste as you go. All good cooks try as they go.'

Pete stopped to sniff his finger. There was now audible disgust in the audience. Pete had managed to transfix them, but before he could continue, Eugene yanked the microphone from Pete.

'OK, lads, that's quite enough…'

Eugene gave us a stern and disappointed look of a father reprimanding his children and shook his head sadly. I nodded in acceptance and resignation. We stepped off the stage and made a walk of shame through the audience back to the bar. Tim had disappeared. We later received news that he had decided to go travelling again. Eugene tapped the mic.

'Well, that was a bit different. Please give a hand for Andy and Pete.'

There was a lacklustre round of applause. Eugene swiftly announced the next comedian who burst onto the stage to release the pent-up laughter that had been denied to us. Once again, the room was transported to a warm and happier place. I could feel Pete's presence next to me, but I dared not look at him. I stood at the bar, trying to process what had just happened. We were being stared at like we had the plague. I suppose this was what it was like to be famous.

17. Fork

MID-FEBRUARY 1992

The offer of a full-time job brings me to a crossroads but is maybe also an opportunity. Marcus reveals a talent for lyric-writing as a new song is born.

The people from the DHSS were on my bleeding back again. I needed to show evidence I was actively looking for work. Very tedious. I didn't have time to look for work. And although it was sporting of them to cover the rent, it only went so far and didn't cover the seven nights I needed to spend each week socialising and networking. The comedy routine wasn't exactly bringing in the bacon, but a solution of sorts presented itself through a random phone call from a college friend from City Poly.

'Not sure if you're interested but there's a job going at this new independent record store in Soho.'

I felt an icy hand clutch my heart at the mention of this three-letter swear word. Dan continued.

'They are looking for someone who knows about music, so I recommenced you. Good money too. £220 per week. You've got to work five days, including Saturdays. Interested?'

That was a lot of money. Plus it was a job in music, of sorts. There would be no more money worries allowing me to record the demo. The icy hand relinquished its grip, but a knot of dread tightened in my stomach at the inevitability of my answer.

'Right… when would this be starting?'

'They're looking for someone to start in March.'

'Christ. March is only two weeks away.'

I looked over at the sofa while considering my options. Pete was asleep with his mouth open and hands down his pants. I looked down the corridor towards the kitchen, the leaning tower of pizza boxes, overflowing sink and spaghetti stuck to the wall. I sniffed the air to check the general stench – it was still putrid. I did a quick cost-benefit analysis. It would get DHSS off my back, but what about the band? I felt a sudden resolve that this would be purely temporary. And I did need something to kick against; a bit of structure, for focus. It would be a couple of months max. Most importantly, it would facilitate the recording of a demo.

'OK, I'm interested. What next?'

'Great. You need to go and meet the manager, Tracey, for an interview, but don't worry – it will be a formality. The shop is called Selectadisc, and it's on Berwick Street.'

'Selectadisc?'

I laughed – what a silly name.

'Can you go in this afternoon?'

'OK, yes, I suppose I can…'

I hung up and stared at the wall ahead. I had never noticed before, but it was covered in dirty fingerprints, a chart of knuckleheaded groping that had unfolded over the past few years. I studied the various smudges and smears aware that I had just made a life-changing decision – a full-time job. I reminded myself this would only be temporary, but already I could feel an urgency creep within me. How depressing, was this de-studentisation? Or was it taking control of a car skidding on ice headed towards a tree? At my driving lesson in Crowborough, the instructor taught me that in a skid you had to turn in to the skid, to get out of the skid. It was counter-intuitive. It was funny how this thought came to mind now.

I decided to break the news to Pete. It would be our *Withnail and I* moment.

'Pete, wake up.' I prodded him.

Pete opened a puffy eye.

'I've been offered a job.'

Pete sat up. He had woken from a pleasant dream into a nightmare – dry red wine caked his mouth.

'A what?'

'A job.'

He dry-retched and then nodded gravely. A confused look of horror and disappointment etched upon his face. Not that much different to normal at least, I thought.

'So, does this mean the commune is a no-go?'

'Probs.'

He nodded, sadly internalising the gravity of his situation. Had he pinned his hopes on the commune? People on communes must need laughs; maybe a comedy career would work out for him after all. He started rummaging in the ashtray.

*

I left Pete to it. I had a shower and got the Tube to Tottenham Court Road and made my way through the streets of Soho to my interview at the shop. It felt refreshing to be in a new environment, especially such a vibrant community as Soho. I felt energised not just by my surroundings but by new horizons. February had been a cruel month so far and change was as good as a rest. There were only so many mornings you could wake up with your nose in an ashtray.

It was an optimistic kind of day and everything felt clearly defined. However, in contrast, the shop was dark. There were no windows to the outside world and some very discordant metal music was playing loudly. It was like walking from day into night. Or heaven to hell. Three people were behind the counter putting records in sleeves, opening boxes and looking at delivery notes. Two of the employees were male, and one was female. I guessed the female was Tracey, so I made a beeline for her. She took no notice of me. I coughed. Still, she took no notice. I coughed again, but she obviously couldn't hear above the infernal din. I shouted an 'excuse me'.

'Yes?' she said, not lifting her head to look at the person to whom she was talking.

I continued shouting. 'Oh, hi, it's Andy. I'm here for an interview. Are you Tracey?'

She lifted her head and looked me up and down. She didn't seem overly impressed. She asked me a question, but I couldn't hear what she was asking.

'I'M SORRY, CAN YOU REPEAT THAT?'

She repeated the question.

'Sorry, I can't quite hear you.'

It was like two people talking in a storm. Our words being carried away by howling guitars. Turning down the volume didn't seem to be an option. The two other guys behind the counter were preoccupied and had yet to acknowledge my presence. Tracey tried again.

'I SAID, WHAT MUSIC ARE YOU INTO?'

'Um… gosh, where to start…?'

I had been going through a Lenny Kravitz phase. His two albums *Let Love Rule* and *Mama Said* were hardly off my stereo, but instinctively I knew that might not go down well. I decided to be economical with the truth.

'Well, when I woke up this morning the album I put on was Nirvana's album *Nevermind*.'

Tracey nodded. 'OK, you got the job.'

God, that was easy. I was invited behind the counter and went downstairs to the office for a cup of tea, where she explained a few rules:

1. She was called Gaffer.
4. The customer was not always right.
5. Swearing was encouraged.
6. Strictly no chart stuff.

'There's one more rule,' she said, 'the golden rule. People don't leave Selectadisc. It's a job for life.'

I nodded, feeling numb.

'We're going to be the best independent record store in London.'

She had one last question.

'What football team do you support?'

'Spurs.'

She shook her head sadly. 'See you on Monday 2 March. 9 a.m. Don't be late.'

17.2

I now had less than two weeks. I returned to the flat in a shocked daze. There were no signs of Pete or his belongings. Had he left? Maybe it was for the best – he needed to get cracking on his flowing beard and commune set. I also needed to make stuff happen. It was now or never. I felt like an elastic band being stretched, soon to either shoot off or snap. I knew what I had to do. I knocked on Marcus's bedroom door. I hadn't seen much of him and felt things had become a bit estranged between us since Pete had arrived.

'Come in,' said the voice behind the door.

Marcus sat on his bed in his brown uniform with his red bass guitar on his lap. It was unplugged, but he had been practising. I smiled sheepishly. He nodded hello. There was no time for small talk – I got straight to the heart of the matter.

'We need to record a demo.'

A smile crept across his face. 'I know.'

'Fancy a jam?'

He didn't need to answer in the affirmative – it was a given. I returned to my room and grabbed my guitar. When I got back, Marcus had a surprise for me. He bashfully produced a piece of A4 paper and handed it to me.

'What's this? Not your P45, I hope!'

'It's just something I wrote. See what you think. Might fit one of the songs?'

I unfolded the paper and read. The title of the song was 'Razor Blades And Lightning'. It detailed a near accident with his manhood while shaving in the bath – it was quite literally a close shave.

'With a flick of the wrist and it could have been
Blood in the bath not from my chin.'

It had drama; it had humour; it had pathos; it was subtle. It was everything a Pointy Birds song should be, with a rhyming couplet prophetically articulating a desire or longing maybe never to be satisfied:

'Could've been on a glistening beach
sipping white rum well within reach.'

I had to doff my cap. It was lyric-writing of top order.

'Marcus, this is brilliant. It might fit that song we don't have lyrics for yet?'

Marcus knew the one I meant.

'Let's give it a go.'

The song was a bit of a mongrel. An old chord progression by Stu that I had nicked and added a chorus and vocal melody to, but it needed lyrics. The bittersweet sentiment of 'Razor Blades And Lightning' would be a perfect counterpoint for the more upbeat vocal melody which I had lifted from the verse of 'Sowing The Seeds Of Love' by Tears for Fears, which they had stolen from 'I Am The Walrus' by The Beatles. The best pop songs often had a dark underbelly lyrically; otherwise things could become too sugary sweet or worse, enter cheese territory. Not that there was anything wrong with a bit of cheese. But it had to be good cheese. 'Razor Blades And Lightning' was like a well-aged stilton. The words fit the melody like a Cinderella slipper, and at the next rehearsal we added a guitar riff that gave the song a Pearl and Dean or James Bond vibe. Bish bosh, we had another hit in waiting. The decision that 'Razor Blades And Lightning' should be one of three songs we would record as part of our first demo was a no-brainer. We needed to find a studio and an engineer and record a demo that would blow the music industry's socks off. There was only one man for the job: Ernie.

18. Ernie's

FEBRUARY 29–MARCH 1 1992

Our first time in a studio to record a demo. The keyboard riff rift resolves itself temporarily. Some musings on the creative process and more pondering of the future.

The final weekend before starting my new job at Selectadisc, we played our last residency show supporting Paint. It doubled up as the perfect rehearsal ahead of getting in Ernie's studio. Dave and Josh travelled down from their respective universities for the gig, and we impressed a packed and very drunk Friday-night crowd, winning over a few new fans along the way. The band was tight. We rocked, and it was clear these songs were ready for posterity.

The following morning, we drove down to East Sussex, and Ernie greeted us outside his small semi-detached house on the edge of town. Ernie was a friend of Josh's older brother and ran a recording studio from his home in Crowborough. He was about ten years older than us and had played in numerous legendary local bands. There was something of the Elvis Costello about him. He was shy and quiet, and in this leafy suburban commuter belt of golf courses and conservative clubs, he could parade his rebellion with a black leather jacket, spiky hair and national health specs. Locals probably suspected he might have a tattoo. No doubt he enjoyed his role as the only punk in the town, as much as a couple of pints of Harvey's in The Wheatsheaf, where he might offer a few war stories about the times they nearly made it, playing the Tunbridge Wells Forum.

From the outside, his home looked like a regular dwelling, but it soon became apparent that he had spared no detail in converting his one-up-one-down into a recording studio. The sitting room was set up as a live room for the band to play, the walls and ceilings covered in egg cartons for soundproofing, and spaghetti junctions of leads were cabled all around the house. The toilet doubled up as a vocal booth, and his bedroom was the control room. Luckily the kitchen had been spared, so cups of tea were not a problem. There wasn't much in the way of regular furniture or soft furnishings. It seemed unlikely he brought many ladies back for romancing and dancing.

Ernie had made sacrifices in a bid to capture the spirit of rock'n'roll, but what Ernie didn't realise yet was that The Pointy Birds were here to help him achieve his task. I felt for his neighbours, but he waved away any concerns explaining that an old deaf couple lived next door. And Crowborough needed waking up a bit – after all, he had to live up to his punk reputation.

Immediately, Ernie got busy setting up microphones and running leads to record the drums and various instruments. I watched in admiration as he scuttled back and forth, hunched over the amps, getting the mics in the right position and checking leads were working, and sound levels were correct like a mad scientist ahead of an experiment. There was no joking around, just serious intent for the job in hand. Even though we were paying him, it felt great that he was taking us seriously. When I became prime minister, I would put him on the honours list for services to rock'n'roll. Ernie OBE had a ring to it.

We unpacked and made ourselves at home. Tea was made and a packet of chocolate Hobnobs was seductively unwrapped. We were tuned up and ready to rock. I wasn't so bothered about playing any instruments so delegated guitar to the superior skills of Dave and Josh. My role was of singer and conductor. We had chosen to record three songs – 'Liquorice', 'Nostradamus Blues' and 'Razor Blades And Lightning', which we decided to race through as a warm-up.

As the band played, I jumped up and down as only a lead singer with no inhibitions could. In addition to vocal duties, my job was to enthuse, encourage, cajole, motivate and inspire the other members of the band while they played – keep their energy levels up. It involved lots of eye contact, winking, tongue waggling and air guitar. Although it was quite a cramped space, it was necessary to find my inner Freddie Mercury. This demo was our CV. And if it sounded shit, I only had a future working in a record shop. But I had no doubt we were nailing it. When we finished, silence filled the room. Ernie gave nothing away, but I knew he was impressed.

Ernie called us through to the control room to have a listen. He had secretly recorded our warm-up without telling us. We assembled into the cramped space as he explained that the vocals and guitars were just guides which we would redo later as there were a few bum notes here and there, but this was to give us an idea of how the recordings might sound. He pressed play. We sounded vast and unwieldy and incredible. Computer screens and effects units surrounded us, displaying different information as the music boomed out of the speakers and monitors. Ernie swung around in his wheely chair pressing buttons and adjusting levels on the mixing desk like Hans Solo at the helm of the Millennium Falcon. I had no idea what anything did, but I could tell he was in his element. I suppose Paul made a decent R2D2. I scanned the rest of the band. Marcus was C-3PO, Dave was Chewbacca and Josh would be a toss-up between Darth Vader and Obi-Wan. I was Luke Skywalker, obviously.

Ernie could isolate each instrument or even different parts of the drums. Each component of the song had a dedicated track on his desk which could be adjusted in volume and embellished with effects. He wanted to get the perfect take of each instrument, and then we could polish up and add effects afterwards. To give us an idea, he gave us a tantalising glimpse of how he could add distortion to the bass or reverb to the vocal. He then stripped away everything but the drums.

Alone they sounded terrific, and there were a million ways we could adjust their sound. For example, if we wanted a punk feel, there would be a more prominent snare in the mix, or maybe we wanted the drums a little warmer and lower in the mix to give the track a mellow groove. I soon realised the art of this was about knowing what you wanted; the options were limitless.

'It's all in the mix,' Ernie kept saying.

The final say of how each instrument and song should sound usually led to a fight within the band. Bands fell out over the final mix as much as they did when the drummer slept with another member's girlfriend.

We left the control room inspired and returned to the live room to record (or 'track') each instrument. The idea was to record all the parts for each song and then give Josh and Dave free reign to let rip on guitar and keyboard on a spare track which we could then edit into the song accordingly. The songs would benefit from a blend of Dave's intricate guitar picking and Josh's funk guitar and piano. The one non-negotiable thing for me was the keyboard riff in 'Liquorice'. Josh may have been a virtuoso, but I needed to clip his musical wings – less was more. But when it came to laying down the keyboard, Josh couldn't help himself, jamming throughout the song. My keyboard riff was nowhere to be heard. I had tried the diplomatic approach, but now I felt my blood start to boil.

'Josh, can you play the sodding riff as it's meant to be sodding played.'

Josh pulled a face. 'But it's so dull. How about this instead?'

He did some fancy stuff. It sounded good, but it was wrong.

'No, you need to do this on repeat.' I played the riff angrily.

DA DA-DA DAAAA

DA -DA-DA DA

It didn't sound quite so fancy-pants. But it worked.

Josh released a long, drawn-out sigh and played the riff badly. Once again he added a few extra notes. He was taking the piss out of the riff, and this was causing a rift about the riff.

'Why don't we put it to the vote?'

I didn't want to do that. 'You can't create good art by committee.'

Josh scoffed sarcastically. 'So, you saying it needs to be a dictatorship?'

The room went quiet, and the rest of the band members stared at the floor. I knew I was right on this, but Ernie had a suggestion.

'How about you keep to the riff, and then let rip with a keyboard solo at the end? Then you got the best of both worlds.'

'Fantastic idea, Ernie,' said Marcus enthusiastically.

Josh shrugged his shoulders.

'What, something like this?'

Josh started riffing on the keys. The band started up – it was perfect.

'Josh, just do what you did then. Ernie, can we do a take now?'

Josh kept to the DA DA-DA DA script and then let rip for the solo at the end taking the song to a new level. High-fives all around. Maybe Ernie was not just an engineer but a potential producer. Every band needed that fifth member to realise the sound of the group, a George Martin to our Beatles. Josh still didn't look 100 per cent convinced, but this was a moral victory. He was a stubborn foe, and I still had some work to convince him that The Pointy Birds were destined for the toppermost-of-the-poppermost. And I really needed him aboard, after all, Josh's surname was Levay so our songwriting credits could be 'Levay Macleod' which wasn't a million miles from 'Lennon McCartney'.

There was now palpable magic in the studio as we worked on improving the songs, trying out new ideas. In 'Nostradamus Blues', Dave overlaid guitar parts we'd never heard before that elevated the song. Josh contributed some weird and wonderful magic with his tremolo during the verses. He also beefed up the James Bond riff on 'Razor Blades And Lightning', and added a soaring keyboard and guitar solo that gave the song a fitting climax. How much longer could he call us crap, since we had his fingerprints all over the songs?

At the end of two very long, satisfying days we had recorded and mixed three tracks. Ernie produced two tiny speakers and wired then up to the desk.

'This is the test,' he said. 'If it sounds good through these crappy things, it will sound good through anything.'

We all huddled around the speakers with cans of beer to listen to the final results like kids around a campfire. The speakers hissed and crackled, and then the opening bars of 'Liquorice' began. It sounded all compressed like the song was being broadcast long-wave from a pirate radio station out at sea, but we had captured the energy of the band and the freshness of the songs. My heart soared. We had done it. We had created something out of nothing that would last forever.

I looked around at the others – Marcus C-3PO and Paul R2D2 were dancing. Marcus's hands had turned into ears as part of his signature dance move. Dave Chewbacca and Josh Obi-Wan (or was it Darth Vader?) were chin-stroking enthusiastically in time to the music. Ernie Hans Solo sat at the controls with a stern expression on his face, his ears hard at work, but his head nodding in quiet satisfaction. Not since winning the obstacle race on sports day at Watlington Primary School, aged 8, had I experienced such a sweet taste of success.

Surely, with these recordings, someone out there would believe in us. We just needed a manager and then it would only be a matter of time before these songs turned into hits that would become timeless classics. I suddenly felt a strange sadness – the dream was at last turning into a reality, but the sense of achievement and euphoria I was experiencing by reaching this milestone on the path to superstardom was being accompanied by a peculiar sense of loss, like a mourning for the dream itself.

18.2

At the end of the recording session Josh drove us back up to London in his mum's clapped-out estate car which somehow managed to fit all five of us, plus amps, drums and instruments. Ernie gave us the reels from our recording session on quarter-inch tape and waved us off having run off some cassettes too, but frustratingly Josh's tape deck in the car had broken so we couldn't listen to the songs on the way home. I was desperate to hear them again. I had already forgotten what they sounded like and wanted the reassurance they were still great. It was like the excitement of having a crush on someone and wanting to see their face. I held the reels in my hand and stared at the label with pride.

The Pointy Birds – Ernie Sessions (Feb 1992)
(1) Liquorice (4:20)
(2) Nostradamus Blues (3:11)
(3) Razor Blades And Lightning (2:45)

It had been such a rewarding weekend, and as Josh navigated the various B-roads, we sat in silence as the Sussex countryside whizzed by, reflecting on the previous two days. Spring was in the air, and summer was on its way. I released a profound and happy sigh of satisfaction as I sat squashed in the back of the car with my brothers in arms as the last of the evening sun flashed through the trees. This was what it was all about – life on the road. There would be more of this soon when we hit Route 66. But the moment was ruined by a nasty and sinister smell.

'Disgusting, who has chuffed?'

I wound down the window. I felt Marcus shaking with guilty laughter.

'Sorry, that's last night's kebab repeating.'

Eventually, we hit the A2 as the sun began to set under a rose-tinted sky. London appeared on the horizon like pieces of Lego, reminding me that I was starting a new job in the morning. My heart sank as the knot of dread tightened in my stomach. In those twinkling city lights of the capital lay my destiny, the place where dreams could be made or broken. Which way would it go? A life in retail or superstardom? Would I be living the dream? Or a nightmare?

FAST FORWARD >>

The business of promotion, the trying to make it, the relinquishing of control, the reality…

19. The Best New Band In Britain

SPRING/SUMMER 1992

I start full-time employment and tout our new demo by night. A door opens into a seductive new world, and a chance to ingratiate myself with an indie-pop star goes wrong.

My new job at Selectadisc was a shock to the system. The early starts were killing me, and I hadn't given the best impression of myself to my new colleagues, Gaffer, Norwich and Big Phil. I was constantly tired, hungover and late – if I wasn't yawning, I was sighing. Plus, I had to suffer the regular ignominy of bollockings on the shop floor.

'JESUS CHRIST, HORACE. I JUST FOUND THE LEMONHEADS IN VARIOUS ARTISTS!'

Didn't they realise how hard it was to file alphabetically with a hangover? I needed to get famous and quick to escape this monotonous world of filing vinyl pain.

But our fortunes were to change towards the end of March. It had been a particularly late finish at Camden Palace, and I could count the hours of sleep I had had on one finger. I punched the alarm clock quiet and crept out of my bedroom, feeling like shit. That was the last time I played the *Withnail and I* drinking game. Marcus's bedroom door was closed with no signs of life on the other side. I made my way zombie-like to Golders Green Tube and headed southbound on Northern line to Tottenham Court

Road trying to avoid the reflection of Straw Peter staring back at me, and then entered the square mile of Soho with a pounding head.

A light rain fell, releasing musty smells of piss-stained pavements and overturned bins. Two pigeons pecked at a puddle of vomit outside a kebab shop, and I felt my stomach do a triple salchow lurch. I noticed the time. Shit, I was a whole twenty minutes late. Again. I entered the shop and acknowledged my work colleagues with a sheepish smile and mumbled something about someone jumping in front of the Tube.

'Another one?' was the sarcastic reply.

I picked up my unfeasibly large pile of vinyl and started filing. Having both double and blurred vision made filing alphabetically extra tricky. I thought of that Japanese show *Endurance* where contestants competed to see who could last longest under various forms of physical and mental torture. They might be able to go forty-eight hours without urinating, but I bet they'd struggle to file for nine hours non-stop on no sleep and a hangover from hell five days a week. How on earth was I going to make it until the end of the day? At least I would get some respite when someone put in an order for a cup of tea or a toastie from Bruno's.

Luckily, Massive Attack's album *Blue Lines* was on the stereo. Perfect hangover music – soothing and soulful. I couldn't deal with hardcore nosebleed guitars this morning. The album seemed to stimulate the residual alcohol in my system, and I felt a brief respite from the pain and was soon lost in the music as I filed records. I rewound to last night – Camden Palace had been the usual five floors of fun.

In recent weeks, we had met a Canadian girl called Laura, who seemed pretty well connected. She knew Steve Mack, the singer of That Petrol Emotion, one of my favourite bands that featured the two O'Neill brothers, principal songwriters from The Undertones. 'The Petrols' were a big part of the reason I wanted to be in a band. I had first seen them perform their songs'

Big Decision' and 'Swamp' on The Tube in 1986 and then eagerly booked tickets to see them live at Brighton Polytechnic, which didn't disappoint. I became instantly smitten by their indie-pop charm. And Steve Mack, with his non-stop goofy smile on stage, embodied the fun that was possible as a lead singer.

But Laura's main topic of conversation was her friend Brett who sung in this band called Suede. I had never heard of them, but she said they had record company interest and we should see them live. She gave me a copy of their demo, and on listening to it, I felt my heart sink. I didn't want to admit it to myself, but it was better than ours. Our demo had gone down well. Mum and Dad had said they *definitely* liked it. And some friends seemed to be genuinely impressed – surprised even – we had given a good account of ourselves. But there was something a bit more sexy about Suede's efforts in comparison.

But still, we were making inroads, mixing business with pleasure, turning our dreams into a reality. The trouble was, right at this moment, I couldn't remember what my dreams were beyond curling up into a foetal position and going back to sleep. I leaned my head against the filing cabinet and tried to resist the seductive pull towards sleep. Maybe I could snatch a quick five minutes shut-eye. But this particular dream was interrupted by my current reality – an angry Norwich waving a white inner sleeve in my face.

'JESUS CHRIST, HORACE. I JUST FOUND NICK CAVE FILED UNDER K!'

I wiped the dribble from my mouth and gave the blurred vision my best hurt puppy look, but it didn't wash. Norwich stomped off, and I heard him apologise for the delay to the customer followed by the sound of a till being slammed shut. He returned to processing his Warners box muttering angrily to himself about not being able to get the staff. I decided to avoid him for a bit.

The clock tick-tocked agonisingly slowly to lunchtime at the pace of a snail in no hurry. At last, I could get out for some fresh air. Plus, I felt the first seeds of hunger growing, like new buds in spring. The elicit promise of a jacket potato would satisfy. I took down the lunch orders on the back of a flyer.

'Don't be ages, Horace.'

I nodded, knowing I would try and be as long as possible.

'Also, can you pick up *NME* and *Melody Maker*?'

I left the shop and wandered dreamily down Berwick Street through the market and entered Bruno's Cafe. I put the lunch order in and sat down with a cup of tea and the newspaper. My eyelids were heavy – it was the effort of a Russian weightlifter to keep them aloft. I looked at the clock through narrowed eyes – six long hours to go. After a quick power nap, I returned to Selectadisc with the jacket potatoes and their requisite fillings, stopping off at the newsagent to pick up the *NME* and *Melody Maker*. They had just arrived, and the front cover of *Melody Maker* featured a band I didn't recognise staring back at me. Who were they? They didn't look grunge or shoegaze. The headline said: SUEDE: BEST NEW BAND IN BRITAIN

Bloody hell. It was Laura's mate's band. I knew them. Well, I knew someone who knew them. I raced back to the shop with the jacket potatoes and newspapers somewhat revived by this exciting news. I entered the shop with speed not witnessed by my colleagues before.

'Look at this… I know them…' I spluttered. 'On the cover… look… Suede on the cover…'

I was met with three confused expressions. I knew how Lassie the dog felt when she tried to explain someone had fallen in a well.

'They're kind of Smiths meets Bowie. I've heard their demo. It's brilliant,' I said, taking immediate ownership of the band.

My three colleagues seemed impressed by my insider knowledge as they took in the front cover. Suede stared back up at us all pouts and come-to-bed eyes. I had never actually seen them before, but it was an arresting image – a definite contrast to the grey comfort of grunge and shoegaze.

Phil broke rank. 'Look like twats to me.'

The waft of jacket potatoes with various fillings seemed to have distracted them. They grabbed their orders and returned to their respective places behind the counter. They seemed unbothered by this front cover, but to me, it was both earth-shattering and ground-breaking news.

The rest of the afternoon was not just a physical blur, but a mental one too. After work, I returned to the flat as quickly as possible and handed the paper to a still hungover Marcus. His blood-shot eyes widened.

'Bloody hell!'

'I know!'

A brand-new band on the cover that we sort of knew meant we were only one degree of separation from the big time. This cover had propelled them to indie-pop stardom. And if it could happen for them, it could happen for us.

19.2

Not only was my rock'n'roll career now about to take off but thirteen years of Tory rule was about to come to an end too, and not before its time. A ginger-haired saviour was here to rescue us – his name was Neil Kinnock, and as leader of a resurgent Labour Party, he was to take the country to the promised land. With the Labour Party back in power, the nineties were going to become the new sixties. Numerically, at least, a nice symmetry existed between the two decades, with Neil Kinnock our Harold Wilson. A political, musical and cultural revolution after the bravado and shoulder pads of the eighties. One long party, basically.

The election took place on a sun-filled Thursday in April. Luckily it was my day off work, and a group of us headed to

Golders Hill park with an acoustic guitar and alcohol to sing songs and celebrate. Kinnock's victory was a foregone conclusion. We could get to the polling booth and vote later. But like many younger voters, I was guilty of both premature celebration and being too drunk to make it to the polling booth. To everyone's horror, the Conservatives were returned to office in the small hours with a slim majority for the fourth consecutive time since 1979. John Major was to stay on as Prime Minister, and the Conservatives were to stagger on for much of the nineties embroiled in sleaze and spoil our party. Labour needed a re-think. The only silver lining was that at least the Tories gave artists and comedians lots of material and weren't to disappoint with sexual antics involving tangerines.

*

Meanwhile, Suede's ascent began. Through Laura, we got on guest lists and into after-show parties to their London gigs as tickets sold out, and venues doubled and tripled in size. After each gig, people surrounded the band members, keen to speak to them. They were in the process of becoming famous. Their dream was coming true. What on earth was that like?

It was exciting to be part of this world, and we were able to pretend their success was happening to us. Marcus and I would find ourselves drunk and silly in the back of a taxi at 3 a.m. after one of their gigs on the way to someone's flat for the post-after-show-after-show party. We'd exchange winks knowing we were now on the periphery of the periphery of the Suede inner circle. We had managed to get on head-nodding terms with Brett, the singer and exchanged a couple of witty one-liners with Matt, the bassist. And one night after their show at the Underworld, fuelled by several bottles of San Miguel, Marcus and I cornered Matt at the bar and wowed him with our rabbit jokes which he seemed to enjoy until he looked at his watch and said he had to go.

It was strange, the effect their presence had on me. I became all giggly and excitable like a first crush at school. They represented the dream and made it seem real and doable. But it wasn't just me; there was a noticeable increase in the energy and volume of the room when they appeared – people made more effort to be funny and engaging; laughter more pronounced, hair twirled around fingers flirtatiously. What was this sorcery which then depleted as soon as the band departed the room?

This world was full of people working in the music industry – A&R execs, PR agents, managers, journalists, or 'liggers' as they were known. Ligging was the ability to get up close and personal with the band and was an art form in itself. It got a bit annoying, often the person I found myself talking to would get distracted and start looking over my shoulder. Their eyes would glaze over like I wasn't interesting enough. And no matter what I did, I couldn't seem to hold their attention – even some of my funniest stories about our family dog Max, the golden retriever, fell on deaf ears.

But didn't they realise the next big thing was right here in the room, under their noses? It was almost as if I didn't exist. But I would show them. The Pointy Birds would soon be hosting their own after shows, and then they would all want to speak to me, then they would laugh about the time Max got stung by the wasp. Maybe I needed to learn how to lig better because we needed to compete, we needed to get into that inner circle before they got too far away. If I could get five minutes with Brett and talk to him about my vision for The Pointy Birds, plus a few of my funny stories, then surely a support slot on their next world tour would be in the bag.

19.3

My chance was to come sooner than I realised. It was yet another hungover day in the shop after another late finish. That was the last time I drank a bottle of Jewish sherry. The pleasure wasn't worth the nine hours filing pain, and I hadn't helped my cause by scoffing a jacket potato with chilli and cheese from Cookies a bit too quickly. I wondered around the shop in a daze taking my thoughts and my vinyl with me trying to avoid annoying customers asking me stupid questions. I had a couple of sleeves to file in the Acid Jazz section when two customers wandered towards me, and with a shock, I realised it was Brett and Matt from Suede, both in big fur coats and shirts undone to the navel. They were taking some time out to stroll the streets of Soho and enjoy being famous. Brett clocked me although I could tell he couldn't quite place me. He had big hoop earrings and a long fringe that covered one eye. He peered at me with it.

'Hey,' I said.

'All right, mate,' he replied, obviously not quite sure how he knew me.

I was too hungover to deal with this. I had never been one-on-one with Brett before, or any pop star. I was from Crowborough, famous people didn't live there, apart from David Jason but he didn't count. I noticed one of Bretts's nipples was on display. I was surprised as it was quite chilly out. Or I suppose *nippy out* was more appropriate in this instance. I wasn't expecting to be suddenly confronted by a nipple, especially not a famous one.

I looked away, conscious I was staring at his nipple too long and an uncomfortable silence lingered while I racked my brain what to say. Behind me, I could feel my Selectadisc colleagues watching. They did not miss a trick – having celebs in the shop was a biggie, especially a celeb that was currently our biggest seller. I knew this would be several thousand brownie points. Trouble was the cat had got my tongue. I tried to speak.

'Yeah, I've just been, um…'

Brett's visible eye widened in expectancy awaiting what I was going to say, but my mind was a complete blank. There was so much I wanted to say, but for some reason, I couldn't speak.

He represented everything I wanted to be. The gulf between us suddenly felt huge. He fronted a band that had just got a multi-million-pound record deal. He was on the cover of every music magazine and selling out bigger and bigger venues to an adoring and growing fanbase. By contrast, I worked in a record store misfiling vinyl. I tried to speak again.

'Yeah, I just… um…'

I coughed to clear my throat, but still, I couldn't think of what to say. Matt smiled politely and then looked around the store distractedly. Brett kept his gaze fixed on me like he was watching an insect flicked over on his back, struggling. Curious if he would flip back over and whether to give him a helping hand. The pause was going on way too long now. I noticed that both Brett's shoelaces were undone, which seemed a little incongruous with the rest of the pop star get-up. Maybe he was trying to make untied shoelaces cool, but what if he tripped over them? It wasn't practical. He might hurt himself. My gran once told me that people who didn't tie their shoelaces were drips.

This pause had become way too pregnant, and someone needed to give birth. My mouth had gone dry, and speaking was suddenly physically very tricky. I silently cursed my stupid self. Why was my body rebelling? Was it trying to scupper things to save me from a life of stardom that deep down I knew would lead to ruin? That was ridiculous. Of course I wanted to be a rockstar. Beads of sweat coated my upper lip.

'Yeah, I just got this bug thing… terrible diarrhoea.'

Brett recoiled, germs were clearly not his thing. Matt's eyebrows lifted at this news.

'Yeah, nightmare,' I continued. 'Was up all night – on all fours. Coming out both ends.'

Both of them danced a step back.

'Well, get well soon, yeah, mate?' said Brett.

'Yes, get well soon,' said Matt.

'Yeah, sure – better get on with this filing shit,' I said.

Brett and Matt hurried off with their untied shoelaces and bared nipples. That had been my chance to get us on the Suede tour – and I had blown it. I was not a pop star. I was just a wannabe who worked in a record shop. They were up there, and I was down here. My only saving grace was that the conversation, or lack thereof, had not taken place within earshot of my work colleagues. The few words we had exchanged would have to be our little secret. I returned behind the counter, deeply depressed, though my colleagues seemed impressed by my famous friends. I wasn't going to let the truth get in the way.

'So, Horace – hanging out with pop stars now?'

I feigned disinterest. 'What? Oh right, yeah, that was just *Brett*.'

'Oh, Brett, is it? First-name terms?'

'Celebrity bum chums.'

As they teased, I fixed a smile on my face knowing that if we didn't get offered the Suede tour, it would be due to my ill-advised description of an anal ailment. The worst performance of my life. My only hope was that he didn't recognise me as that bloke from The Pointy Birds. And I suppose if worst came to the worst, I could always have a twin brother.

20. Enter Ricky

SUMMER/AUTUMN 1992

Paul drops a bombshell, and we find a new recruit. Start gigging the deluxe toilet circuit and our demo makes its way to Ricky.

I had sent our demo out to the various Camden venues and management companies but was yet to receive a response. It felt like we needed a manager to get a manager. And then we had a breakthrough. A music promoter called Nadir got in touch. He had promoted a couple of Suede gigs, and our demo had made its way to him through Laura. He seemed to genuinely like our music and started offering us shows at slightly more prestigious venues, a level up from the bog-standard toilet-venue shows; plus we would be playing with more established bands. My brother Dave had now graduated from Leicester University and moved to London, so we were ready to rock'n'roll as a four-piece with Josh still in Cardiff for another year but available to step in for the important shows.

But just as we were about to start retreading the boards, Paul the drummer dropped a bombshell. He was leaving the band to go and study abroad in America. He had explained to Marcus at Sainsbury's how it was a huge opportunity. But what about *this* huge opportunity? It seemed the most wrong-headed decision in the world. We were on the verge of superstardom. We needed to find a drummer and fast.

As luck would have it a chance encounter with our next-door neighbour was to provide a solution, if but a temporary one. I had crossed paths with him a few times, either entering or leaving our flat and had always exchanged smiles but never pleasantries. But one afternoon, he popped the question.

'You in that band?'

'Yes, sorry…' I assumed he was going to complain about the noise.

'No, it's great, I've been getting into some of the tunes actually.'

'Really?'

'Yes, there is one about a squirrel?'

He was a man of taste.

'Yes, that's one of our oldies.'

'I used to be in a band back in the day actually,' he said bashfully.

'Really? What did you play?' I asked, already knowing the answer. Fate was in the air.

He wiggled his two index fingers in the air to denote drumsticks.

'But I'm more of a table-tapper these days… My name's Luke by the way…'

'Hi, Luke. I'm Andy, but you can call me Horace. It just so happens we're looking for a table-tapper…'

20.2

Although Luke was greying at the temples and could maybe do with losing a bit of weight, he had everything you could hope for in a band member. He was a nice guy, he turned up on time, loved the songs and even contributed to the cost of rehearsal, but as a drummer, he lacked one key ingredient – natural rhythm. But in the plus column, he also had transport and a printer for flyers; plus his girlfriend was a stylist. The songs were strong enough to carry him anyway. We just needed him to keep a steady but straightforward 4/4 beat, and we would do the rest.

With a full line-up in place, Nadir booked us a series of gigs through the autumn. The Subterranean in Ladbroke Grove, followed by an indie club night at the PowerHaus in Islington and then the big one – supporting the Cardiacs at The Venue in New Cross. Students would be back from summer holidays, and it was a chance for us to show what we could do. My only cause for concern was with our new drummer and general lack of live experience, I had doubts as to whether we were entirely ready for this level of exposure, but as Joanna Lumley said, 'Say yes to everything'.

With these three gigs on the horizon, it was time to go shopping, and so Marcus and I headed straight to Camden market. And that's when I saw it – a turquoise sequinned shirt with wing collars. It was skin-tight, so I would need to keep it unbuttoned to the navel, but that was all the rage and would show off my hairy chest. Brett from Suede would kill for this kind of shirt. I also purchased a banana-yellow tutu, not unlike the one Mick Jagger had worn at their concert in Hyde Park, in July 1969, two days after I was born, the same day Brian Jones was found dead in a swimming pool in Hartfield, East Sussex, a few miles from Crowborough.

My mum had heard their concert from her bed in the Chelsea and Westminster hospital. The music must have drifted into me, and maybe the spirit of Brian Jones too. In this sense, I was revisiting my roots, and if a tutu was good enough for Jagger, it was good enough for me. Marcus had been busy shopping too and done me proud with a collection of different coloured flamenco-themed shirts, with frills that thrilled. Combined with his spectacle frames and a blond ponytail, he trod the finest of lines between academic, rockstar and bullfighter, and no one was rocking that look.

But even though we had splashed the cash on new outfits very much on-trend, we were met with stubborn resistance, to put it mildly – Dave and Josh were having none of it and put forward a stupid, illogical argument that it was *about the music.* They seemed happy just wearing jeans and a T-shirt. The classic band photo shot of four miserable blokes standing around on a pavement in black and white was all you needed. Granted, that studied cool had its place, but I wanted us to be colourful and to put on a show. But for Dave and Josh, it was akin to sticking hot needles into their brains. They weren't budging, so we had to go with a democratic half-glam half-indie look. At least we were halfway there.

20.3

The Subterranea could hold up to four hundred people, and Nadir had booked us in as headliners. We decided to do this show as a four-piece with Josh agreeing to travel down from Cardiff for the more important October shows at the Powerhaus and The Venue with the Cardiacs.

We arrived for the soundcheck, and the sound engineer seemed quite excited to tell us his news.

'Hey, you were just name-checked on Radio One. Steve Wright in the afternoon. They were discussing gigs on tonight in London, and they mentioned this one.'

'What? They said our name?'

'Yes, they said The Pointy Birds are playing the Subterranea. And then they discussed silly band names.'

I felt my tummy churn with excitement. There was more news. Laura had asked for a plus one because Brett from Suede was coming too. The singer of the *best new band in Britain* was on our guest list and coming and see us. It was a chance to redeem myself and impress him enough for that support slot. But the thrill of this news mixed with a concern we were playing with an untested drummer who was rhythmically challenged.

My fears were justified. As we started playing to an empty

room a few hours later, I listened to the noise we were making with objective ears, and it was not good. We were missing our old drummer Paul. The lack of rhythm meant the songs had lost all shape. We were also missing some of Josh's musicality. Plus, my guitar had gone out of tune and was too loud in the monitors. As we played, the twelve members of our audience didn't look impressed. Laura was standing on her own, thank god Brett hadn't shown up to witness this carnage. Although I was also slightly disappointed he hadn't shown. Did he have somewhere better to go? But then, halfway through our final song, Brett appeared.

As we brought 'Applaud That Tree', a new tune we hadn't completely figured out, to an end and the last guitar notes rang out with Luke adding a made-up-on-the-spot-out-of-time drum roll, there was a palpable feeling in the room that we had at last put a sick animal out of its misery, having tortured it for thirty minutes. A ripple of lukewarm applause broke out and then people darted off to get the last Tube.

I jumped off the stage and made my way uncertainly over to where Laura and Brett were deep in conversation at the bar. Brett nodded hello as Laura did a never-mind face about the gig. I mumbled something about it being shit and that we were bedding in a new drummer. Brett didn't say anything, but I could tell he was impressed by my hairy chest. An awkward silence descended and not wanting to repeat the whole diarrhoea fiasco I made an excuse about having to pack up the gear. When we had finished loading up, I returned to the bar, but they had gone.

20.4

I decided to give Luke the benefit of the doubt – he hadn't had long to learn the songs, and maybe he was nervous, and everyone deserved a second chance. Plus we didn't have an alternative, but there was clearly work to be done and there needed to be significant improvements. At least Josh would be down for the next gig to add some musical sprinkles.

The PowerHaus in Islington was a trendy indie club night where *NME* journalists hung out, and new bands were spotted and signed by record labels. Even though we were the opening act, it was a coup to get on the bill. We were supporting this band called Echobelly and word had it that they had interest from Nude Records, and label head honcho Saul was possibly going to be down to see them, among other labels.

They had taken an eternity with their soundcheck adjusting levels and playing songs over and over again, meaning we only had five minutes to soundcheck before doors opened, which wasn't nearly long enough. We then had five minutes to grab a drink and 'take a shit' before we had to jump back on stage.

I popped outside to get some fresh air. The queue was around the corner, and I heard a journalist mention his name on the door.

'Yes, it's Ian Watson from the *Melody Maker*. I should be on the Echobelly guest list.'

I had never seen a music journalist before. It was like being on safari. He was a bit like a scruffy student with national health specs and big hair. I watched him order a drink. He then sat on a stool at the bar in prime position to watch the bands. The first of whom would be us. This realisation made me feel sick – maybe he would review us too?

Before I knew it, we were on. I noticed Josh had placed his keyboard to the side of the stage so the audience couldn't see him.

'Come on, Josh, plenty of room on stage.'

'No, I'm quite happy here, thanks.'

I went to help him move the keyboard into view, but he wouldn't shift. It was almost as if he was embarrassed to be seen playing with us. During the gig, I looked over at Josh, giving him encouraging glances, but he wore a pained expression like he was committing a crime against music. He wasn't wrong. I felt a similar frustration.

The bottom line was that Luke couldn't play the drums – they were beyond his musical abilities. It was also dispiriting to play to a packed venue, the vast majority of whom were paying us no attention. We had briefly piqued the interest of Ian Watson. He wandered over during our first song to watch us. He cocked his head like a puppy as if trying to understand and then returned to his stool at the bar and started reading a newspaper.

We finished the set and exited stage left and hung about in the bar as it got more and more packed for Echobelly. They went on stage to a big cheer and played a tight set, but I knew we were better. We just needed a proper drummer and a decent soundcheck, and then labels would want us, not them. This was the start of a fierce rivalry, made more acute by the fact that Echobelly barely seemed aware of our existence.

20.5

Luke was loving being in the band. His girlfriend told me it had turned his life around. She had never seen him so happy and thanked me for giving him the opportunity. This nugget of information made the conversation I needed to have with him a bit tricky. We decided on balance that it was better to keep going with him in the hope he might improve. Plus we still didn't have an alternative.

The Venue in New Cross had sold out. All six hundred tickets had gone, so the size of the audience wasn't going to be a problem. The type of audience, however, was a different matter. I didn't know much about The Cardiacs, but maybe I should have done some research. A few friends who had heard of them thought it was a strange fit with The Pointy Birds. The Cardiacs were an intellectual prog-punk band led by Tim Smith that inspired devotion among their followers, a demographic that was mainly middle-aged men with shaved heads and stern looks.

Full marks to Nadir for getting us this support: we would be playing to our biggest audience yet. It was a chance to turn some heads and inspire some devotion in our direction. The time was right for my new banana-yellow tutu. And I was determined the band should dress up too. Josh gave me a lift to the venue, which gave me some quality one-on-one time with him to discuss the dress code for the evening. With Dave being most resistant to dressing up, my tactic was to work on Josh first. He could wear one of Marcus's frilly numbers, then Dave would have to toe the party line and could borrow my frilly turquoise shirt. Josh was a bit more concerned about the headliner audience.

'Have you heard The Cardiacs? Not sure it's the best fit. Their gigs are more like a rally. There is not much in the way of nob gags.'

'I'll win 'em over.'

But our conversation was cut short with a pigeon refusing to get out of the way of the car. There was a flap of wings and then a thud. We got out to find bloody entrails and feathers in the car engine.

'Why didn't it fly out the way they normally do.'

'God, hope that wasn't a premonition about tonight's gig.'

But it was.

Dave and Josh had made some effort on the dressing-up front. Dave wore a striped T-shirt and Josh had brought a black cap. It was a start but not far enough. And pre-gig in the dressing room there was a standoff about putting on the frilly shirts. It was clear the only way to solve it was to pay them handsomely or force-dress them. We didn't have any money, so it would have to be the latter. Josh called our bluff by putting on the orange flamenco shirt and then taking it off just before going on stage. I looked out at a sea of stony-looking faces. My tutu hadn't broken the ice, so I decided to tell them about the pigeon.

'Hello, we're The Pointy Birds. We ran over a pigeon on the

way here tonight, so I hope that won't be a metaphor for how this gig is going to go.'

There was a deathly silence before Luke cued up a perfectly out-of-time comedy drum roll, but the assembled stony faces betrayed no emotions. They were tough nuts.

Post gig, I stood at the bar feeling a bit lonely. Our songs, the jokes and my tutu had failed to win the audience over. And now that The Cardiacs had transformed the venue into a spectacular celebration of clever post-prog punk with visuals and confetti, I could see why. The only thing to file in the plus column was when one of the six hundred middle-aged men with a shaved head and a stern look came over to me, put his hand on my shoulder and looked me straight in the eye.

'One word. Brave.'

20.6

Luke was so pleased to be in the band. He kept smiling and winking at me whenever I caught his eye, and on one occasion he mouthed a *thank you.* But I had to give him the news his drumming services were no longer required. His bottom lip trembled, he nodded in acceptance and then ran off down the street. I took no pleasure in making a grown man cry, but the band came first. Reduced back to a four-piece we needed to do something positive, so I booked us back in at Ernie's. We had four songs ready to record, and we could use a drum machine. After two days we left with four more recordings, two of which we were particularly pleased with.

'Benefit Office' was a proper grown-up indie-pop song and our best recording yet. It had a beautifully structured sequence of chords and the cleverest of key changes courtesy of Dave, embellished by a fab guitar solo at the end which Josh pulled out of the bag first take. It was a pleasure to sing, and I had packed the lyrics full of rhyming couplets, of which I was quite proud, especially the fact I had rhymed 'Paris' with 'office'. And 'Jeremy Beadle' with 'devil'. We also recorded a ballad called 'Lift Me', which although a bit slushy and sentimental had number one in America written all over it.

We circulated the demo, and within a few days, Nadir's friend Ricky rang offering his services as a manager.

21. Rocking Horse Studios

AUTUMN 92

A productive day in a recording studio not without some steep learning curves.

And so life began with Ricky. He had got us a day in a glamorous, state-of-the-art studio in Catford called Rocking Horse Studios where Suede had recorded their *Drowners* demo that had got them their deal with Nude Records. The plan was simple – record two smash hits that Ricky would pass to Nude Records, as he had done for Suede, and the rest would be rock'n'roll history.

We caught the overland train from Charring Cross to Catford. It was a cold, wet, miserable day, but these were perfect conditions to go into the studio. The worse the weather, the better for producing great art. It was no surprise that the grey drizzle of Manchester and Seattle had produced two of the biggest global music movements in recent times, in baggy and grunge respectively. The sun, sand and surf of Sydney was not conducive to creating good music – why reflect on your existence when you could hang out at the beach?

As we trundled past the delights of Lewisham and Peckham Rye, the stomping ground of my formative years, I rested my head on the grease-smeared window of our carriage and reflected on my earlier conversation with Ricky. He had rung to give directions to the studio, but he wanted to run through a few things too.

'How many songs are you planning to record?'

'Um, not sure yet, um…'

'Don't do any more than two, OK?'

'All right.'

'And make sure they are all worked out, yeah?'

'Um… OK…'

'Don't wing it. You need to know exactly what you want to achieve with each song, yes? Otherwise, you will waste valuable studio time.'

He sounded quite strict. No doubt it was wise advice, but he was taking the fun out of it a bit. He hadn't finished.

'The bedroom is the place to write, and the rehearsal room is the place to finetune and work arrangements out. You got limited time, so the studio is not the place to experiment with half-baked song ideas.'

Ricky went quiet on the other end of the line to let this sink in. I decided to inject some positivity.

'Wait 'til you hear "Rocket Child". It's a future number one.'

'Really?'

The excitement returned to his voice, but the truth was that apart from 'Rocket Child', we didn't have any other songs worked out, definitely not ready to be recorded. Our other song 'Man Who Kisses Horses' was a couple of chords and a melody line – quarter-baked at best.

From the outside, Rocking Horse Studios didn't look very glamorous, or state of the art, sandwiched between a fried chicken shop and a newsagent on the main high street as traffic from the south circular hurtled by. We checked the address and then rang the buzzer. A strange voice answered.

''Allo, Chinese takeaway?'

'Er, is that the studio?'

'No, you got wrong place.'

The voice disappeared.

We double-checked the address – it was correct. We pressed the buzzer again. This time there was a familiar sound of Ricky's giggling.

'Sorry, couldn't resist. Come on up. We're the door at the top of the stairs.'

I didn't realise Ricky would be at the studio too. The door opened and we climbed up a dark and dingy flight of stairs to a door with a sign saying Rocking Horse Studios. The door opened a fraction. Ricky's eye peered out.

'No milk today, thank you,' he said in a cranky voice.

The door clicked shut. I could hear the laugh again on the other side of the door. We waited for a moment, and then the door swung back open. Ricky greeted with a big smile plastered across his face. We shuffled in and plonked our instruments down. I introduced the band to Ricky – our new manager, who would make things happen for us. We shook hands. Ricky took immediate control.

'Right, lots to do today so let me give you a quick guided tour and then we'll get cracking.'

The studio wasn't quite what I was expecting. I had conjured pictures in my mind of polished wooden floorboards, black leather sofas and a white grand piano, like in John Lennon's 'Imagine' video. In contrast, it was a cramped and dingy space with a smell reminiscent of our flat in Golders Green – a blend of body odour, cheesy socks and dirty underpants – the natural result of the male species spending quality time together in a confined space with no fresh air.

Still, Ricky was all twinkly-eyed and waggy-tailed with enthusiasm like an indie Willy Wonka as he showed us around the cramp confines of our new abode. There were two small rooms separated by a dividing window – a small control room for the sound engineer and an even smaller live room for recording the band. It wasn't much of an upgrade to Ernie's, but Ricky's excitement was contagious. At the controls was a rather pale and tired-looking individual smoking a cigarette, who, like most engineers, and vampires, didn't see much in the way of daylight.

'This is Martin. Or George Martin as I like to call him,'

sniggered Ricky as he massaged Martin's shoulders. Martin acknowledged us with a nod and puff of smoke from his cigarette.

'He can work wonders on this desk. You are in excellent hands. Martin engineered Suede's demo right here in this room.'

We all nodded, impressed. The seedy sound of their demo supported the argument that music was a reflection of its environment. Ricky continued in his tour guide role. I suppose this was what managers did.

'So, first things first – I'll put the kettle on while Martin gets you set up, and then we'll talk through what you want to do and then let's get cracking, shall we?'

It sounded like a good plan. Ricky appeared with cups of tea, and then we played through 'Rocket Child' so they could get an idea of the song and program a drum beat. I was surprised that this was something Ricky was going to do. Maybe he could drum? He hit the different drum pads with his fingers – a snare, a kick drum, hi-hat, cymbals and toms. Through the speakers, it sounded pretty good, and I was impressed. He was like a kid in a sweet shop and explained they could add all sorts of effects to give it a bigger sound, but for now, we would manually program the basic beats and then loop them.

We all nodded. Ricky continued.

'So, Josh, this is your song – a simple 4/4 time signature?'

Ricky started hitting the drum pads. A basic bass drum and snare beat came through the speakers.

BOOM-TISH. BA-BOOM-BOOM-TISH. BOOM-TISH. BA-BOOM-BOOM-TISH.

The beat stopped, and we all looked at Josh. He was scratching his chin. 'Nearly, it's a bit more boom-tish, tish-boom, boom-tish, tish-boom.'

'Ah right, so a TISH BOOM at the end?'

Ricky rattled off a new beat.

BOOM-TISH.

BA-BOOM-BOOM-TISH.

BOOM-TISH.

BA-BOOM-TISH BOOM.

The loop stopped, and we all looked at Josh again.

'Nearly, it's a little more on the offbeat.'

'OK, so like this?'

Ricky did a BOOM TISH variation. Josh pulled a face.

'Not quite. It's more. Boom-Tish. Tish-boom. Boom-Tish. Tish-boom.'

'Ah, so like this?'

Ricky tish-boomed and Josh pulled another face like he wasn't sure, so I left them to it.

While they worked on the drumbeat, this was my chance to put the finishing touches to the lyrics. Penning these final lines in the studio was what it was all about. These scribbles would be part of the album artwork for the inlay sleeve, and the originals would be worth a small fortune in years to come – auctioned at Sotheby's for north of a mil. The only worry was with all the excitement of actually being here my mind was a bit blank. I was confident inspiration would flow when the time came, but the sand was shifting through the hourglass a bit sharpish.

Eventually, the drums were in place. They sounded good but somehow had got a bit lost in translation, and I was wondering quite how the vocal melody would work against this different beat. Some of my words would need to change or be sung with a different emphasis to scan. Not quite knowing what those words were meant I had work to do. Maybe I should have worked all this out beforehand.

It was now Marcus, Dave and Josh's turn to track their instruments, and the atmosphere in the studio was one of a quiet industry as each member recorded their guitar parts. I could tell Ricky was impressed by the song and our ability to work quickly and get things down first take. I was also surprised at how comfortable Ricky was in the studio. He knew all the lingo and his way around a sound desk, and as the engineer twisted knobs and adjusted levels, he consulted Ricky who made further technical suggestions. Gone were the jokes, replaced by a work ethic and determination to get these tracks sounding as professional as possible.

All it needed now was the vocals – the icing on the cake. I would be like Morrissey revealing the vocal line and melody of the song to the rest of The Smiths. But as I donned the cans and saw a sea of faces looking at me through the dividing glass with expectant, excited faces a sudden seed of doubt crept in. Marcus winked and gave me a good luck thumbs-up. His hands were ears again. Dave gave me the thumbs-up too. Ricky's tail was wagging. Even Josh was scratching his chin with some enthusiasm.

The track started to play in my earphones. The guitars sounded huge, like a rocket taking off. All I had to do was lay down a vocal that turned it into a sure-fire number-one hit. Simples. But as I started to sing, I could tell by the looks on people's faces that I wasn't achieving my goal. It's weird how you can learn a lot about yourself in moments of crisis, and after the eleventh vocal take one thing I didn't want to do was start crying. Marcus was doing his best to remain positive. Josh's told-you-so face had turned into a why-are-you-butchering-my-song face. The engineer had his head in his hands. I caught Ricky's eye. A look of frustration flashed across his face followed by, worse, a look of disappointment, but he rallied. He pressed a button on the sound desk, and his voice came into my headphones like a concerned parent trying to encourage a toddler on their first day at school.

'How are you doing in there?'

'All right,' I lied.

'Do you want to give it another go? We can always record in sections, one line at a time?'

I nodded. I didn't want to resort to that. It felt a bit like riding a bike with stabilisers. I wanted to blow people away with my vocal first take, leaving everyone in the studio reeling, but instead I was letting everyone down and ruining the song. Confidence was draining like water from a bath.

'I'll give it another go. I think I know what I am doing now.'

I looked at my notes and tried to make sense of my jumble of scribbles. It was a vortex of gobbledygook. At Ernie's the reason the recordings had come out well is that we had practised the songs and knew what we wanted. The recording studio was not the place to write and rehearse. Ricky was so right. The engineer flicked a switch, and then his voice came on in the headphones.

'You OK?'

'Sorry, I'm having a bit of trouble getting in the zone… um, not sure what's wrong.'

Was there anything lonelier than the humiliation of not being able to perform? This was even worse than having stage fright at a urinal, or even 'it's not you, it's me' in bed. The engineer muted my headphones, and I could see everyone discussing the situation in the control room on the other side of the dividing glass. I couldn't hear their conversation, but their grave faces conveyed the gravity of the situation. Houston, we have a problem.

I tasted something strange and metallic in my mouth. The biro I nervously chewed had leaked ink down my chin and onto my shirt – the proverbial insult to the injury. What an idiot I was. I wasn't a rockstar in waiting, I was a deluded shop assistant with dreams of grandeur and a leaky pen. I felt my bottom lip tremble. It would feel good to release the floodgates. Ricky's voice came into the headphones concealing his concern and panic.

'How about we work on the chorus? And then we can jump back in on the verses later?'

It seemed a sensible plan and achievable goal. I held back the tidal wave of tears and felt a new resolve to salvage this session. I had to dig deep.

'Yes, good idea.'

'OK, Mart. Cue the chorus.'

The music started up in the headphones. I just needed to get the timing right. Also, I had to hit a high note.

You Can Do It, Duffy Moon.

The chorus kicked in, and I went for it.

'OOOOOOH, ROCKET CHILD.'

Immediately, Ricky and Marcus's thumbs shot up. The chorus stopped, and Ricky's voice came into the headphones. He sounded relieved.

'Sounded great – let's do a few more takes and we can pick the best one.'

I did as was told and could feel my old friend confidence return – welcome back, my old mucker, how I missed you. I was Spartacus breaking free of his shackles. I finished a final take, took off the headphones and returned to the control room triumphant. The engineer pressed play. Heads in the room were nodding. Ricky had an idea.

'Have you thought of BVs? Would sound amazing.'

'BVs?' We looked at each other non-plussed.

'Backing vocals. I think it needs something. You know, something a bit 'Sympathy For The Devil'.' Ricky broke into song. 'Woo woo-hoo. Woooooo.'

'Sympathy For The Devil' was a staple at Camden Palace. When they played that everyone got on the dance floor. The band looked at Josh. It was his song, or used to be.

Ricky continued his sales pitch. 'Might lift it a bit? Can I show you what I mean? If that's all right with you, Josh? If you don't like it, we'll take it out.'

Josh shrugged his shoulders in acceptance; this was now a collaboration.

'Sure, let's give it a go.'

Ricky scampered through to the live room and I followed him. We both donned some headphones and shared a microphone just like Paul McCartney and Stevie Wonder in 'Ebony And Ivory'. Not sure who was who though.

'You sing the chorus, and I will riff around you and harmonise.'

Ricky gave a thumbs-up. The engineer pressed record, and the backing track fired up in our headphones. As I sang, Ricky started harmonising and adding some flourishes. He had a surprisingly good voice and effortlessly hit the notes. I wasn't sure if we sounded good or bad, but it gave the song a defining chorus and Ricky was undoubtedly enjoying himself, clicking his fingers and wiggling his hips. It was hard to tell what Josh was thinking. He was somewhat inscrutable, but pretty soon the chorus was a wrap, and I now had an idea for the verse and found myself manically scribbling lyrics. It was a chance to redeem myself. You couldn't sit around waiting for inspiration, you had to work hard, just like Benny and Bjorn spending nine hours in a hut in Sweden to slay the dragon and emerge victorious with 'Dancing Queen'.

The words were pouring out of me. I was making connections, rejigging things, happy accidents, lines discarded, darlings killed. The song, like a fossil, was revealing itself. At last, I knew what I was doing. I was ready to record the verse. I knew this would only need one take, and I was right, nailing it first go. I had turned 'Rocket Child' into a hit. Ricky and Marcus seemed pleased too, but I noticed the engineer was non-committal and Josh and Dave were more muted in their enthusiasm. The song had altered quite a bit – could they hear something I couldn't?

Now it was time for 'Man Who Kisses Horses'. We didn't have long left, but it was a far simpler song, and after the difficult birth of 'Rocket Child' we raced through it. We looped a drumbeat, strummed a chord on repeat and gave free rein to the rest of the Pointys to express themselves, recording everything first take. The song sounded like a TV theme tune for a holiday programme in the eighties. I wasn't sure if that was a good or bad thing. I delivered my vocals first take redeeming myself further in front of the band, Ricky and the engineer.

It had been a long productive day, and we had two new songs

in the bag. We caught the train back to London with Ricky. I had seen another side to him too – he was creative and a problem solver, but also driven and ambitious. And now, the entertainer re-emerged as he got to know the different members of the band. Josh explained he was studying philosophy at Cardiff University and Ricky was quick to make a connection.

'Brilliant, I did philosophy too. Are you a Kierkegaard or Jung man?'

'Well, I'm quite a fan of Wittgenstein,' said Josh surprised that Ricky knew his philosophers.

Ricky nodded appreciatively and then spoke. 'Interesting fact. Did you know Wittgenstein went to school with Hitler?'

Josh was impressed by this nugget of information as Ricky started giggling and then began a routine.

'Yes, imagine being at school with Hitler. "No, Adolf, sit down. Do that again, or it's the naughty step".'

Ricky exploded with laughter at his joke. I didn't know who this Wittgenstein character was, but Ricky certainly had a knack for going off on a tangent and finding the fun in any conversation. Josh had opened his mouth to reply, but Ricky had changed gear and subject. He couldn't help himself – conversations seemed to go off-piste into utter hilarity quickly. And it was hard to compete with his huge laugh. Perhaps it was insecurity, or perhaps he just found everything funny. Life was a comedy, and he had front-row seats.

22. New Stuart Copeland

AUTUMN/WINTER 1992

Post-studio blues followed by a much-needed confidence boost at work. Final piece of band jigsaw slots into place. Ricky brings someone mysterious to our rehearsal and reveals plans.

I returned to work, feeling deflated – not because I was back to reality after the high of being in a recording studio, but because I had listened to the fruits of our labour and the results were beyond disappointing. What had we done to 'Rocket Child'? The rhythms, melodies and lyrics all altered unnecessarily, pulled this way and that. The song had been humiliated like a dog dressed in human clothes. And as for 'Man Who Kisses Horses' – well, that was just weird, the aural equivalent of adding custard to fish and chips. These songs were no acquired taste; they weren't going to mature with age, and they certainly weren't going to win anyone over on a third listen.

There was only one course of action. The recordings needed to be swept under the carpet, airbrushed from history and erased from memory. 'Rocket Child' would probably need to be dropped from the set for a while too. We couldn't unhear the things we had done to the song. Best it was not spoken of like a member of a family arrested for doing something unspeakable. We would probably never hear from Ricky again. Who could blame him? My future as a retail assistant was secured. My work colleagues had noticed the forlorn face, the bowed head, the more pronounced sighs as I filed records feeling very sorry for myself. They gave me a respectful distance assuming there had been a death in the family and, well, there had – the death of my future career as a rockstar.

As the morning dragged on my depression thickened and morphed into anger – mainly at myself for wasting an opportunity. We had gone into the studio unprepared. I needed to revisit our previous Ernie demos and remind myself of our true potential. I needed to know we weren't shit and needed this reassurance as soon as possible. I knew what I had to do. For once I had caught up on the filing, the others had processed the boxes and customers were thin on the ground. Sensing an opportunity, I joined my colleagues behind the counter. The final track on the album finished playing on the shop stereo. Big Phil pressed eject and took the CD out. Usually, he lined up CDs ready to play, or a customer would request to hear some vinyl (a task I was not yet allowed to perform). Phil rifled through a few CDs and then blew out his cheeks.

'What next? Any suggestions?'

No one seemed to have any strong opinions. The Gaffer and Norwich were at the counter, chatting with the rep from Rough Trade. The current shop favourites had been exhausted, and there were no new releases until Monday. It was now or never. I plucked up courage and asked Phil, like Oliver Twist asking for more porridge.

'Could we play our demo?'

'Your demo?' Phil's eyes widened, and his eyebrows formed a high double arc. I was undeterred.

'Yes. The Pointy Birds.'

His eyebrows stayed aloft, and then a small smile crept across his face.

'Gaffer, Norwich – what do you reckon, should we give The Pointy Birds a spin?'

'Who?'

'Horace's band.'

They looked at each other. It was Gaf's call.

'Go on then, Horace, we need a laugh.'

I ran to my bag and got our demo tape, and with shaking hands inserted it into the cassette player. My fingers trembled and my heart pumped as I pressed play. This tape was a compilation of the seven songs recorded at Ernie's. Although I was proud of them, my colleague's opinion suddenly really mattered. They listened to a lot of music, and they knew quality. If the tape survived until the end of the first song it would be an achievement.

'Benefit Office' began, and a customer approached the counter with some vinyl. Norwich dealt with the customer as Gaffer continued in her conversation with the Rough Trade rep, and a strange thing happened – everyone went about their regular business with The Pointy Birds playing in the background. Only Phil stared ahead with a puzzled expression on his face like he was trying to tune in to some alien frequency from outer space. I was now desperate for some records to file. Out on the shop floor, I could see a customer nodding along. He was a Japanese guy with long, dark hair in a ponytail. He was flicking through record sleeves in the 'Soul & Blues' section. A bit strange as we were hardly a soul-blues band, but maybe he was a man of many tastes. I noticed his foot tapping. It was like our music was on the radio.

'What's this track called Horace?' shouted Gaffer.

'"Benefit Office".'

'Not bad, Horace, not bad. I was expecting a lot worse.'

A customer appeared with some vinyl. Phil took the records and wandered off to find the stock. I could hear him whistling – only bloody whistling. The fact he whistled to everything was irrelevant. No one had pressed the stop button – we were *so* going to make it. Gaffer piped up.

'Hey, Horace, you got a fan. Sean wants to know what this is.'

Sean was the rep from Rough Trade Records. A mop of curly hair and a friendly face. I usually wasn't allowed to speak to the reps that came into the shop. He was from up north.

'Aye up, Horace, what's the name of your band?'

'The Pointy Birds.'

'This you?'

I nodded.

'I like it, Horace.'

'Thank you.'

'If you need a guitarist, let me know.'

'Yeah, sure thing.'

I returned to the filing feeling supersonic. Phil was whistling and now Sean the rep was wanting to join the band! What next?

The Japanese customer came up to the counter. I was still technically not meant to serve the customers, but the waves parted, and he made a beeline for me. I decided to take some initiative. My colleagues watched open-mouthed as the customer popped the question.

'Who is this playing?'

'It's The Pointy Birds,' I said.

'Cool, do they have an album out?'

'No, not yet.'

'OK, is this the single?'

'Er, no, it's a demo.'

I could hear muffled laughs from the others.

'Tell him, Horace.'

'It's, er, my band actually.'

'Really? It's really cool.'

'Thanks.'

The laughter continued. I ignored it.

'Are you playing live soon?'

'Yes, soon, we're just sorting out some dates.'

'Cool – look, here is my card. Let me know when you got a gig.'

'Thanks.'

'Shame it's not out yet, I would have bought that.'

As he turned and walked out of the shop, I looked at his card.

He was a DJ and producer. I resisted punching the air – our first proper fan. If a groovy Japanese DJ producer liked it then so could anyone.

'Right, what next?' said Big Phil rubbing his hands together. 'How about some hardcore?'

22.2

The reaction to our demo was just the tonic. I placed a short but snappy advert in the *NME*.

Pointy Birds seek pointy drummer. Time Wasters only.

I thought this might attract a drummer with a sense of humour as well as a sense of rhythm, but no one fit the bill, and we had to deal with a series of prank calls at 3 a.m. from timewasters wasting my time. But it didn't matter because the answer had been quite literally staring me in the face in the form of the rehearsal space's receptionist Adrian, a quietly spoken kid with cool rock'n'roll hair. I remembered he had once mentioned in passing he played the drums; he might be the solution. The answer was right under our noses like the smell of weed that permeated the studios.

I picked up the phone, dialled the number for the rehearsal studio and Adrian picked up. There was no time for niceties. I got straight to it and said we needed a drummer.

'You interested?'

'Yeah, sure.'

'What kind of music you in to?'

'All sorts, my hero is Stuart Copeland from The Police.'

The perfect answer. We arranged to meet. Drummers were a tough breed to get right – either your best mate with no timing or a brilliant liability, but everything about Adrian was perfect.

He had a mellow personality and relaxed attitude, he could rehearse any time as he pretty much lived at the studio and had control of the booking diary, plus he liked our songs. And, most importantly, he was a supremely talented drummer who, like his hero Copeland, had the timing of a metronome. Adrian may have been shy, but behind the kit, he brought the songs to life and gave them power, pace and precision, adding flourishes that were subtle and unexpected. He didn't bang the drums. He played them.

I couldn't wait to give Ricky the news that we had the new Stuart Copeland on drums and could now hit the live circuit. I still hadn't heard from him since Catford and feared he had gone cold on us. But this was the perfect way to bounce back with some positive news. I also needed to tell him to bin the Catford demo – it wasn't a faithful representation of who we were, and we had learned never to wing it in the studio again. I recalled the Catford session with a shudder – it was vitally important no one ever heard it. I rang Ricky, but he beat me to it with his news.

'People are loving "Man Who Kisses Horses".'

'What?'

'Yeah, Michael, the guy who runs the Blow Monkeys label and paid for the session, loves it…'

'Really?' It hadn't even occurred to me he would play it to people, let alone people might like it.

'It's Echo & The Bunnymen meets Teardrop Explodes…'

High praise indeed. Maybe 'Horses' did deserve a second listen? I noticed he hadn't mentioned 'Rocket Child'. I decided not to mention it either. I couldn't deny it was nice to hear the enthusiasm in his voice, but Ricky wasn't finished.

'And I think I've got you a live agent – Mike Greek at Wasted Talent. Top agent. Top agency. Do loads of big acts.'

Ricky was getting me excited. We used to get our golden retriever Max excited by rubbing his back, near his tail, and this would cause him to race around the sitting room in circles with his tongue hanging out. I felt like doing the same. Even though I wasn't exactly sure what a live agent was or did. Ricky continued.

'He loves the demos, and he's interested in taking you on. He wants to come and see you live when you're up and running.'

It was time for me to hit the ball back over the net.

'Well, I got news on that front actually. We found a drummer. And he's good. *Really* good…'

22.3

Willesden Green. We arranged for Ricky to come to a rehearsal to see us in action with our new drummer. Our rehearsal studio was in Willesden Green and run by a Rastafarian collective. There was a friendly, relaxed atmosphere, and we were something of a curiosity to the owners Eddy and Malcolm, with our 'indie' ways. Occasionally, as we rehearsed, there would be a gentle rat-a-tat-tat at the door, and Eddy and Malcolm would ask if they could come in and listen to the music. They would sit rolling a Camberwell Carrot-sized spliff and head nod to the music with the occasional 'Ire, man. Ire, man' until ganja smoke filled the room. At this point, it made perfect sense for the songs to slow down and take a more laid back direction, especially as the nods of appreciation from our small audience increased as the songs slowed down. Then Malcolm would ask to have a go on the drums and Paul would sleepily get off his stool and hand over his sticks and lie down – he needed to be horizontal. Next, Marcus would hand his bass guitar to Eddy in exchange for the spliff and lie down next to Paul. Finally, I would succumb, and we would spend the rest of our rehearsal watching Malcolm and Eddy jam deep reggae before we got the munchies and each scoffed an extra-large doner kebab on the way home. There was nothing devious or dastardly about what they were doing, but it wasn't a very productive way to rehearse and seemed a bit steep at £35 per hour. Plus, we were putting on weight. We needed to get a bit more professional for Ricky's visit.

We got in early, and Adrian explained to Malcolm and Eddy that we had important music industry people coming down, so please no carrots. We had an hour warm-up before our guests arrived. This time the rat-a-tat-tat was followed by Ricky's head popping around the door. He had brought a someone with him – a tall, odd-looking individual with an intense stare and a roving eye. Ricky introduced him as Gordon but didn't explain who Gordon was or what Gordon did. I wouldn't have been surprised if Ricky had said he was a policeman. Gordon nodded a hello, and I got the impression he wasn't thrilled about being dragged out to Willesden on a wet and windy Tuesday evening.

'Don't worry, he doesn't bite – do you, Gordon?

Gordon was non-committal.

'Well, not often.' Ricky started giggling. 'Except that time. Remember what you did to that last band when you didn't like their music?'

Ricky stifled his laughter. We all stood with fixed grins. It was hard to share the joke. Was it at our expense or Gordon's? If he was trying to put us at ease, it had the opposite effect. Ricky hadn't finished.

Ricky pointed at Gordon. 'Look… not happy… Egor… oh dear…'

Gordon stared ahead with a poker face giving nothing away.

'Shall we play?' said Marcus, keen to move things on.

Adrian counted us in, and we started with 'Lift Me', our slightly soppy but future transatlantic number-one hit song. Ricky always name-checked it from our Ernie demo. And so did Marcus's mum. Adrian had given the song more power and made it less sentimental. Out of the corner of my eye, it looked like Ricky was genuinely into it – nodding his head, tapping his feet and nudging Gordon, who betrayed no emotion. It was weird to play to an audience of two, but this was an important gig and in our world still a relatively big audience. We finished the song to whoops and hollers from Ricky. He seemed particularly excited by the addition of Adrian on drums. Gordon remained unmoved. We played through the rest of our set, and when we finished, Ricky made some suggestions.

That song needs to lift more on the chorus.

That section needs some work.

Maybe some tambourine on the verses.

It was constructive criticism, and his suggestions were met with wary nods from the band, his singing stint at Catford still fresh in their minds. It was time to move the conversation from the creative to the commercial and talk business. He felt we were ready and started explaining his role going forward, which seemed to be less manager and more builder. We needed to *build* stagecraft, confidence and repertoire. He would *build* a team around us – a live agent, a promoter, a label, a publisher, an accountant and a lawyer, then we could start *building* an audience to *build* a career. It all sounded great, but the devil was in the detail – how exactly were we going to do this? Ricky revealed the cherry on top.

'I got you a gig. Fancy playing the Underworld?'

There were excited and impressed noises. The Underworld was one of the coolest venues to play in Camden. My only concern was the size – it was big. Who were we supporting?

'The Passiondales.'

Ricky looked at us expectantly, waiting for the band's next question.

'Who are they?'

'It's my band,' said Ricky.

There was a small silence as air hissed out of a balloon.

'You are in a band?'

'Yes, just a bit of fun. Anyway, do you want to do the gig? Will be hilarious.'

There was a general nodding of consent.

'Brilliant! How many people could you get along? If you really push it?'

'Um, dunno. Fifty, maybe?'

'Brilliant!' said Ricky.

The gig was agreed, and although supporting Ricky wasn't what we had in mind, it was still a chance to play a cool venue and impress people that needed impressing. Gordon was yet to say anything, but on leaving the rehearsal room, he acknowledged our presence with a brief nod, which felt like a result.

23. The Underworld

WINTER 1992

Go shopping ahead of gig supporting Ricky's band and my new cardigan becomes star of the show.

Ahead of the gig, I revisited the look of the band. This gig was our first proper outing with Adrian on drums, and first impressions mattered. With 50 per cent of the band not willing to dress up, it was wise to default to a more indie factory setting. And with Kurt Cobain rocking a cardigan, pipe and slippers look, I temporarily ditched the frilly shirt in preference for more grungy attire, plus with winter on its way a shirt undone to the navel was not practical, or warm.

Also, I had become enchanted by the slacker charm of a six-piece indie-rock outfit from California called Pavement led by the ever-smiling Steve Malkmus. They were like a naughty Velvet Underground – and their debut album *Slanted And Enchanted* was on repeat in the shop. We had gone to see them live, and on stage, they were an utter shambles. Paradoxically, they were also in total control. It didn't seem to matter if songs went wrong, guitar strings broke, amps didn't work, drummers exploded – that was all part of their shtick, and somehow the band found their way back home on each song. Like Picasso, you had to know the rules to be able to break them. It was good to remember that being in a band was all about not caring what people thought plus being good and having FUN! They also rocked a scruffy look that suited us down to the ground.

With these thoughts in mind, I paid a visit to Camden Market, and that's when I saw it. If ever an item of clothing was both calling my name and had my name on it, it was this beauty. An Aran chunky-knit cardigan with multi-coloured stitches woven throughout. I think the technical term was speckled. It appealed to my Scottish roots and fit me snug as a bug in a rug. And I could wear my sparkly sequinned shirt underneath, so best of both worlds. But the reaction was not quite as expected. Marcus danced a step when I got back to the flat, and my colleagues at Selectadisc laughed openly at it. Had I made a rash decision? My leather jacket had elicited impressed noises and looks; the cardigan produced mirth. Not just from people I knew but strangers – stifled sniggers and sarcastic comments. I decided to ignore them. My new Highlands get-up was just ahead of the curve, ok it clashed slightly with Marcus's flamenco shirts, but apart from that, we were ready to rock.

23.2

The Underworld sat underneath the World's End pub opposite Camden Town Tube and was a regular haunt for new music lovers putting on great gigs, club nights and after-show parties. I had seen bands like Eat and The Afghan Whigs play live there and couldn't wait to tread the boards myself, but I was still concerned about the size. The capacity was at least five hundred, and I wasn't sure if this was the venue The Passiondales should be headlining unless they had a following I didn't know about. Maybe this was why Ricky was so keen for us to bring people. But at least it gave us a chance to play a prestigious venue in front of the various industry types that Ricky had said he would invite. In his words, we were *ready*. And we had to treat every gig like it was the most important gig regardless of turn out as who knew who might be lurking in the shadows.

It was also a chance for my co-workers at Selectadisc to check us out. I had been bigging up our prospects, and it was time to deliver. I also put in calls to old college and school friends, as well as my new Japanese fan. Josh travelled down from Cardiff for the gig slightly mystified that things were happening for the band, having heard we had a fab new drummer, gig and potential live agent, but remained unswerving in his belief that our days were numbered.

We arrived at The Underworld for the soundcheck. Ricky greeted us outside and showed us around the venue enthusiastically, like the proud owner of a hotel. Inside felt spacious, especially with no one in it – plenty of room for tumbleweeds. Ricky's band had finished soundcheck and seeing the stage set up with instruments got the butterflies fluttering – the hopes and fears of what the night might bring. But with new drummer Adrian on board, I felt strangely confident this gig was going to go well. I could hear the ringing of a metaphorical phone – destiny was calling.

'Look, I'll show you – they even got a green room,' Ricky said excitedly. We followed him backstage. He opened the door to an empty room with some chairs in it. 'Plus you got a dressing room.'

He pointed excitedly at a piece of A4 paper sellotaped to another door. It read:

POINTY BIRDS DRESSING ROOM

It was a nice touch, and a dressing room was a first for us. Ricky pushed opened the door with a 'ta-dah…!'.

The room was the size of a small broom cupboard, but it was the thought that counted. On another door was a similar piece of paper which read:

THE PASSIONDALES DRESSING ROOM

Ricky pointed at the sign like an excited school kid. 'I've always wanted our name in biro.'

Their dressing room was more extensive and furnished with an old sofa and some chairs around a table adorned with a bowl of sad-looking fruit and an array of snacks. It felt very glamorous. Ricky opened a fridge packed with bottles of cold beers. We eyed them mischievously, every support band's prerogative to snaffle the headliner's rider without being caught.

Ricky was more hyper than usual and slightly distracted like he had bitten off more than he could chew. In addition to being the lead singer in the headline act and managing the support band, he was also manning The Passiondales' merchandise stall. If he shared my anxiety about the size of the venue, he didn't show it and seemed keen to make us feel at ease. I suppose he wanted to create an atmosphere where he was a friend first, manager second. Probably entertainer third.

We finished our soundcheck, and as usual, things had overrun. The stage manager, who was large and hairy and looked like he doubled up as a Hell's Angel biker in his spare time, was not ambiguous in his instructions.

'You got give minutes, so take a shit and then you're on stage. If you go on stage late, I will cut your set. You got to be off by 8.15.'

I nodded. It all felt a bit police state. The doors had still not opened, and there were no signs of life in the venue. I thought of protesting, but he didn't look like a stage manager willing to negotiate. We did our necessary ablutions, had a quick team talk outside our dressing room cupboard and climbed back on stage. I could see Ricky eagerly waiting with his sidekick Gordon. They were our sole audience. I still wasn't sure what the deal was with Gordon. Who was he and why didn't he speak?

Annoyingly, there was no sign of our fanbase or any other audience. Had doors even opened yet? I was slightly relieved my three work colleagues from Selectadisc weren't here to witness this non-event. An empty venue didn't square with my bragging that we were on the verge of the big time. But even though this current audience was 0.4 per cent of the total venue capacity, Ricky was yet to see us live, and I needed to show him we meant business. We took to the stage, picked up our instruments and the stage lights blinked on. It was no longer possible to see our two audience members, for the brightness of the lights. It was probably for the best. Would be dispiriting to look at such a large, empty venue. We had to put the glad rags on and play as though the place was packed and our lives depended on it.

I tapped the mic to check it was working, Adrian counted us in with four clicks of his drum sticks and we launched into 'Benefit Office'. The first of the seven songs from our Ernie demos that we would be playing tonight. Gone were the days of introducing the band as we sauntered through 'Pube On My Lip' and more jokey numbers such as 'Married To A Squirrel'. As for 'Rocket Child', it was still in recovery and not ready to be released back out into the community. We now had proper indie-pop songs – no fillers, all thrillers. 'Benefit Office' sounded immediately good on stage, and we relaxed into the song.

Enthusiastic applause greeted the end of the song. It sounded like a few more people were in the room. I couldn't tell how many – we were possibly into double figures. I decided to introduce the band. I had recently seen Doctor and The Medics at Camden Palace, and the singer had got a big laugh when he introduced his backing singer to the audience. I decided to steal the joke now.

'And on keyboards, we have Josh, without whom the rest of the band would still be virgins.'

Josh flashed daggers at me as the familiar sound of Ricky's hyena laugh echoed around the venue. It was flattering that he found the joke, and me, so funny. Ricky was the perfect audience for my music-meets-comedy shtick. The banter between the songs gave the audience an insight into the personality of the individual band members. OK, not every band needed to have 'knock knock' jokes, and there was something to be said for a bit of mystery, but some interaction between artist and audience was essential. I felt cheated if the band ran through the set and didn't say anything. The greatest singer-songwriters told stories to explain the provenance of each song, and if they could make you laugh on top, then it was love. Was there anything more charming than footage of Neil Young telling stories and playing songs from his 1970 album *Harvest*? No.

We raced through the rest of our seven-song set peppered with jokes and banter. I could hear all the different band members and the song sounded faithful to the recordings – better even. Adrian's meticulous metronome drumming took us to another level – it was tight, rhythmic and subtle. As we finished each song, the audience seemed to be getting louder, and the reaction quite positive. We ended the set with 'Blowing Your Brains Out', an old song that had originated from a series of chords I'd jammed with Stu. He had come up with some lyrics for a chorus:

Have you ever thought of doing away,
with the things that make your life seem grey?
Have you ever thought of ending it all…
Blowing your brains out against a wall!

The clever bit was that the music stopped on the word *all* at the end of line three, then everything went quiet as I uttered the immortal line:

'Blowing your brains out against a…'

We would leave things hanging and then the band came crashing in on the word *wall*, which sounded a bit like brains splattering against a wall.

Initially, I felt slightly fraudulent singing what seemed to be a deeply troubling suicide anthem, when that was the opposite of how I felt inside – I wanted our songs to be life-affirming, so the protagonist in the song chooses to live and not die. I didn't want to compare myself to Shakespeare, but it was effectively a musical 'to be or not to be'.

Like Abba and The Smiths, the best pop had a dark underbelly, and with this song, we had tapped into the zeitgeist and created our own Generation X anthem. We were in good company with Beck singing 'I'm a loser, baby, so why don't you kill me'; Kurt Cobain wanted to call their new album 'I hate myself, and I want to die'; and Radiohead had cashed in with 'I'm a creep I'm a weirdo'. Self-loathing had become de rigueur, and these tunes provided a catharsis that people needed.

We brought 'Blowing Your Brains Out' to a climactic end, and huge applause broke out. We still couldn't see anybody beyond the hot white lights on stage, but when we left the stage and the glare of the lights, I was impressed by how many people had shown up. It was by no means full, but the word respectable could be applied. How had Ricky pulled this off?

We cleared our instruments off the stage satisfied with a job well done, and Marcus and I headed for the bar feeling like popstars. Ricky was first to appear through the throng.

'That was brilliant, guys – loved it. I want to introduce you to someone. This is Mike Greek, live agent from Wasted Talent.'

We shook hands and exchanged smiles.

'Hi, I loved it too,' said Mike. He seemed like a grown-up in the room. Someone you might go to in a crisis, suave and sensible like a pilot.

'I'll leave you guys to it,' said Ricky. 'Oh, actually, Horace, can I borrow your cardigan?'

I looked at Ricky, trying to work out if he was joking. I felt slightly disarmed by this strange request. Ricky explained.

'I want to wear it on stage. Be hilarious.'

He started laughing, but I didn't get the joke.

'What you reckon? Go on, it'll be a laugh.'

I looked at Marcus and Mike confused – they shrugged their shoulders. I took my cardigan off and handed it to him.

'Brilliant. Wish me luck!'

Ricky disappeared back into the crowd, leaving us to get acquainted.

'You guys fancy a beer?' said Mike.

We nodded eagerly and followed Mike to a quieter part of the bar for a post-gig business meeting. Mike handed us a couple of cold beers and then broke the ice by telling us how much he loved the demo, demonstrating he was a real fan by knowing the correct titles for each song. He particularly liked 'Benefit Office', which reminded him of Lloyd Cole.

'Wow, that's a massive compliment,' said Marcus.

'You like Lloyd Cole?'

'Yes, we are massive fans. *Rattlesnakes* is an album we have on rotation at the flat, isn't it?'

Marcus nudged me, and we exchanged winks and then clinked bottles of beer. Over the hub-bub, Mike explained the role of a live agent. He would be in charge of our live career – booking us gigs, routing tours, negotiating fees. I had never heard anyone refer to what we were doing with the word *career*. Mike also used words like market share and name-checked his roster of successful artists – it sounded an exciting and seductive world. Marcus and I both nodded eagerly and slurped our beers not knowing what to say but feeling dizzy with joy that at last, people were taking us seriously. Success was lifting the hem of her skirt and showing us a bit of leg.

I noticed my Selectadisc work colleagues had turned up and were at the bar and so I joined them for a drink. They started chanting Horace and singing 'Blowing Your Brains Out', and I felt a huge surge of affection for them. They had come out to see the band. And dare I say it, they were fans! I would make more effort at work now, especially as I would be leaving soon – no more yawning or lateness or misfiling. And the nickname

Horace was growing on me too, or maybe I was growing into it? It definitely worked as a stage name.

The Japanese DJ also appeared through the crowd. We shook hands, and he said he enjoyed the gig and asked when the next one would be. Did life get any better than this? The lights dimmed. It was time for The Passiondales. I was curious to see Ricky in action. The band appeared on stage minus Ricky and started playing an instrumental number building up suspense for his imminent arrival. A few moments later, Ricky appeared on stage wearing my cardigan and waving to his fans made up of students, family and friends. Eventually, the music stopped, and Ricky went into a monologue about the cardigan. I didn't understand the joke. Not sure anyone else did either. Although when I looked around at Marcus and Mike, they were both smirking.

Ricky launched into the next song – his voice was good, and he was a man after my own heart who was trying to combine music and comedy. But maybe he shouldn't be doing either. I stood watching the rest of the gig wondering why he was still in a band. He just needed to smell the coffee and focus on managing us, that was his best chance of success because one thing was for sure: he didn't have a future as a performer in the entertainment industry.

24. The *NME*

FEBRUARY 1993

We appear within the pages of the UK's leading independent music publication. Three-Hurdle Theory goes under the microscope.

Suede had gatecrashed the Brit Awards and then the top ten with their new single 'Animal Nitrate'. It was weird to watch them on TV replicate what we had seen them do in the sweaty clubs, but now their performance was being watched by millions rather than a few hundred. Although this was exciting and showed how quickly things could escalate for a new band, I was concerned they might be getting too far away from us. But now Mike had jumped on board the good ship Pointy Bird as our live agent it would be a case of the tortoise chasing the hare.

Mike was as good as his word and booked us some gigs. As much as he enjoyed our live set, he explained we needed to develop our stagecraft, so the idea was to play a few low-key supports with like-minded bands to get tight and then would go for some bigger, buzzier shows. He deflected my questions about getting on Suede's forthcoming UK tour saying that would be very *competitive* and *in demand.* That wasn't a no. And Ricky had said Saul at Nude Records was *interested* and wanted to come down to *check us out.* Surely with Ricky and Mike's connections it was only a matter of time before we were signed and on the road?

Our first show was a return to the Camden Falcon supporting a band I had never heard of called The Rumblestrips. We were to follow this with a run of shows supporting another band I had never heard of from New Zealand called Magic at a new venue in Kensington called The Orange. Mike had also booked us a show at the Borderline in Soho which was renowned for showcasing acts before they became famous. Having an agent booking shows for us made me feel validated and more like a professional artist.

Our gig at the Camden Falcon went well, and we made amends for that previous appearance with Mad Cow Disease. I felt a bit sorry for The Rumblestrips having to come on after us. We had blown them away. There was now no stopping us and about a week after the Falcon gig the phone rang at Selectadisc.

Norwich answered and shouldered the phone.

'Horace, it's Ricky on the phone *again.*'

I grabbed the phone excited about what news he might have.

'Guess what?'

'What?'

'You are in the *NME.* They reviewed the Falcon gig.'

My blood turned to ice.

'Well done. Gotta go.'

Ricky's voice vanished, and I replaced the phone. The receiver clicked into place.

'That was quick,' said Norwich. 'What's wrong? You look like you've seen a ghost.'

'We are in the *NME,*' I said in a shocked monotone voice with a faraway look in my eye. This was how it felt to have your dreams turn into reality.

'Well done, Horace.'

Norwich went off to tell the others, and I resumed filing with lots of questions spinning in my head. It was Tuesday morning. Was the *NME* out yet? It didn't usually appear until Tuesday afternoon earliest. The wait would be torture. Had Ricky read it? How did he know? What did the review say? Thank god we had played a blinder. I had to tell the others. I would put a call into Marcus when he was on his lunch break from the frozen aisle.

The morning tip-toed agonisingly towards the afternoon. Time moved slowly in the shop, but now it took on new tortoise-like proportions. I was desperate to get down to the newsagent and pick up a copy of the paper. My whole future depended on this article. A good review propelled bands into the middle of an A&R bidding war. An unsigned band with the *NME* behind it made you hot property. So far our only exposure in the press was a *Time Out* listing for our gig at the White Horse which had described us as ‘spiky punk with a tinge of jazz’. It was a strange way to describe our music until another band, also called The Pointy Birds, got in touch to say we had stolen their name and the listing referred to them. Still, it was a thrill to see our name in print.

Lunchtime came and went and while on the jacket potato run I made numerous detours to the newsagent, but still the *NME* hadn’t arrived. The guy behind the counter said it was strange as they were usually delivered by now and maybe there was a problem at the printing plant or distributor. He made some arbitrary joke, but it was no time for games, horseplay, tomfoolery. Could he not ring the pressing plant or the delivery company to find out why the delay? Couldn’t he see the urgency and desperation in my eyes? But he shrugged his shoulders like he didn’t care. I returned to the shop with the agony of not knowing. I tried ringing Ricky to find out more but annoyingly couldn’t get hold of him.

For the rest of the afternoon, my life was on hold. Normality could not continue. I wasn’t in a fit state to file – I no longer remembered the alphabet. I had rung Marcus but not got through. Maybe I could ring the *NME*. It was now 5 p.m., and I was beginning to accept that if the papers hadn’t arrived now, it would be until tomorrow. Oh, the torture ahead of me – the endless hours of waiting and wondering, the sleepless night ahead. At this point, Gaffer, who had gone out for a cigarette, returned excitedly waving a copy of the *NME* and *Melody Maker*.

'Oi, Horace! Put on a brew and we can have a read!'

She carried not just these papers, but my destiny in her hands. She laid the newspapers out on the counter.

My heart was thumping so loudly in my ears that I couldn't hear anything.

'Which mag you in, Horace?'

'The *NME*,' I said, my voice breaking into falsetto as I tried and failed to keep cucumber-like with coolness. I could feel my body shaking and control of both bowel and bladder loosening. Norwich and Big Phil joined us, and for a moment there was silence as Gaf flicked through the pages one by one. Images of familiar indie-popstar faces flashed up – Miles Hunt from the Wonderstuff, Barney from New Order, so weird that any second now I was about to join their ranks. Eventually, we hit the live section containing all the reviews of the best gigs in the last week. The *NME* was the number-one taste-maker, and they didn't mince their words. If they said you were good, you were good. And they didn't just set the agenda here in the UK – it was international. Every country followed.

My eyes scanned the pages. How big would the review be? Was there a photo to go with it?

Where was it? Where was it? *Where was it?*

'Here you go, Horace. The Pointy Birds.'

Gaffer's finger landed on a review of The Rumblestrips + Pointy Birds at The Camden Falcon. It ran for about an eighth of the page, and I was a bit disappointed that we had shared the review with The Rumblestrips when they didn't deserve the coverage.

We fell silent, digesting the words, but there was some mistake. The journalist was describing another band. He was using words like 'bland' and 'inoffensive' which couldn't refer to us, surely. And then it got worse:

> *'...with a seriously over-acting singer...'*

A seriously over-acting singer? He had singled me out! And not just an over-acting singer, which was bad enough, but a seriously over-acting one. Could it get any worse? The words seemed to increase in size and glow like hot coals. I felt dizzy and could feel myself float upwards like I was having an out-of-body experience. I looked down upon the four of us reading this terrible review – a futile attempt to try and escape the reality of the situation. With each poisonous word, a nail in the coffin of my dreams, and the death of my ambition.

The only slight positive was a comparison to Blur's poppier moments, a band who had already died a death. And to add insult to injury, The Rumblestrips had got a glowing review in comparison 'in this tale of two singers'. But they were shit. My shock turned to anger. What cloth-eared journalist wrote this? Mark Sutherland? How could they let someone with no music taste be a music journalist? It was mean and spiteful. Well, two could play at that game. I would find out where he lived. Never had I wanted to defecate through someone's letterbox as much as I did right now.

'Don't worry about it, Horace,' said Big Phil with a paternal hand on my shoulder. 'We still love you.'

'No one ever leaves Selectadisc, Horace, better get used to it,' said Gaffer, 'now that your dreams are in tatters.'

Her laugh echoed around the shop. The grim reality of her words resonated. This review was the moment everything ended. I smiled and tried to laugh it off, but this hurt, it was a definite flesh wound.

Twenty-three years of my life had come to this point. All those hours watching *Top Of The Pops*, taping the Top 40 on the radio every Sunday evening, dancing in front of a mirror with a hairbrush-microphone. For what? For this! I seemed to be experiencing the five stages of grief simultaneously: shock, denial, anger, depression. But acceptance? No. The consequence of this review, the ramifications of people reading it – Mum, Dad, old school and college friends, my Japanese fan, Saul at Nude, Ricky, Mike, the entire music industry, the rest of the world. It was official – in print. We were 'bland and inoffensive with a seriously over-acting singer'. Could it get any worse? I imagined Josh's 'told you so' face. I returned to my filing and heard some giggles. Norwich was doing an impression of me – limp-wristed and wiggling his bum with a pretend microphone. That wasn't me, was it? I couldn't wait to get home. I needed to curl up into the foetal position and give this some serious thought.

24.2

Luckily, the next day was my day off which I spent productively behind a closed bedroom door under my duvet. The phone hadn't rung – people were obviously too embarrassed to speak to me. Even naysayer Josh was conspicuous by his silence. I needed a period of self-confinement, introspection and navel-gazing. I needed to put my stupid Three-Hurdle Theory under intense scrutiny – I had swallowed it hook, line and sinker without really contemplating what it meant. I needed to unpick it, test it. Rewind to that first hurdle. What did I want? Did I still want to be a rockstar? Did I want the reality of it, including the judgement and disappointment? The heartache and the misery? The making of music was fun, but the business of trying to make it was a lot harder than it looked.

Or maybe I hadn't jumped the second hurdle and worked out if I was capable of making it at all. Perhaps we didn't have what it took? I didn't possess enough natural talent. Maybe Josh was right, and Stu was right, and that arsehole journalist was right. We were rubbish. Or maybe this was the third hurdle in action – the 'do it' element – the hard graft on the treadmill. I just needed to dig deep and keep climbing to the scenic views at the summit of fame and fortune and fun. But it felt like I was a long way down the mountain and my legs were weak.

Maybe I was missing the Four Ds – drive, determination, dedication, desire. I just had one big D – delusion! I'd had a happy childhood, and that was the fatal kiss of death – nothing to kick against? I didn't want it enough. Would I sell my grandmother down the river for a hit? Probably not. And even if I would, did I have the essential ingredient of not caring what anyone thought? Maybe I was too thin-skinned for this lark.

The Three-Hurdle Theory was all about knowing what you wanted and going for it and not caring what people thought, but could it be I *didn't* know what I wanted and *did* care what people thought? Maybe I just liked the idea of being a rockstar, the hairbrush microphone. But if I didn't want to be a rockstar, then what did I want? And if I wasn't a rockstar-in-waiting, then who was I? Was Horace the rockstar a construction that needed dismantling – a wrong narrative that needed correcting? Could it be that beneath it all, I was, god forbid, just ordinary?

24.3

I hadn't heard from Ricky since the review. No doubt he had moved on, I thought. But then he rang with a different take on things.

'Doesn't matter. Only one person's opinion and better to be written about than not being written about.'

Was it? I wasn't sure. He doubled down and echoed the same line that Dad had said to me when he read the review.

'There's no such thing as bad publicity.'

Wasn't there? I wasn't sure. Having someone write 'seriously over-acting' in print for the whole world to see was a bitter, humiliating pill of publicity to swallow. But Ricky's positivity won me over. The clouds began to part, and the sun peeked out. Suddenly, the famous saying popped into my mind that seemed to put everything in glorious perspective: what doesn't kill you makes you stronger.

I could feel my blood tingle with excitement, and the Three-Hurdle Theory made sense again.

'Who cares what other people think!'

Yes, I had to dig deep. It was all in my hands. I just had to work hard, focus, keep on the treadmill. This review was but a minor setback, the merest of hiccups, the tiniest of bumps in the road.

The more I thought about it, the more I realised it was positive. Ricky was right. My dad was right. Thousands of people were reading about the band. We were on their radar. I could feel my skin thicken like the Hulk – Horace the rockstar was back! I suddenly felt liberated and as happy as a puppy playing in the sun. If part of Ricky's job as a band manager was to make his artist feel better about themselves following some bad news, turn a negative into a positive, he had played a blinder.

25. A Vision Of The Future

UNKNOWN DATE

We receive some independent advice from a futures expert that helps put things into focus.

It was time to get back on the horse. And to quote Simon Le Bon, I was hungry like the wolf. I was so hungry I could eat the horse I had just jumped back on. Paradoxically, the bad *NME* review had made me want it more than ever. That journalist had got it all wrong, and I now had something to prove. I was more eager, more driven. We needed to gig, to write and get back in the studio, especially now we had such a good drummer in Adrian, and luckily we had the gigs through Mike to keep us going.

My only concern was any negative impact the review might have on the rest of the band, especially Marcus. I needed to gee him up with the old Three-Hurdle Speech and repaint the glorious vision of the future, but he didn't seem to be biting. I needed to call in the experts, get a fresh perspective and a few pointers or signs. And that's when I saw the sign, a real one, hanging outside a stall at Camden Market:

TAROT CARD READING
£5 for 5 minutes

It was just what we needed and although Marcus poo-pooed Tarot cards as gobblygook along with star signs, he agreed it might be a laugh if nothing else. I didn't disagree with his scepticism – but at the same time, the fact I could pick up a phone and someone in Australia could hear me instantaneously without me even needing to raise my voice was yet to be adequately explained to me. If that was possible, then so was anything. And this was not to mention we lived on a spinning ball hurtling through infinite time and space. And if a 1-year-old Chinese baby could do the Rubik's cube in under a minute which defied all explanation, then surely someone peeking into the future using cards wasn't so mind-blowing?

A Tarot card reading might show us an exciting glimpse of the future as rock'n'roll stars and get Marcus back on board. We entered the tent, and the smell of Petunia hit us like a truck. A woman wearing in a long flowing dress and the jingle jangle of cheap bangles greeted us, and we held our guitar cases aloft.

'Where shall we dump these?'

'Oh, in the corner is fine and then come and join me on the mat, my lovers.'

She had a Cornish accent. I didn't want to generalise, but the fact she hailed from the west country didn't surprise me. We did as she said and sat cross-legged on the floor and tried to make ourselves comfortable as she dealt out the cards. Marcus made his feelings known it was all somewhat questionable through a singular raised eyebrow and series of sneers and sighs.

'Right, let's see what we have here then shall we, my petals?'

We sat quietly as she turned over a row of cards, and then she spoke.

'The cards are saying you are something to do with music? Are you in a band?'

She was good. OK, maybe the guitars and our silky locks were a slight give away. I nudged Marcus, impressed. His right eyebrow remained aloft, and it didn't look like it was coming down anytime soon. She turned over some more cards, followed by a sharp intake of breath.

Marcus leaned over to me and whispered a bit too loudly into my ear. 'Let's go. This is bullshit.'

I shushed him to be quiet. More cards were turned until they made a pattern on the mat, then, at last, she spoke. 'I can see that you are on a journey. You are climbing a mountain and assembling the pieces you need like a jigsaw.'

She wasn't wrong there, although she was slightly mixing her metaphors. She turned over another card.

'I recommend focusing on getting your songwriting and live act as tight as possible and then record a great demo.'

This advice had grabbed Marcus's attention. His eyebrow started to lower.

'You will also need guidance in the commercial side of things to negotiate the choppy seas of a cut-throat business.'

This was not what Marcus or I was expecting. She continued.

'Do you have someone that can help you with that side of things?'

We kind of nodded. She continued.

'A good manager can take care of the business while you focus on the creative side of things, which I am sure you are supremely talented. A good manager is hard to come by, so don't necessarily take the first one that comes along.'

'How will we know if we have found the right manager?'

'Let's see, shall we?'

She turned over another card – it was 'The Fool'. She smiled and nodded sagely.

'The fool is a potent card. Don't be alarmed by the name. Foolishness can be very optimistic as it means being free from the constraints of normal life…'

She widened her eyes and leaned closer.

'…but you need to use this power wisely. It portends important decisions ahead. You are entering a new phase in your life, and you need to make choices. To succeed, you must find new ways to bring about the achievement of your goals…'

We were both nodding vigorously, but it was slightly vague. I wasn't exactly sure what she meant.

'Right, so does that mean we are going to make it?'

She smiled enigmatically. 'It depends what you mean by making it, my lover.'

It was obvious – the promised land, hitting the big time, the land of milk and honey.

'Um… being successful?' offered Marcus.

'I suppose that depends on your definition of success. The cards are saying the road is long and winding but with patience and hard work, you will get there.'

Hey, she was nicking my Three-Hurdle Theory. Marcus was getting restless and needed clarification.

'So, when you or rather the cards say we will get there, where exactly do you mean?'

'Well, that depends on where you are trying to get to, flower.'

We both were a bit frustrated at the lack of specifics. She elaborated.

'It is for you to decide your ultimate destination. What is your main goal in life? Is it a personal goal to reach enlightenment and self-knowledge?'

She left this hanging before offering what she clearly thought was the lesser alternative.

'Or is it the material goals of fame and fortune?'

There was a pause.

'Um, the fame and fortune one?'

She smiled in a slightly disappointed way. 'Let's turn over a card, shall we…?'

She turned over another card and then spoke. 'I can see things are going to happen. I think there will be a big success. Especially for someone in or around the band.'

I resisted punching the air. She was talking about me obviously and my subsequent solo career. I looked at Marcus; he couldn't resist a bashful smile thinking the big success referred to him.

'Brilliant, do you know exactly when I, er, I mean we will get there?'

'I'm sorry, the cards don't give an ETA. It's not a train service, you know.' She turned her attention to me. 'Can I ask why you want fame and fortune? Did you move house a lot when you were younger?'

This took me back. 'Yes, I did, actually.'

She nodded.

'Why?' I asked.

'Oh, nothing.'

She couldn't leave it there, but she planned to. 'I'm sorry, my lover, but time is up. I could tell you more, but you will need to pay. The main thing going forward is that if you are positive and have a sunny outlook, good things will happen.'

This sounded reasonable.

'And don't let the knives turn in on themselves.'

'What does that mean?'

'That means the band needs to keep busy. If you don't keep the band busy, the knives will turn on yourselves so keep busy – rehearsing, getting better, doing gigs, always improving – puts the knives outwards.'

Marcus was nodding furiously in agreement like he was in one of his politics lectures. His brain was being stimulated to the potential of it.

'Have you ever thought of becoming a band manager?' he asked.

'What, me?' She laughed. 'No, what do I know? I'm just a fortune teller from Truro with special psychic powers.'

We picked up our guitars and left the tent and jumped on the Tube back to our flat in happy silence, reflecting on the conversation. *The road was long, but with patience and hard work, we would get there.* Although she hadn't specified exactly where we were going or when we would arrive, it was great to know we were on our way. And all we needed was a sunny outlook, some knives and to keep busy. The Tube burst out of the tunnel, and the carriage was engulfed in daylight as we approached Golders Green station. I exchanged winks with Marcus. A sure sign he was back on board.

26. Yeah! Yeah! Yeah!

SPRING 1993

A bit on Stereo MC's followed by some thoughts on rhyming couplets, the songwriting process and the perfect three-minute pop song. A new song comes together that might be our best yet.

With US grunge bands still reigning supreme and Suede single-handedly trying to inject a bit of glamour back into the British indie scene, it seemed as if 1993 was going to sound much like 1992, but hip hop/electronic dance collective from south London called Stereo MC's had other ideas, and were enjoying critical and commercial success with their album *Connected.* Although released in September 1992, album sales grew exponentially with the band releasing several hit singles from the album, eventually headlining Glastonbury and scooping best album and band awards at the Brit Awards in 1994.

But in spring 1993, *Connected* was omnipresent on the radio, TV and dance floors soundtracking everywhere I went. Their simple message of getting 'connected' seemed to resonate with a post-rave generation who were dealing with day-to-day realities of paying bills and putting the bins out and how this squared with the love-ins that they experienced high on drugs at 3 a.m. in the late eighties. There had to be a better way, and Stereo MC's along with The Beloved combined a dance-infused blueprint of uplifting melodies, beats and bleeps with the quest for a higher form of spirituality. But without the drugs, maybe.

But it was in their rhyming couplets that Stereo MC's made

me smile. Not Since ABC's 'Lexicon Of Love' had a band scaled the dizziest of heights and finest of lines between good cheese and bad cheese. And lead singer/lyricist Rob Birch was a tightrope walker extraordinaire. Dubious lines like 'don't take a genius to know about Venus' should have been banned for crimes against lyric writing, but backed with the euphoric rush of their music and his confident vocal delivery the line never made more sense.

Lyrically, I had been guilty of a few Venus toe-curlers ('Love, Love, it's hit me like a boxing glove' or 'the poster on the wall says it all' were two particular low points that maybe even the best music couldn't rescue), but now I wanted to emulate the likes of Dylan, Morrissey and countless rap artists that elevated the rhyming couplet. Their lyrics stood on their own two feet without even needing the oxygen of good music. This didn't mean all rhyming couplets had to be worthy – quite the opposite – whether literary or throwaway, Michelin star or beans on toast, both forms were valid. The rhyming couplet was the place where music met comedy and the jewel in the crown of the perfect three-minute pop song.

Although there were many reasons I wanted to be in a band, not least because it could lead to the three As of applause, adulation and affirmation and the three Fs of fame, fortune and fun, I could feel my motivations change. A door had opened to the majesty of the songwriting process itself, and the ambition of what bands did. There was no more satisfying feeling when a song started to take shape – a rhyming couplet slotted into the melody. The sussing of a middle-eighth – the pinnacle of the song, where the verse and choruses had been carrying us to – at its cleverest also teeing up a key change so the final verse and chorus could hit an extra gear. And when this happened between different band members contributing and improving on an initial idea, it was truly magical. Eventually, the song would reveal itself like a fossil as though it had always existed.

To unearth this precious tone – that for three minutes

transported the listener and moved their head, their heart and their hips – was there a more noble endeavour? Going back centuries, writers like Shakespeare and Chaucer hadn't done a bad job of moving people with their words. And Mozart, Chopin, Bach and all that mob had proved they could pen a decent tune. But in the twentieth century, words and music combined with a voice and evolved into this most glorious art form of them all. Paintings, sculpture, architecture moved me not – well, a bit. I could appreciate the Sistine Chapel, and Renoir had his moments, but 'Teenage Kicks' by The Undertones, 'The Whole Of The Moon' by The Water Boys and 'Total Eclipse Of The Heart' by Bonnie Tyler were among our greatest feats of human engineering. Clifton Bridge in Bristol was not to be sniffed at, but it didn't transport me like the bridge in 'Come On Eileen'. These three-minute wonders were our modern-day Parthenons.

To be legit, the perfect three-minute pop song needed to do three things.

1. It had to capture a mood.
2. It had to tell a story.
3. It had to climb a mountain.

And if you could throw in a few witty rhyming couplets that revealed the dark underbelly of modern life, or unravelled the human condition in a compelling, funny and believable way then it was icing on the cake with several cherries on top. And we now we had a song that did just that. 'Yeah Yeah Yeah' was packed full of cherries. As soon as Josh strummed the chords in rehearsal, he got our attention.

'What's that you are playing?'

'Oh, just something I wrote.'

This ability to prick up ears was the test of a good song. If it grabbed the band's attention on an acoustic guitar, you knew it would sound good in front of 100,000 fans at Wembley Stadium.

Josh had worked out the basic song structure – plus it had a guitar riff to die for and a vocal melody – but no lyrics apart from a 'Yeah Yeah Yeah' chorus. I felt my magpie eyes hungry for the prize. It was a tune we could pilfer and now that Josh was a fully signed-up member of The Pointy Birds whether he liked it or not, what was his was ours. I set to it, and the lyrics tumbled out. Dave added some guitar trickery, and Adrian and Marcus added some tension with a perfectly restrained rhythm section and hey presto, the song came together.

'Yeah Yeah Yeah' was our 'Maggie May'. It was a love story and a call to arms and a cry for help. It told the story of a dreamer bumping into reality and potentially losing the love of his life for his art. Slowly, the song climbed towards its summit as the protagonist tried to convince the girl in the song, and the listener and maybe himself, that one day he would get there. One day the door was going to go 'click'. But whether that 'click' meant the door would be clicked shut in his face or everything in his life would click into place was ambiguous. And there was nowt wrong with a bit of ambiguity in a pop song.

At the heart of the story was conflict. Which would he choose? His art or his love? Or could he have the best of both worlds? And one of the cherries on top was a rhyming couplet to make Morrissey proud, rhyming 'impress' with 'mentally undress'. We needed to road-test it a few times before it was ready to record but 'Yeah Yeah Yeah' articulated exactly how I felt and what I wanted to do. It was the Three-Hurdle Theory set to music.

27. Second Best Band In The Shop

SPRING 1993

A daydream about fame is interrupted, a delivery is made to Rough Trade, more sniggering about my cardigan and a rival shop band appear on the scene.

It was good to get back out there and play live, but there was only so many times we could support New Zealand band Magic. They didn't have a following, and neither did we, so the gigs were a bit of a private affair. And my helicopter-flavoured crisps jokes really needed an audience other than the engineer to have maximum impact. Our hopes were still pinned on Ricky touting 'The Man Who Kisses Horses' to the labels and Mike reeling in those bigger gigs, but morale was starting to ebb and patience was wearing thin. At least as a live band, we were getting better. Suede's debut album was about to be released with expectations high it would go to number one. Nude Records ran adverts for a big UK tour. We had to get on that as support. It was perfect timing – with Josh graduating and Adrian settled in on drums, we were ready, willing and able.

Meanwhile, Selectadisc was getting busier and busier. The fact newer recruits got promoted over me was a testament to the fact that everybody believed in me. I had bounced back from the *NME* review with a new focus and belief, and there was no point training me up if it was only a matter of time before

I would be moving on to rock'n'roll stardom. With new staff, I got a bit of a break from filing vinyl and had to process the odd Warners box and serve the customers, which was a bit of a pain. Still, I managed to hold on to my tea-making and jacket-potato collecting duties, which allowed me frequent excursions out of the shop, plus fresh air and daylight, and with more staff, the catering side was becoming a full-time job in itself.

It was fair to say I had settled into life at Selectadisc. I might even go so far to say it was a laugh and my work colleagues were now good chums. We spent the day listening to music, talking about football and films, taking the piss out of customers and then enjoying a beer after work at The Green Man pub. I had converted a long plank of wood into a tray which carried up to seven mugs of tea. This was not only an efficient use of my time but brought a bit of merriment to my colleagues. If I could brighten their day with jacket potatoes, general silliness and 'the plank' then I was happy with my role as shop jester. Selectadisc had become a form of work experience and tied into my evening job as rockstar/entertainer.

The Pointy Birds would definitely come back to the shop and do a signing when we made it, or better still play on the roof and bring Berwick Street to a standstill. Other shop keepers would be talking about it.

'What's with the kerfuffle outside Selectadisc?'

'Haven't you heard? The Pointy Birds are playing on the roof!'

The Beatles had done it, so why couldn't we? We had the songs; we had the charisma. We had the jokes. A rooftop concert was definitely on my bucket list. I loved the old footage of John Lennon counting in the band before the Rhodes piano kicked in and he sang the first line of 'Don't Let Me Down', not just because it was The Beatles performing on a roof but because I was watching a future version of myself.

I would look over to Marcus and the rest of the band and count them in, and we would hit the E minor chord to introduce

'Benefit Office'. The gentlest London summer breeze ruffling our hair as we went through the motions of a song that had been number one everywhere in the world. Marcus's iconic frilly flamenco shirt now worn by millions. His own spectacle frame merchandise brand. Down on Berwick Street below, crowds would be gathering and getting bigger. The police would have to cordon off traffic, helicopters in the sky capturing the aerial footage that then beamed out as breaking news. Yes, this was all to come. This glorious vision of the future so vivid and so real, normally interrupted with one of the following:

'HORACE, WHAT THE FUCK! I JUST FOUND BILLY BRAGG FILED IN VARIOUS ARTISTS!'

Or

'HORACE, CAN YOU MAKE ME A CUP OF TEA?'

Or

'HORACE – THE FILING IS PILING UP!'

But today, the daydream was interrupted by a different request. Gaffer needed me to deliver a box of vinyl to a guy called Stuart who ran the Rough Trade record store in Covent Garden. He was an ex-employee from the Nottingham branch of Selectadisc. This task represented at least an hour's escape. I could possibly stretch it out to an hour and a half with the off-detour meander. Off I went whistling to life's possibilities. I caught my reflection – my hair was about the right length, and I looked the part in my cardigan. I breathed in the spring air through my nose and filled my lungs. Oh, the freedom, the potential of a life lived to the max. It wasn't long now. I cut down through the Berwick Street market, taking in the sounds of the trader's songs.

'Pound-a-mush. Who wants a pound-a-mush.'

'Strawber-strawberryyyyyyy.'

I loved mixing it with the real Londoners. They got up at 3 a.m. and their day, like mine, was hard graft, although the skin on my hands was arguably softer. I cut across Soho down Old Compton Street and Chinatown over to the Seven Dials. Everywhere I went, people zig-zagged in front of me. I was in the middle of the greatest capital in the world. I could never tire of the hustle and bustle of central London. As a kid driving around In the back seat of my parent's car, the twinkly lights enchanted me. I loved the atmosphere, and On cue Russ Abbot's hit song 'Atmosphere' came to my lips. Yes, I enjoyed a party with a happy atmosphere too, and it was the perfect song to sing as I entered Covent Garden.

Eventually, I arrived at my destination, stopping for a cappuccino and a slice of cake at a local cafe. The twenty-minute journey had taken me around fifty minutes. Rough Trade was a small dark bunker of a shop nestled underneath a skater shop in a quaint courtyard of shops called Neal's Yard. I had to descend spiral stairs to a much smaller version of Selectadisc – music blared out too loud, customers rifling through the vinyl racks and posters of upcoming gigs Blu-Tacked to the walls. Behind the counter sat two guys a bit older than me. One of them looked me up and down and muttered something under his breath. His colleague sniggered – some private joke. It was not very welcoming, but I decided to ignore it and plonked the box on the counter with a cheery smile.

'Hi, I was told to give these to Stuart?'

They both looked at me but didn't say anything. Again one of them muttered something, and the other laughed. I narrowed my eyes. I had the measure of these two and decided against giving them both a Paddington Stare. Sensing there was nothing more to be said I turned to leave. One of them spoke.

'Like your cardigan, Horace.'

I decided to pretend I hadn't heard it and climbed the spiral stairs to the sound of their cruel laughter. What was so funny about my cardigan? I was sick of people taking the mick out of it. I returned to the shop in a less good mood despite stopping for a Mr Whippy. Gaffer was waiting behind the counter. I immediately got the impression she had been on the phone to this Stuart character. I wasn't in the mood for any more cardigan abuse.

'Took your time, Horace.'

'Yes, er… um …I …'

'Enjoy your ice cream?'

How did she know? And then I realised the schoolboy error of an ice cream moustache.

'Did you meet Stuart?'

'Yes, kind of…' I mumbled, wiping the evidence away from my upper lip.

'He's in a band too, you know.'

I nodded. Good for him, I thought. I bet they're shit.

'Yeah, they are starting to do quite well.'

Damn.

'They're called Tindersticks.'

27.2

Tindersticks were a six-piece band that featured an array of current and ex-Selectadisc employees from the Nottingham branch of the shop. They had previously released an album under the name of Asphalt Ribbons, but now with a name change, they had signed to a small independent record label. And following my visit to Rough Trade things started taking off for them. They released a single 'Marbles' on limited 7-inch vinyl, which sold out as *NME* made it their single of the week, followed by glowing live reviews and the offer of a European tour with Nick Cave. There was also talk of a debut double album in the autumn. It looked like Stuart might be leaving his record shop before me.

Although he might have laughed at my cardigan, I couldn't help but be seduced by the lo-fi charms of their single 'Marbles' as it shuffled along with a spoken-word monologue, spooky David Lynch keyboard and sleepy groove, plus it was the best title for a song ever. And the fact this was another success story in our orbit meant that surely our turn was next. The only slight annoyance was that up until this point we were the Selectadisc shop band and now there were two Selectadisc shop bands. And with all their success and attention, I worried The Pointy Birds were no longer my colleagues' favourite. But then an opportunity presented itself to put it to the test.

'Hey, Horace, do The Pointy Birds want to support Tindersticks at the White Horse? It's a "Marbles" single launch party.'

Gaffer had put a good word in for us and although accepting this offer might formalise the notion that we were the second-best Selectadisc band, I was quick to say yes. It was still a gig, and this was a chance to redress the balance and maybe teach Stuart a lesson for laughing at my cardigan. Plus, it would be good to return to our old stamping ground and show that indie promoter how much we had improved. I told Ricky and Mike, who were impressed that we had reeled in such a buzzy show.

I decided against wearing my cardigan for the gig. I didn't want to unnecessarily draw attention away from what we were doing on stage. Plus with spring in the air, the weather was warming up, so there was no need. We arrived at the White Horse and the promoter was as I had left him, busy with his Blu-Tack putting up and taking down posters. I nodded hello and he looked at me like he was trying to place me.

'Pointy Birds. We played that time it snowed? You said we were quite possibly the worst band you had ever seen?'

'Did I? You must have been bad then.'

'Yeah, we're playing tonight actually. Got invited by Tindersticks… so… there you go…'

I left the sentence hanging. I didn't need to explain that we were clearly on the up. The promoter didn't reply; his attention had returned to the posters. I left him to it, victorious, pleased I had righted a previous wrong.

The Tindersticks had arrived all suited and booted – kind of a Reservoir Dogs vibe to them. I decided to avoid Stuart just in case there were any smart remarks about my choice of sparkly shirt. The pub was packed, and although we would be playing to a decent audience, I couldn't help feel like second fiddle. We played through our songs well, but the reception was a bit muted. This audience was clearly there for The Tindersticks. I decided to stick around and see what all the fuss was about.

It was a masterclass – I watched spell-bound as they created this subtle and soulful cinematic world. The obvious reference points were Tom Waits, PJ Harvey and Nick Cave and the Bad Seeds, but it was the violin that was the star. Never had an instrument sounded so sad and so beautiful as the band played whiskey-soaked ballads that examined the underbelly of urban life reflected in gems like 'City Sickness', 'Patchwork' and 'Jism'. I had to give it to Stuart. OK, he had laughed at my cardigan, but I could forgive him that one indiscretion. He had put together one hell of a band. I guess The Pointy Birds were just a different flavour.

28. Emergency Band Meeting

E.B.M. takes place at ULU with Ricky and Gordon to discuss why we aren't famous yet. Watch new band from Sheffield with lead singer who is pretender to my throne.

Terrible news came in. Suede had confirmed The Auteurs as support on their forthcoming UK album tour. The bloody Auteurs! Ricky was to blame – he was the manager, and it was his responsibility. A ticking off was long overdue. We had now played four shows in a row with Magic, and enough was enough. Even though there was a logic to getting the band tight, we were like a stretched elastic band about to snap. Where were the buzzy gigs and the record labels? Where was the bidding war? We were ready and ripe for the picking like a juicy peach. We needed to be plucked from the tree sharpish.

I filed records in a sulk. And to make matters worse the debut Radiohead album was out, and it was ordinary. These third-rate bands releasing albums. I couldn't understand it. OK, Radiohead had one decent song, but the rest of it was pedestrian indie by numbers landfill. And they were all so po-faced. Where was the humour? The gags? The puns? How come these bands were getting deals, and we weren't? They had got lucky with 'Creep', but there was no way they were going to evolve into anything interesting and sustain a career in music.

I got home and told Marcus about The Auteurs – he wasn't happy. I then popped the question.

'What do you reckon to Ricky?'

Marcus pulled a could-do-better face. We needed to go and see him – find out what was going on. It was time for an Emergency Band Meeting.

*

I put the call in, and we headed to ULU after work to have our showdown with Ricky. He greeted us in the reception with the usual waggy tail, and we made our way up to the student union bar. A band from Sheffield called Pulp were sound-checking, and Ricky told us how the phone hadn't stopped ringing since lunchtime, and the show was now a complete sell-out.

'Great frontman. Tells stories and writes funny lyrics. You should check them out later – complete star. I've put you all on the house guest list.'

We thanked Ricky, but I felt a throb of jealousy. Who was this pretender to my throne mixing music and comedy?

'He's called Jarvis Cocker.'

Ha! Well, that was a non-starter. No way he would make it with a stupid name like that.

The union bar was heaving with drunken students, indicating all sorts of hijinks and drinking games since lunch. The floor had turned into an ice rink slippery with beer. Much spillage came from one group of freshers who clung on to each other like they were shipwrecked. Singing and swaying, bleary-eyed and red-cheeked, they lunged one way and then another way careering into other students who joined their ranks – an amorphous mass defying the laws of gravity. Another group were partaking in the grand final of a game called 'Pennies Up The Bum'. The rules were relatively simple – the more pennies you could carry between your buttocks over a certain distance and drop into the pint glass was the winner. At more advanced levels the game got quite sophisticated with more elaborate rules to allow for obstacles courses and different sized containers and pennies, not to mention currency. I had played 'Pesetas Up The Bum' once before on holiday in Majorca and found I was quite good at it, but those days were behind me. I was a serious entertainer now.

We found a table in the bar away from the main noise and Gordon joined us. Ricky explained it was a world-record takings behind the bar and now security was in the process of kicking everyone out before the Pulp fans arrived en mass, but some of these students were proving a stubborn foe. It wasn't the ideal time or place to have a band meeting. Apart from the general noise and distraction of paralytic students, Ricky seemed preoccupied with the Pulp gig – the soundcheck was over-running, the box office didn't have all the guest lists, big queues forming outside and his pager kept bleeping. And we were forever interrupted by pie-eyed students high-fiving Ricky.

I was also slightly nervous about what we needed to discuss. Seeing Ricky, I realised this meeting was going to be harder than I thought it would be. I was not too fond of confrontation. It was much easier to moan and groan behind someone's back than articulate grievances direct to the person's face. The two elephants in the room were the Suede support and Nude Records deal. Marcus got straight to it.

'We can't be supporting Magic all the time.'

'Why not?'

'They're shit.'

He had made his point eloquently. Marcus had no trouble conveying the band message, and it was useful to hide behind the tricky bass player. Ricky narrowed his eyes and nodded like he agreed. I decided to add a bit of nice cop to Marcus's nasty cop through the medium of eighties comedy-drama films, and one of my favourite movies of all time – *Gregory's Girl.*

'Yeah, it's just… there's a scene in *Gregory's Girl* where Andy and his mate are getting sick of everyone kissing girls, and they're not.'

Gordon blushed like I had touched a nerve. I continued.

'So, they go up to Claire Grogan in an attempt to chat her up and say, did you know when you sneeze it comes out your nose at a thousand miles an hour?'

Ricky looked confused. Marcus took over and cut to the chase. Why weren't we on the Suede tour? And what about Saul at Nude? When were they going to sign us?

Ricky listened intently, and when Marcus had finished, Ricky said he agreed we needed bigger shows and that he would be putting pressure on Mike. But we had more chance of being signed if there was a bit of a buzz and the gig was packed. We nodded and then hit the ball back. But wasn't this the job of managers and agents to help us create that buzz? Plus it was hard to get a buzz going if we kept supporting Magic. Ricky's pager was buzzing manically.

'Sorry about this. I need to sort, back in a moment.'

Ricky rushed off, leaving us with Gordon. Frustrating as we had just got to the crux of the matter. We exchanged raised eyebrows and sat in silence, waiting on Ricky's return.

Eventually, Gordon spoke. 'Sorry about this. Busy night and as usual everyone wants a piece of Ricky.'

I had never heard Gordon's voice before. He was surprisingly softly spoken for such a large chap. He continued.

'He's got so many projects on. I keep saying he probably needs to focus on one.'

I nodded. What projects were these I wondered, but Gordon hadn't finished.

'Love your music by the way.'

'Oh, thanks.'

''Benefit Office' is such a great tune.'

'Yes, that's my favourite too.'

'I love how some of the rhymes don't rhyme. Like Paris and office.'

I was starting to like Gordon. He then broke into a line from the song. '"And do you promise you're not the devil. Worse still you're not Jeremy Beadle."'

Wow, he was a real fan. I thought he had been suffering in silence. Amazing how a bit of flattery could change your perception of someone. Gordon was clearly a man of high intellect, immaculate taste and generous spirit. An unfortunate Rottweiler face betrayed the enthusiastic labrador beneath.

Ricky returned, apologised and we got back down to business. Ricky had an answer – the key was our next demo. Labels were nibbling but not yet biting, but we could reel them in with a fantastic new demo. He was happy to get us back in the studio, but did we have songs? Were they ready to record?

Yes, yes and thrice yes was the answer. Or maybe 'Yeah! Yeah! Yeah!' was the more appropriate answer for that was the name of our new song. Plus we had another new one called 'Umbrella'.

We had the ingredients and had worked out the recipe. We just needed to bake them in the oven, and they would sell like the proverbial hotcakes. A plan formulated to hit the industry again with a new demo and some superior gigs. We clinked glasses and settled in for a few rounds before the Pulp gig. The conversation moved from the tricky subject of our careers to easier topics like censorship in art. Ricky engaged with enthusiasm and was particularly passionate that the comedian's job was to hold a mirror up to society. It was a search for the truth, and no idea should be sacred. He had clearly thought this all through and was articulate about the subject. It was nice to hang out at the bar getting to know our management team. We would be spending a lot of time together when things took off.

Pulp were due on stage, and so we made our way from the bar towards the gig, a large hall with a huge stage which held up to eight hundred people. I was keen to see them and in particular this frontman, Jarvis. With several pints of lager swishing inside me, my critical faculties were a bit blunted, but he was a man mixing music and comedy, proving a gap in the market. His rhyming couplets were witty, he told funny stories between the songs and even introduced the band. I would need to watch out for him. The highlight was a track called 'Babies' which told the story of hiding in a cupboard watching his girlfriend's older sister having sex as the band played a hybrid of indie-bedroom disco and electro-pop with elements of Scott Walker, Abba and The Smiths. They rocked a kind of art-school-meets-nerd-studied cool and generated a lot of love from their audience who dressed like the band. But as the gig wore on, I started feeling a bit resentful. That should be me up there, not him. I surveyed the crowd with a scowl like I had a bad smell under my nose. Jarvis was good, but Horace was better. And there wasn't room in the town for both of us.

29. Camden Falcon

SPRING 1993

Secretly entertain a new admirer in the hope they can further our interests. Our rivalry with Echobelly continues at a star-studded gig at the Camden Falcon.

It had been over a year since I joined Selectadisc. Not that I was planning to celebrate this anniversary. The fact remained if I had to fill out a passport application, my job description would be shop assistant and not popstar. But although the dream continued to prove elusive, a more immediate concern was that Ricky had gone quiet since our meeting at ULU. Maybe he was sorting shit out, but it had been over a week and the phone had stopped ringing. I was starting to regret going to see him. Had we been a bit too high maintenance? After all, Ricky was working for us commission only. Had our demands frightened our biggest believer away? Finally, the phone rang, but the call was not one I was expecting. Gaffer answered and held the receiver towards me.

'Horace, phone. It's someone called John. He says he manages Suede.'

Gaffer gave me a you-better-tell-me-what's-going-on-right-now kind of look. I took the phone as my colleagues gathered around listening in.

'Yes… oh, hello? …Right. …Great. …OK. …Um, OK, sure. …When? …Tonight? …Yeah, OK. …Bye.'

I put the phone down pleased as punch and then noticed I had an audience.

'That sounded a bit cryptic, Horace. Spill the beans.'

'Yeah, that was the manager of Suede. He likes our demo and wants to come and see us rehearse tonight.'

29.2

I had met John a few times at the early Suede gigs and exchanged a few words and winks. He was very approachable and down to earth, considering he was managing the hottest band in the country. He arrived at the rehearsal studio in Willesden Green looking the part – a big fur coat and dark circles under his eyes. He looked a bit like Droopy the dog with a slightly melancholic face, but you could tell he had a passion for music. We played through the songs from the demo. John watched and listened intently, and when we finished, he spoke.

'Have you got management?'

'Well, this guy Ricky… er, he's the Entertainment manager at ULU, he's kind of looking after us…'

'Yeah, I know him.'

We all nodded.

John continued. 'So, have you signed a contract with Ricky then?'

'No!' said the rest of the band quite forcefully in unison.

John explained how he liked the demo and liked us, but he was busy with Suede. They were about to tour America, and he was sorting out international label partners with Sony, but he wanted to play the demo to Saul, the MD at Nude Records and the man who had signed Suede. John thought Saul would love it. Getting a deal should be a formality. The only issue was whether he could put the serious time in that we as a band, and as artists, so obviously deserved.

I could tell by the serious nodding from the rest of the band that if John had offered his services, they would have bitten his arm off right there and then, as would I. John coming to our rehearsal felt a bit adulterous. We had arranged it behind Ricky's back. As John spoke to us, I could see Ricky in slow motion slapping his thigh in laughter as a bucket of water toppled off the top of a door and soaking another unsuspecting victim. But if ever there was a no-brainer this was it. John could take us all the way.

The only thing was John hadn't offered his services. Yet. So, it would have to be a waiting game. He would come and see us live, and then maybe we could have another conversation, and in the meantime, he would play the demo to Saul. It was all a bit tenuous but enough to get us all very excited. If John was playing hard to get, then he had played a blinder. We wanted John. We wanted John bad. The next day John rang the shop again.

'Do you know this band Echobelly?'

Ha, yes, our fierce rivals. We knew them well.

'They are playing the Camden Falcon – might be able to get you on the bill. It's this Thursday?'

'Yeah, great. I'll check the band is available.'

'Cool, and I'll bring Saul down.'

I replaced the receiver. Things were clicking into place.

29.3

We confirmed the support with Echobelly but I didn't know the etiquette with Ricky. Should I tell him about the gig? Or would this scupper the chance of John taking us on and a deal with Nude? Ricky had done loads for us, but I still hadn't heard from him and things had ground to a halt. Was this the cutthroat side of the business? I much preferred the refuge of my mind where I could play and rhyme words – the shed in my head. I decided if Ricky rang, I would tell him. Or maybe I would let him know later but not get around to it. That way, my intentions were honourable, and my conscience was clear. It was a nice problem to have two people bigging us up to Saul.

My thoughts turned to the opportunity of a lifetime. Having seen Pulp, I knew for sure there was a market for music and comedy. But for this gig we needed to prove ourselves musically. There was plenty of humour in the witty rhyming couplets but I needed to ease off on the jokes. Adrian, the drummer, had changed the dynamic slightly anyway. He wasn't one for the comedy drum roll. For this gig, the music should do the talking. Perhaps the better we got live, the less I needed to rely on jokes anyway. I had been compensating before now because I knew we weren't there yet musically. Or maybe there was a more psychological explanation behind my jokes – constantly moving around as a kid, always being the new boy, the neediness to be accepted, to be liked, to play everything for laughs?

And was Ricky a bad influence in this department? The slightest attempt at a joke was met with a huge belly laugh like it was the funniest thing he had ever heard. I couldn't deny it was a nice feeling to know that my helicopter-flavoured crisps joke would elicit such a positive reception, but was he the only one laughing? It was almost the endeavour of trying to be funny that made Ricky laugh rather than the joke itself. He seemed to find every joke equally hilarious. And thinking back, the most common audience reaction we got after each gig was that we were so funny. It was frustrating the response was never 'you are so good'. But the better we got musically, the more I wanted people to take us seriously, and this was the moment to prove that musically we had arrived.

29.4

The Camden Falcon was like our home ground, even though the previous two attempts hadn't gone that particularly well, tonight was third time lucky. We would get that record deal and vanquish our main rivals Echobelly in the process. Or at least make them aware of our existence. As per usual, they had taken ages with soundcheck, but we were now a well-oiled machine and knew how to turn things around in our allotted five minutes. We put our glad rags on – I plumped for my turquoise sequinned sparkly shirt undone to the navel, some beads and a splash of aftershave, and we made our entrance into the front bar. The place was packed with people spilling out onto the pavement outside. We had fifteen minutes to kill before we had to get ready for showtime. Three guys had congregated around a pool table and were checking out the gig poster. We could overhear them discussing us.

'Pointy Birds? Who are they?'

'Never heard of them. Stupid name.'

Marcus winked at me and then approached them. He never missed an opportunity for a quick sale.

'You should check us out.'

'Who?'

'The Pointy Birds. I'm in them. We're on in fifteen minutes. You won't regret it.'

The three guys looked at each other. They would need some more information to be convinced.

'What do you sound like?'

Marcus pondered the question. The answer was crucial. 'I'd say we sound a bit like Gallon Drunk. I don't know if you know them?'

This had made them smile.

'Yeah, we know them well. We're Gallon Drunk.'

'Wow, what are the chances of that? We're big fans!'

Marcus fluttered his eyelashes and the real Gallon Drunk, flattered by his advances, decided to join the queue that was now snaking its way down the road outside the venue. I congratulated Marcus on a nice bit of band-on-band networking. A constant stream of taxis pulled up, dropping off suited-and-booted music industry types, and the guest list was over-subscribed. At last, we had made it on to an A&R buzz gig. I could feel nerves start to jingle jangle inside me. It was time for the much-needed pre-gig toilet visit.

En route, I clocked Damon Albarn from Blur in the main bar. Was he here to see Echobelly or us? Either way, having a minor indie celeb at our gig was a result. He was staring at me – probably impressed with my sparkly shirt and hairy chest combo. He could spot a star rising when he saw one. The last time I had seen him was collapsed in a heap after their disastrous gig at the Town and Country Club a year previously. And now he was back from the dead rocking a new look – all decked out in mod gear – Harrington jacket and Dr. Martens, like he was in the film *Quadrophenia*. Well, that look was never going to catch on. Our eyes met, and I brushed passed him. I heard him say something derogatory to his loser mates. I decided to ignore him. Tonight was my gig, not his, and the future was ours, not theirs.

Post ablutions, I made my way through to the backroom to check guitars were in tune and to have a quick team talk with the band. We were due on in five minutes. I noticed Ricky wasn't about. Did he even know about this gig? I felt a pang of guilt for not telling him, but we still hadn't heard from him and now we had bigger fish to fry. I saw John busy in conversation with various silver-haired executives. The place was heaving. Full of faces I didn't recognise, but if there was one thing I was good at in life it was being a frontman in a band, and I had my trusty weapon of supreme confidence by my side. No prearranged jokes tonight. Let things be organic – feed off the crowd, and show the silverbacks I could work on my feet. Focus on the songs; keep it tight and polished. And no nob gags.

We had learned that part of becoming a great live band is coping when things go wrong as they invariably do. The golden rule is: don't panic. Technical hitches can be out of your control, and you must turn them to your advantage. It's all in the preparation, and the more gigs you play, the more mistakes you make, the more lessons you learn, the more prepared you are. A decent guitar tuner makes a big difference. Having a spare guitar solves strings breaking. Checking pedals have batteries and leads aren't faulty adds to a smooth running of the night so you can focus on the actual performance of the songs and the stagecraft – sequencing the songs in such a way that creates drama and takes the audience on a journey. Bringing people in with the opening song and blowing people away with the finale. And most crucial of all was having fun – to enjoy it.

Before the gig, I had bought a harmonica harness so I could add a bit of rhythm guitar to beef up 'Nostradamus Blues' while I blew the relatively simple harmonic part. But nowhere on the harness instructions did it say about avoiding long curly hair. As we launched into 'Nostradamus Blues' as our opener, I could feel something pulling at my hair and soon realised it had got tangled in the harness. I cursed my stupid self for not tying it back in a ponytail. And to make matters worse, I had washed my hair with shampoo making it extra fluffy and bouncy. We brought 'Nostradamus Blues' to a close and I needed to be set free. Luckily, Marcus was on hand to help untangle my locks. It wasn't the best look and slightly undermined the new level of professionalism I was trying to project. Still, it seemed to have the effect of an ice-breaker, amusing some sections of the audience.

Eventually, Marcus successfully separated me from my harness. We had squandered a bit of goodwill, but the majority of the audience had stuck around curious to see if I would be set free. Now we had one more song to win them over. But during the next song, the adjustable microphone stand started to lower ever so slowly as I sang, and as I was on rhythm guitar, I had no free hand to tighten it. I motioned to the sound engineer that we needed him pronto on stage to tighten it to its correct height. But he wasn't paying attention. I could detect this too was amusing the audience, so I had no option but to go with it as if all part of the act. By the end of the second song, I was on all fours singing into a mic two feet from the ground.

I noticed the real Gallon Drunk leave the room. Maybe not everyone wanted a band that combined Tommy Cooper-style slapstick with their music. The audience had thinned a bit. I needed to win the rest of the room over with some good banter. But all these strange faces were slightly intimidating. Should I introduce the band, or tell a joke or a funny story, or just play the next song? I felt paralysed. I decided to plump for the wasp joke.

'This guy walks into a pet shop and says I'd like to buy a wasp please. The guy behind the counter says, "Sorry sir, we don't sell wasps." And the other guys says, "Well, you got one in the window!"'

There was a groan in the room as Adrian decided against the comedy drum roll. He counted us in, and the third song started. More people started to leave – this gig wasn't going according to plan. I cursed that stupid harmonica harness. This was a chance to blow people away, and we had blown it. By the end of our set, we had about fifteen stragglers left who seemed to enjoy what we were doing – curious to see if there would be any more comedic mishaps. Maybe they liked the music too. On the upside, we had fifteen new fans, but as a percentage return, 7.5 per cent of the audience was not high enough.

Fifteen minutes later, Echobelly took to the stage in a packed room with a polished performance and no mishaps, and no one left the room. There was only one winner. Echobelly went on to sign a deal with Epic and remained unaware of our existence. In contrast, a distinct lack of record company execs handed me their business cards, John and Saul avoided my eye and the next day I chucked the harmonica harness in the bin.

30. The Marquee

SPRING/SUMMER 1993

Some musings on Blur, some memories of Simple Minds and then a stressful soundcheck ahead of our biggest gig to date. Ricky saves the day.

Blur had somehow managed to get on the cover of the *NME*, which irked. Having just seen Damon prancing around the Falcon in his new look, I enviously devoured the article. They had created a whole new narrative. Damon seemed to be waving the flag for postmodernism. His argument I had heard before – nothing can be original, history is dead and in this sense everything is rubbish. The only thing that matters is what you pick to rip off. It was a reboot of the old *talent borrows genius steals*, and it was as clever as it was depressing. They were also celebrating their Britishness and issuing a call to arms against bands from America. Gone was the baggy grunge shoegaze indie look and overnight they had turned into mods. Union jacks, British Bulldogs on leads, Dr, Martens and sugary tea. The whole gamut, kitchen sink and nine yards. It was a shameless last throw of the dice. It would never work in a million years. Plus that should be me on the front cover.

I returned to work, annoyed that the fickle finger of fame was refusing to point in our direction. The tide had turned against us. The phone still hadn't rung since the Falcon. I cursed that stupid harmonica harness. Also a slight regret we had done the gig and not told Ricky. I still hadn't heard from him. He must have found out, and I wouldn't blame him for moving on. Considering everything was going against us I felt strangely optimistic. It was when the dream seemed furthest away that I wanted it more.

Big Phil was at the stereo. He inserted a CD, and a song started playing. It was a song that I had recently heard snatches of on the radio or blasting out from a shop, but infuriatingly I kept missing who the band was. I raced over.

'I love this song, who is it?'

Big Phil was busy processing an E.M.I. box while whistling along to the melody. He threw the CD single cover on the counter I picked it up. Whoever it was I was about to become a massive fan. I looked at the sleeve cover. Blur's 'For Tomorrow'.

'First single from the new album. You like it, Horace?'

'It's all right,' I lied. I loved it.

'Yeah, thought I'd give it a spin. The new album is called *Modern Life Is Rubbish*,' said Phil. 'Should be called *Our New Album Is Rubbish* if you ask me. Wankers.'

'Yeah, right.'

I returned to filing while the song played.

Jesus, of all the bands, but god, I loved this song. That chorus was so damned catchy. Maybe it was time to come out of the closet as a Blur fan? After all, 'There's No Other Way' and 'Bang' were works of indie-pop genius. I may as well admit that to myself now. I had to give it to them – they were a great singles band. I suppose my issue with Blur was that true artists planted a flag in the sand, they stood for something, but Blur didn't know if they were baggy, grunge or shoegaze, and now they were mods. But maybe that didn't matter? Perhaps they were just figuring that out, discovering their sound in public? Maybe it was their success that I resented and craved. And this ambiguity over their identity was cleverly captured in their name – Blur. It even seemed reflected in Damon – encapsulated in his voice. He sounded like a posh-cockney. Was he middle class or working class? And did that matter? Dividing lines in society were becoming increasingly blurred. Their name reflected this too. People weren't black and white – put a magnifying glass on anyone and contradictions would flare up. It was hard to know what to think.

In a philosophical mood, I went over to Big Phil for a chat.

'It's weird, the only thing I have a strong opinion about is that I have no strong opinions on anything.'

I was quite pleased with this. Phil shook his head like he didn't know where to start. 'You do come out with some grade-A nonsense, don't you, Horace?'

*

The day continued in the diminishing hope that the shop phone might ring. Eventually, it did, and I was pleasantly surprised to hear Ricky's voice on the other end of the line.

'Guess what.'

'What?'

'I got you The Marquee.'

'No way?'

'You like Simple Minds?'

Did I like Simple Minds? I had been their biggest fan back in the day.

'It's supporting Derek Forbes from Simple Minds' new band, The Fly.'

I knew all about Derek Forbes – he had been their bass player in the early years and left the Minds shortly after 'Don't You Forget About Me' went number one around the world. It was exciting news, indeed. But Ricky wasn't finished.

'Plus, I got you some more time in the studio. Sorry for the delay but I had to pull a few strings and…'

'Wow. Brilliant.'

'Cool.'

God, I felt guilty. I had to mention the Echobelly gig, absolve myself, but Ricky had more to say.

'Oh yeah, there's one other thing. Some of the students here are filmmakers, and they want to make a doc about an up-and-coming band. I said you might be into it…'

'Right, OK…'

'It's part of their degree. They will film you in the studio, live footage, kind of fly-on-the-wall-style documentary, and will shoot a promo video for you too.'

'Wow, this all sounds… amazing.'

'So, that's three yeses?'

'Three yeses!'

30.2

In the mid-eighties, in my mid-teens, I developed a bit of an obsession with Simple Minds. I had gone to see them play live in 1986 dressed as lead singer Jim Kerr. Other bands such as The Cure, The Smiths, Echo & The Bunnymen inspired similar devotion, but I was surprised it was a decision only I had made out of the 50,000 fans that crammed into Milton Keynes bowl. Maybe it was the fact Jim Kerr wore a big white shirt with a waistcoat and belt, coupled with black leggings and a beret that put his fans off. It was a weird look, kind of half-Frank Spencer, half-leprechaun, but I was smitten and undeterred. I borrowed my gran's beret on the strict condition I didn't lose it, one of Dad's big white shirts and some of Mum's black tights and a belt. I made the journey by train from Sussex ignoring the sniggers. The fact that little flowers embroidered Gran's beret mattered not a jot. I was displaying my allegiance.

My school friend and fellow Simple Minds obsessive Tim joined me on the train but decided against the full Kerr regalia and plumped for the jeans, T-shirt, Simple Minds jacket combo. He was lead guitarist Charlie Burchill to my Jim Kerr, and anyway, my pal David Rome from Glasgow, who we were meeting at the gig, had told me on the phone he would definitely be dressing up. He was a big Minds fan from their home city. But when we met him, he said that he couldn't find leggings big enough. Fair enough, he was six foot six and tights were probably limited in extra-extra-extra-large, but he could have improvised. It was when someone grabbed my beret during the 'na na-na na naaa's' of 'Don't You Forget About Me' and flung it into the mosh pit that I knew I had made an error of judgement which would lead to a right bollocking when I returned home beret-less.

Simple Minds started letting me down after that, as stadiums got bigger and they started hanging out in cornfields and singing about children from Belfast. Still, at their peak, they were true pioneers, emerging from the Glaswegian art-punk scene in the late seventies. They embraced electronic dance music in the early eighties before bringing these influences together for *New Gold Dream*, their finest album which Kerr described as 'ambient dance music'. It propelled them into the UK singles charts with 'Promised You A Miracle' before global stardom beckoned. Derek Forbes baselines were integral to the sound of Simple Minds driving their tunes with the odd bit of slap and tickle for good measure. And now almost ten years later, I might hang out at the bar after the show and get a few tales from someone whose eyes had seen the glory.

30.3

SUMMER 1993

As news spread we were playing The Marquee, the phone started to ring, and friends and family came out of the woodwork. People had heard of The Marquee, associated it with success – anyone who was anyone had played The Marquee, and now if The Pointy Birds were playing there, they must be about to make it too. It was a satisfying sense of achievement to have got this far and reached a summit of sorts. All previous gigs, good or bad, were now irrelevant; as the old saying went, a comedian was only as funny as his last joke. No matter how many knock backs there was *always tomorrow*. Of course, this also meant there was a danger of people not smelling the coffee and still trying to make it in their fifties, well, that wasn't going to happen to me.

The only slight issue was that we were under strict instructions to be at the venue for 4.30 p.m. load in, soundcheck at 5.30 p.m., which was tricky due to our various day jobs. Luckily it was my day off, so the plan was to borrow Mum's Peugeot and collect drummer Adrian and the gear from the rehearsal studio in Willesden and then meet Marcus, Dave and Josh at the venue. Ricky also said he'd come to soundcheck to make sure we sounded all right in front of house. And Marcus got his younger brother Glyn to come down from Coventry to help with load-in. He would be part of the crew as our first ever roadie and make us feel even more like rockstars.

Glyn was quite possibly the biggest Pointy Birds fan and something of a lucky charm. Younger than Marcus by seven years, gigs always went well when he turned up. He had been down to London on the odd occasion and stayed at our flat, and a few years back I had taken him into central London to show him the sights while Marcus worked a shift at Sainsbury's. We grabbed four tins of Stella and sat drinking beer in the afternoon sun on the benches at Leicester Square. He was not only the perfect audience for my rabbit/wasp/helicopter jokes, Russian Presidents trick and some of my funny stories about our family dog Max but also the exciting vision that the future held for The Pointy Birds as rockstars. He kept shaking his head in disbelief and wonder. I could see from the combination of sun, alcohol and chat Glyn was in a happy place.

'How old are you again, Glyn?'

'Thirteen,' he hiccupped. 'Well, thirteen and a half.'

'Shit, I thought you were much older.' I decided against opening another can. 'We'd better get back to the flat.'

Glyn staggered to his feet with a big goofy grin on his face. Marcus wasn't going to be happy that I was returning his younger brother under the influence, but one thing was for sure, from that moment on Glyn could be classed in the highest category as a believer. And now a few years later, he was of legal drinking age and travelling down from Coventry to witness the dream turn into a reality.

The day of the gig I collected Adrian and the gear as planned from Willesden Green and drove into central London for the soundcheck. Driving in central London was a challenge at the best of times. It was a maze of one-ways and bus lanes, and there was no way you could wing it and guess the route. But one thing I hadn't considered was that we needed to be at the venue at peak rush hour. And this seemed to be the peakiest and rushiest of peak rush hours. At 4.00 p.m. I was stuck in a traffic jam heading the wrong way, at 4.30 p.m. I was in the same place in the same traffic jam and at 5 p.m. I was in a new traffic jam going towards Hackney. Ricky rang.

'Where are you?'

'About five minutes away,' I lied.

'Hurry up.'

God, this was stressful. I cursed my stupid self for scoffing at the need for a map. Finding this venue was like finding a needle in a haystack in a maze with a blindfold, and even when we found it, we still had the issue of parking. Fifteen minutes later, Ricky rang again.

'Where are you now?'

'Um, not sure…'

'There won't be time for a soundcheck, so you are going to have a line check before you go on, OK?'

'OK.'

Eventually, at 6.30 p.m., we pulled up outside the venue. Ricky, Josh, Dave, Marcus and Glyn were waiting. Ricky directed me to the parking, and then it was a military-style operation to get the gear in and set up in time to play the gig. We had about twenty minutes to turn everything around. Just enough time for a quick line check and being seasoned pros this was no problem. The only issue was we couldn't find the power lead for the Casio keyboard. Where was it? We rifled through all the bags, but it had vanished or been forgotten. We asked the engineer if he had a spare lead. Considering how little time we had the engineer lacked urgency in contrast to Ricky, who was panicking on behalf of us all. He scratched his head and examined the back of the keyboard.

'I'm not sure I've got this kind of power lead.'

Ricky looked at his watch. 'Well, do you or don't you?'

'I'm not sure.'

Ricky had an idea. 'How about we get some batteries? Does it take batteries?'

The engineer flipped the Casio over on to its back. It was like we were about to operate in an attempt to save its life. The screws to access the batteries were all rusted.

'I think you need a new keyboard.'

This suggestion wasn't helpful. It was almost like he didn't care if we played this gig or not. We would have to do it as a four-piece which was a shame as Josh had travelled from Cardiff, but still doable. Ricky hadn't given up and seemed very keen we should play as a five-piece, maybe he had people coming to see us? We now had ten minutes before stage time.

'Do you have a screwdriver?'

'Not sure.'

Ricky turned to Josh. 'Do you know what size batteries?'

Josh shrugged his shoulders.

'Or how many?'

'Nope.'

He turned back to the engineer. 'So, do you have a screwdriver?'

'I'll need to go check.'

Ricky looked at his watch. 'So, by the time he returns to open the keyboard up to work out what batteries we will have run out of time to get batteries.'

We all looked at the ground. It was a pickle. Ricky lit up a cigarette – I didn't know he smoked. The thought occurred we might be quite a trying band. He exhaled a fume of smoke and then spoke.

'Right, I'll go and get a selection of batteries and then hopefully by the time I return, he will have opened the keyboard.'

Ricky hurried off. He moved surprisingly fast for a smoker. We hung about on the stage waiting. Five minutes later, there was still no sign of the engineer or Ricky. The lights had gone down, and the venue had opened its doors. It wasn't clear if we would be playing. At 7.25 p.m. the engineer re-appeared with a screwdriver and opened the back panel to reveal some mouldy old batteries followed closely by Ricky with a carrier bag full of different-sized batteries, panting hard. We replaced the batteries, Josh did a little flourish on the keys, and the Casio and Pointy Birds were back in action just in the nick of time.

The venue started to fill, and we played to a respectable gathering without a hitch. I hoped it sounded as good out front as it did on stage. I seasoned the set with a few gags and dealt with a couple of heckles. All in all, it was an enjoyable set, and we gathered in the bar after the gig to watch The Fly (who weren't all that) and catch up with old friends. Glyn, Marcus and I swapped winks to convey mission accomplished. Ricky was in particularly high spirits. Gordon too seemed animated and gave me a thumbs up.

'That was brilliant – best gig yet,' said Ricky.

'Really?'

'Not many bands can pull off the big stage, but you are a big-stage band.'

A big-stage band! God, he really was a believer.

'Do you want to play the ULU Summer Ball?'

'Really? Yeah, def.'

'Brilliant – the students are going to love you.'

'Wow, thanks, Ricky.'

Not only had he saved the day with the batteries, but he still believed in us. Not to mention we still had the studio and film.

'Who else is playing the ball?'

'I can't tell you. It's a surprise.'

Ricky's eyes widened.

He didn't need to tell me.

It was Suede.

31. The Director

Return to Rocking Horse studio to record new demo with student film crew in tow. Shoot first promo video, but the director's vision is compromised.

We met the student film crew at ULU to discuss shooting the fly-on-the-wall documentary and our promo video. The director talked a good talk and kept framing me with his fingers as he told me how much he loved the band and appreciated this opportunity. But if their film was meant to be a collaborative project among the students towards their degree, he didn't want their contributions. They were his cameraman, his lighting guy, his assistant, his director of photography. I suppose not everyone could be 'the director' but I didn't warm to him. He was older than the other students with a hard-looking face, he wouldn't be my ideal person to be stuck in a lift with, but he was focused and driven. A free video was a no-brainer, plus I liked the idea of having cameras on us capturing the creative process. We agreed they would start filming our recording session at the studio in Catford the following Friday. We wouldn't even notice they were there.

Apart from Marcus, the rest of The Pointy Birds weren't so thrilled they would be part of a fly-on-the-wall doc. I hadn't thought about whether the recording studio could accommodate this film crew. It was rather bijou in size. And it was evident when the full entourage of crew and equipment turned up there might be some space issues, especially as the entourage had brought an entourage of girlfriends, boyfriends,

friends of friends carrying plastic bags of alcohol. It was Friday night after all and word had spread that there was some kind of party at this studio in Catford.

On a good day, the studio had enough room for around seven people, but now it resembled a Guinness World Record attempt at sardines. There was no way we could record in the studio, with this massive distraction. But more alarming was that the director had arrived chewing and gurning with an intense stare and an imaginary techno tune in his head. He had taken something and was in no fit state to direct his way home let alone a documentary. Luckily, the lighting guy could see the situation was futile and managed to chaperone the film crew and hangers-on out.

By midnight we had the studio to ourselves and we set to work. There would be no sleep till morning, and while London slept we created. We knew what we wanted and recorded everything first take. And as the sun came up, we had three new recordings in the bag – a new version of 'Liquorice', a new song called 'Umbrella', which incorporated backwards guitars, and most pleasingly of all we nailed 'Yeah Yeah Yeah'. We had captured the soul of the song in the performance. If Ricky needed a final bit of ammunition to reel in the deal, then this demo was it. If record companies wanted a band that could write and record hits to a deadline, we were it. I sent the demo to Ricky and followed up with a call.

'It's the best thing we've done.'

'Really?'

'Yes, seriously.'

'Great, can't wait to listen. And how did it go with the film crew?'

I explained that we had rescheduled and were now going to shoot a video at our rehearsal space this Sunday. I decided not to say the director was a bit of a weirdo. I didn't want to seem ungrateful.

31.2

The director turned up at our flat the night before the video shoot to go through everything. He arrived with his assistant and brandished a full bottle of whiskey which he drained as the evening wore on. Midnight approached and we still hadn't established much of a plan. Marcus escaped to his bedroom as the director explained in minuscule detail how he wanted us floating in space and would fix everything in 'post', which I later found out meant post-production. It all seemed very unrealistic, seeing as he had produced no treatment, no storyboards and there was no budget.

He had also missed the last Tube so would be kipping on my bedroom floor. I looked at his wingman wearily – how would we get any sleep with his incessant yakking? To think we had a whole day with him tomorrow. He started to tell us his life story. It wasn't a happy one, and for a brief period I began to sympathise. The director's life experiences had left him with a void he was trying to fill through drugs, drink and the dream of becoming a film director. As Morrissey had sung, he'd had the kind of life that could turn a good man bad. It was important to have compassion for your fellow man, but as the sun started to come up and he showed no consideration for my lack of sleep, I swayed over to a more black-and-white view – he was a complete twat.

At about 6 a.m. his behaviour became more threatening, hurling whiskey-fuelled insults as his assistant, but luckily this was a final prelude before he passed out in a heap. As my head hit the pillow, I wondered if we could call the video shoot off, but there was crew arriving at the rehearsal room. I considered just not turning up, but these thoughts were too stressful to contemplate and sleep took over.

Marcus appeared at around 11 a.m. with a cup of tea.

'You look like shit.'

'Night from hell.'

'He's a nutcase.'

The nutcase was out for the count on the floor but eventually we prodded him awake. It was like rousing a confused and angry bear full of self-loathing. He had more blurred vision than any kind of artistic one. His assistant mouthed an apology, but it was a little late in the day for that. We got on the bus to Willesden and travelled in silence to the rehearsal space and met the rest of the band and crew. Worryingly, he had produced a second bottle of whiskey which was stirring the beast within.

The lighting guy seemed like someone to go to in a crisis or a farce. And this was rapidly turning into both. He had a kind, long-suffering face and had sensible suggestions for us to set up and play, and they would capture it and hopefully eke out a live performance video. A quiet industry took over the room as the students set up cameras and lights in strategic places around the studio. All the while, the angry bear prowled the room like he was stalking prey. He didn't like what he saw. Stuff was happening without him. He clenched his fist and swung at his assistant but missed by a mile. A camera toppled over. The director stared ahead menacingly, as he told his crew what he thought of them.

'YOU'RE A WANKER! AND YOU'RE A WANKER! AND YOU'RE A WANKER! AND YOU'RE A WANKER!'

Then he turned on us.

'AND YOUR BAND IS SHIT WITH A CAPITAL SHIT!'

'Steady,' said Marcus.

The lighting guy guided the director to a chair, and he slumped down like a defeated boxer resisting the inevitable. In a last-ditch attempt to take control, he got up and stood behind the camera and shouted action while we were in the middle of a take and then cut after we had stopped filming. He also wandered around getting in front of the cameras and the footage. On seeing the rushes there was something amusing about us playing and having a drunk director getting into the shot. We had possibly stumbled upon a decent idea for a video reminiscent of the film *Living in Oblivion.* His forlorn face bobbed in and out of the screen randomly. A shame we wouldn't be able to use any of it.

32. ULU Summer Ball

SUMMER 1993

Excitement builds ahead of our biggest ever gig. The secret headline act is revealed, and we conduct our first press interview.

I was a bit miffed that Ricky still hadn't got back about 'Yeah Yeah Yeah' but I suppose he had been busy, and anyway we would catch up at the ULU Summer Ball. Excitement levels were high, all eight hundred tickets had gone, and at last, we would be on the same bill as Suede. This gig was our last chance to wow them and get that deal in the bag. Obviously, Ricky had been sorting things behind the scenes. He didn't need me bothering him for an update every two minutes. And now that Josh had graduated from Cardiff University and was relocating to London, the last piece of The Pointy Birds jigsaw had clicked into place and we could officially claim to be a five-piece band.

But hearts sunk on arrival as we saw the line up on a poster Blu-Tacked to the wall.

ULU SUMMER BALL
Closet Queen 9 p.m.
Bouncy castle 8 p.m.
The Pointy Birds 7.30 p.m.

'So, no Suede then?' said Marcus.

'Closet Queen? Who the hell are they?' I said.

'And Bouncy Castle? Is that a band?' said Dave.

Our questions were soon answered with the news that Closet Queen were a Queen tribute band, and Bouncy Castle was an actual bouncy castle.

'I suppose this is our Spinal Tap puppet show moment,' mused Josh. 'If I've told them once, I've told them a hundred times. Pointy Birds first, bouncy castle second.'

The rest of the band giggled at his joke, but I failed to see the humour. Ricky was nowhere to be seen, so we got on with soundcheck feeling deflated, unlike the bouncy castle which had been blown up in all its glory right in the middle of the venue. I suppose the idea was to give students the option to jump up and down while they watched us play. We finished soundcheck and assembled in the dressing room and nibbled on some snacks in silence as part of our rider supplied by the university. The fridge was packed with cold bottles of beer. I felt tempted to guzzle it all before the gig, but there was a knock on the door of our dressing room. It was a girl from the university magazine.

'Hey, Pointy Birds? I'm here to interview you for the student mag?'

This was the first we had heard of an interview but were happy to oblige, especially as this would be our first-ever interview. The journalist joined us around the table and produced a notepad and Dictaphone.

'You guys OK if we record this? The magazine has a big circulation so it should be good exposure.'

I suddenly felt the weight of responsibility upon my shoulders. Giving a good copy was part of the lead singer's job description. Brett and Damon, Morrissey and Robert Smith articulated what they were about in concise and witty soundbites. I had interviewed myself on hundreds of occasions so was a bit of a pro in this department, although it was unnerving to be doing it for real in front of other people, and knowing I was about to be immortalised in print.

'So, it would be great to give the reader an idea of who you are and what you sound like. What are The Pointy Birds about?'

Gosh, where to start. What were we about? If we were about music and comedy, this was the moment for the comedy. I was still silently seething about the fact we were supporting a bouncy castle and couldn't think of anything witty or amusing to say. I plumped for something a bit more serious.

'I'd say we're about writing classic songs that are universal and timeless.'

Josh stifled a guffaw, and the interviewer nodded her head earnestly waiting for more. My answer felt clichéd and obvious – the kind of thing, if I read from another band, would make me roll my eyes and hate them for being ordinary. Marcus stepped in with some passable answers regarding our influences while Josh and Dave smirked. Adrian said nothing. The journalist followed up with another question.

'Cool, and so what made you want to be in a band?'

I remembered John Lennon's answer to this. He had gone to the cinema and seen Elvis wiggle his hips to lots of screaming girls and thought to himself *that's the job for me.* I decided to nick that as an answer. She looked slightly disappointed in me.

'OK, and so what would you like to achieve?'

I suppose the stock answer was fame and fortune but Josh got in before me.

'To write the perfect three-minute pop song.'

It was a good answer. We all nodded. The journalist smiled.

'And avoid having to get a proper job,' said Adrian.

Another good answer. I nodded and couldn't think of anything else to add. The interview continued and I withdrew feeling frustration that there was so much I wanted to say but hadn't said anything. Part of the reason The Beatles had become massive worldwide stars was that they were so charming and down to earth in interviews. They didn't take themselves too seriously; they laughed at themselves and had fun. I had done the complete opposite. The interview came to an end with a summons from the stage manager and the obligatory five minutes to take a shit.

At least we could look forward to winning over hundreds of new student fans and playing on another big stage, being a big-stage kind of band. We donned our glad rags and made our way along a Spinal Tap-esque maze of corridors to our destination.

From the wings of the stage, I could see Ricky milling about with Gordon entertaining the troops. At least they had made an appearance for our gig. I couldn't spot anyone that looked like they worked in the music industry in the audience. A few students sat on the floor picking their noses. Floor-sitting at gigs was my pet hate and I made a promise to myself I would campaign to have it banned. But at least they were facing the right direction which couldn't be said for those who had got onto the bouncy castle. The audience was also a bit thin on the ground. Where were the eight hundred students? The cursed sun was shining, so probably soaking up the last of the evening rays, or playing Pennies Up The Bum at the bar.

We took to the stage and raced through our set with no technical hitches, the songs had never sounded so good and the reception among the audience was muted but positive. Ricky and Gordon tapped their feet and nodded along and did their best to give some moral support cheering loudly between songs, but I couldn't help feeling something was missing. And not just eight hundred students.

We packed up our gear and made quick work of our rider of free beers and then headed for the ULU bar to watch Closet Queen's lead singer do a passable impersonation of Freddie Mercury as eight hundred students sang along. Ricky was somewhere in the front row, singing along with a beetroot face. Apparently, he was now managing them. Maybe this was karma for flirting with John? There was a market for tribute bands, and Closet Queen was a good name. Was this what people wanted? Maybe Damon Albarn was right about the past being rubbish, and nothing could be original anymore.

33. Mole Rats

SUMMER 1993

I get an accidental promotion at work and Ricky gets us a mention in a glossy magazine. Marcus breaks some dramatic news with ramifications for the band, the flat and the future.

Selectadisc had got so busy I was now serving customers and processing boxes all day. More staff were needed, and as a result, I got a promotion by default as new filers and tea-makers and jacket potato-collectors moved in on my old turf. These included Big Phil's young brother – even bigger Neil, his mate Phil, who soon got renamed Roger, Nydia who became RG after riot grrrl, and Peter who stayed Peter. The camaraderie was great, but now I had to juggle delivery notes and customers, and I didn't get a minute to myself. As soon as I returned to my box, yet another stupid customer approached the counter with a bunch of CDs and vinyl followed by the dreaded request.

'Can I see your Sonic Youth T-shirts?'

Through gritted teeth, I would retrieve the Sonic Youth T-shirts that I had just put away for a previous customer. They came in a range of colours and sizes featuring their different album covers – *Bad Moon Rising, Daydream Nation, Goo* and *Dirty.* And guaranteed the larger customers wanted the *Goo* design, which we only had left in skinny-rib, and the customers on the smaller side seemed to want the *Bad Moon Rising* T-shirts we only had left in extra-extra-large. Undeterred they would try them on and then decide against, and then I'd have to fold them all up and put them away until the next time. I didn't have time for this. I had a Warners box to process. And rockstardom to attend too.

I was still feeling disappointed after ULU when Ricky rang. Big Phil held up the receiver.

'It's nobface.'

I took the call. Maybe Ricky was ringing to apologise, or perhaps to give some feedback to 'Yeah Yeah Yeah'? But when I answered he was in full laughing policeman mode.

'Wait till you hear this. I got you a piece in Vox Magazine.'

'Really?' He had come through again.

'Hope you like Mole Rats.'

'Mole Rats?'

Ricky started tittering. 'I told them you asked for some Mole Rats. It's a piece about bizarre rider requests.' He snorted. 'And it got in…'

I couldn't quite follow.

'Check it out. It in this month's *Vox*. Page 78. Got to go.'

I put the phone down, feeling a bit confused. I nipped out to the newsagent on the corner of Berwick Street Market and flicked through the pages of *Vox*. Sure enough there it was in print, at the end of an article about riders.

'…and maybe the most bizarre request was from London 4-piece The Pointy Birds who asked for some Mole Rats…'

Was this funny? I didn't get the joke. This article was hardly going to launch our career. I felt a knot of anger. We were a serious band but seeing this in print made us look like a joke.

33.2

After work, I returned home to the flat. I was getting sick of living like a student. The front door still needed fixing, the putrid smell was getting worse and the infestations were increasing. On the kitchen table under a pint glass was a six-legged creature with twitching antennae and big, bulbous eyes. God knows what it was. There was a note in Marcus's scribbled hand.

'Found another. We need to have a word.'

It sounded ominous. Did he mean we needed to have a word with the landlord? Or did he mean that he and I needed to have a word? I felt a strange sense of foreboding. Marcus appeared in the hallway.

'You back then?'

I nodded.

'You met our new friend?'

I nodded and held up his note.

'Ah, yes…'

He sat down at the kitchen table, and so did I. Empty bottles of sherry surrounded us and the overflowing sink was giving the overflowing sink in *Withnail and I* a run for its money. We stared at the creature in captivity under the glass. Maybe we should let him go.

Or kill it?

The poor creature was avoiding eye contact. And so was Marcus. I knew something was coming.

Don't do this, Marcus.

Eventually, he spoke. 'Look this MSc has come up…'

Something vice-like gripped my stomach – the dreaded MSc.

'It's an excellent course up in Coventry.'

I nodded and managed a smile as weak as tea.

'It's just that…'

He left the sentence hanging. I knew what he was going to say. He was having trouble getting the words out. Was it because he didn't want to say them out loud? Admit it was over, hadn't gone according to plan. There was so much I wanted to say.

Don't go, Marcus. Don't leave me now, now, now.

The chorus of that Hot House Flowers song replayed in my head. I wanted to explain this was the tiniest bump, a minor hiccup in the road. We got new songs, and we could change the name. Minor Hiccup was quite a good band name.

But I knew it was over.

'What is the MSc in?' I asked.

I didn't want him to say the words. Just a little longer.

Don't leave me now, now, now.

'It's a management consultancy and political research and then, you know, could lead me into… and you know…'

'So, you will be moving back to Coventry?'

Marcus nodded in the affirmative.

I tried to smile, but the muscles in my face were too weak to lift my mouth. The reality of the situation was now dawning on me. Not just leaving the band but leaving London. What about the flat, paying the rent? Real-life was knocking like a wolf at the door or a bear at the window. I had recently had a dream about a bear tapping at my window. Scary sharp claws and sharp teeth drooling. The condensation of the big beast's breath on the windowpane. The proximity of danger. I now understood what the dream meant.

'It's just that I feel it's time to move on. You know, we gave the band a good go… and you know, maybe it's time… and not sure Ricky…'

Now the Carol King song popped into my head as I felt the earth move under my feet. Was I incapable of dealing with a real-life situation without a song lyric? The vice gripped harder. I had put everything on the line for this. I couldn't go back. This is what I want. This is just the start. The future suddenly looked different. Colder. Bleaker. Darker. Would I be able to do it without Marcus at my side? We looked at the creature struggling for air trapped inside the glass. The metaphor was not lost on me.

A new fear gripped me – what was my plan B? What was I going to do if the band didn't happen? It hadn't even occurred to me that it wouldn't work out. I needed to recite the Three-Hurdles speech, but the sound of Vincent coming up the stairs put pay to that. He had recently returned from his travels and was back at the salon.

'Hello, you English pigdogs.'

He produced a pair of scissors. Somewhat smaller than his swords.

No, Marcus, tell me you're not….

The situation was getting all too real. Thoughts spun in my head like helicopter blades.

But we only just started…

This is but the merest of hiccups… the slightest of bumps.

The road is long, but with hard work and patience, we will get there.

You can do it, Duffy Moon.

Marcus looked at me. Our eyes locked.

'Sorry. It's just something I have to do.'

I sat in silence. I couldn't watch as the sound of Vincent's scissors snipped and sliced. Moments later, Marcus's ponytail was dead on the floor like the dream in my heart.

34. Three Fond Farewells

SUMMER/AUTUMN 1993

A final customer is served, the flat is cleaned and one last gig played.

August had seen the release of two British indie albums that sold well in the shop. *Giant Steps* by The Boo Radleys had quickly become a shop favourite. From indie also-rans, they had come good with this epic. It was a strangely beguiling album full of quirky influences, and by the end of the year, it was topping music press albums of the year. Meanwhile, alternative rock band Swervedriver released their album, *Mezcal Head*. It wasn't my cup of tea combining the odd bedfellows of shoegaze and grunge, but it proved popular with enough Selectadisc customers to make it a moderate seller.

Swervedriver had nothing to do with the Neo-Nazi band Skrewdriver, however, who were doing the rounds at the same time. They merely shared similar-sounding names. But when a customer appeared at the counter and asked for the new Swervedriver album, I got the bands mixed up and replied saying that we didn't sell music by fascist Nazi scum. As my mistake was corrected and the bemused customer left with a Swervedriver album in his bag, and my work colleagues collapsed on the floor in hysterics, I knew my legacy was secure as the shop clown. I knew what I had to do. My time had come. I had to set myself free. Gaffer asked me if I was sure. What was I going to do? Did I have another job? She seemed genuinely concerned. I explained my mate Jeff the Chef had offered some cash-in-hand work catering at Ally Pally. *Oh*, she said. *If you're sure?* I was always welcome back.

The Green Man beckoned for an after-work goodbye pint. Weird to think this was the last time. And even weirder to think the future was unknown. This feeling of freedom was exciting, but scary. We swapped stories, discussed music and football and took the piss out of each other. On the third pint, Big Phil nudged me and handed me a leaving present. Norwich and Gaffer grinned in expectation as I unwrapped it to reveal a golden lighter engraved with the words *Respect Hoz' '93.*

It was unexpected and made the fact I was leaving suddenly very real. Maybe quitting wasn't the wisest of moves – how was I going to pay the rent? But it was too late now. I held the lighter in my hand and knew this would be a precious possession I would keep forever. I thanked my now ex-work colleagues with a trembling lip, and as we ordered more drinks, I reflected on how mutual affection had grown from a shaky start. The third listen applied to people as well as music. And the team at Selectadisc had grown on me like the many bands I had grown to love while filing – Afghan Whigs, Buffalo Tom, The Lemonheads, Pavement, Smashing Pumpkins, Boo Radleys, Blur. Even hardcore noiseniks Leatherface had their moments. And maybe Swervedriver. But definitely not Skrewdriver.

A month later the singer of Skrewdriver died in a car crash aged 36.

34.2

With Marcus moving back to Coventry, I decided to move closer to the source and found a flat in Camden on Delancey Street with Jeff the Chef. We gave notice on Golders Green and to get the deposit back we had to leave the flat in the same condition we had found it, which was a tall order given the state of the place. But the bleach came out, and we got scrubbing. We tackled the sink first – remnants of meals past glued to plates – rock-hard baked beans, pasta with rigour mortis, solidified smears of ketchup.

'Oh, I remember this macaroni cheese,' said Marcus fondly.

We peeled away some spaghetti flung against the wall, leaving an imprint of its former life like a fossil. It had grown in our affection over the years, like a piece of art, or a family pet. We recycled sherry bottles, cleaned the windows, bleached the toilet. We even returned the videos we had rented. The deposit would cover the carpet, which was unsalvageable, and the walls needed a repaint. We also discovered the source of the smell – a toxic prawn in the kitchen sink. Toxic Prawn was a good band name. We left one piece of spaghetti on the ceiling as a tribute to our time here. A builder came around to fix the lock on the front door and said, 'I can't do a Pukka job with a wanky frame like that.' Our deposit would have to cover that too.

Apart from my guitars and pedals, my only property was the intellectual kind contained in my ten precious A4 notebooks lovingly filed on my bookshelf. Each one had a different colour binding and represented my life's work to date. Not quite Shakespeare, but what I would rush to save in a burning fire. I flicked through the pages of to-do lists, lyrics, song ideas, drunken ramblings and half-finished attempts at writing, but rather than feelings of affection, I realised they could be used in evidence against me. Much of it was genuinely awful. I knew that being bad was all part of the creative process of becoming better, but was there any point keeping the chaff?

In the spirit of out with old, I decided to whittle them down – only the good stuff could stay. I would create one master volume. From the first notebook, I ripped out the pages that contained crimes against art and screwed them up. It felt good; it felt liberating; it felt sexy. The bonfire of the vanities had begun. I had to show no mercy, and pretty soon I had reduced ten volumes to one single 'best of'. I had a cup of tea, pleased with my work and then revisited this remaining volume, but as I flicked through the pages a realisation that this 'best of' wasn't all that and the cull continued. Only the exceptional writing could stay, and this would form the basis of a definitive masterpiece. It was quality, not quantity that mattered – less was more. Harper Lee – *To Kill A Mocking Bird.* Better to write one classic than add to the morass.

Soon the best of volume had become a single page. This page contained a list of the best ideas, but still, it was another list and too many average thoughts. I knew what I had to do. I had to keep going. Die, words, die. Get to the source. That one idea and focus on that. It didn't take long. I had distilled everything down to the essence of what I needed to do next. Hundreds of screwed-up pieces of paper littered my bedroom like it had been snowing. My ten precious volumes were no more, and all that remained on the bookshelf was a rectangle in the dust.

We had scrubbed the flat to an inch of its life. The majority of stains had gone, but the phantoms and ghosts of parties past remained. We had shown this flat a good time. We would miss the place. The flat looked sad like it was going to miss us too. We wandered through the empty rooms, once buoyant with life and laughter now eerily silent. But we had to move on. We couldn't keep living like this. I felt proud we hadn't needed a lock on the front door – we had nothing worth nicking. Burglars were more of an infestation than a threat. I had even met one once in the hallway.

'Er... I'm looking for the paint shop?' he had said with shifty eyes before scuttling off down the stairs.

Bloody burglars. But as Bob Dylan had sung, 'if you ain't got nothing, you ain't got nothing to lose'. And although we were now probably embarking on a life with locks on front doors and possessions, I would remember this sense of freedom forever.

34.3

Of course, there was a cruel irony that having waited two years for Josh to graduate from Cardiff, we were now splitting up. We decided to go back into the studio one last time to capture the band live. We booked a day at Escapade Studios in Greenwich and ran through the ten-song set. We added mandolins and accordions to 'Lift Me'; we re-recorded 'Rocket Child'; we remixed Liquorice and then left wondering why we were splitting up just when we were starting to master our trade. But it was over. Adrian informed us he had met someone and was moving abroad, and Marcus confirmed his place on an MSc course in Coventry. It was time to call it a day, and the only thing left to do before signing off was a farewell show at the Tufnell Park Dome.

The Dome was a fitting venue to say goodbye. Back to where it had all started. Five years earlier, Marcus and I had queued to see the House Of Love – the latest *NME* cover stars touted as the new Smiths. The energy in the room was palpable, and as the band appeared on stage silhouetted by the lights as if by magic from the dry ice that billowed out around them, the packed audience surged forward and started pogoing. Marcus and I were in the front row, just meters from lead singer and songwriter Guy Chadwick, and guitarist Terry Bickers, the new Johnny Marr. The thrill to be so close to real rock'n'roll stars! They didn't seem like normal humans – more like superheroes. And for the next hour, we jumped up and down as they cast their indie spells and weaved their magic with psychedelic songs of love and redemption soaked in reverb-drenched guitars – 'Christine', 'Shine On' and 'Destroy The Heart'. We left the gig exhilarated, knackered and charmed.

I hadn't been to the venue since, and on arriving for soundcheck, in the cold light of day, it didn't disappoint. It was everything a toilet venue should be with all its miserable charm – the pong of bleach fighting a losing battle with the stench of mould and rats and the thirty-year-old beer-soaked carpet. The unfeasibly grumpy landlord knowing another night of a thumping bass drum was the only thing between him and financial ruin. You could feel the ghosts and phantoms of gigs and bands past in the air – the only evidence of their previous existence in the faded posters that covered nicotine-stained walls, like something from *The Shining*. Incredible to think that the innocent endeavour of three bands playing their songs had the power to transform this desolate and slightly spooky venue into a magical destination. Later on, it would become a place where audiences could be transported, and the dreams of bands could be made or broken like the shards of glass on the floor at the end of the night.

We had one slight problem. Adrian had informed me a bit late in the day he couldn't make the gig. He was off to Ireland. This news meant it would have to be an acoustic set. Typically one of the support bands had cancelled, and the other hadn't brought anyone, so it was just us and our hardcore fanbase and a promoter flashing daggers at me. Eight people through the door was not quite the amount I had promised.

It was a private affair. A bit like a funeral. Norwich, Phil and Gaffer from Selectadisc, Doug, Ben and Paul from City Poly. The Japanese DJ with the ponytail and Glyn. This gig was for them – our fans. They knew the words and had taken the band to their hearts. True believers. To mark the occasion we had done a limited pressing of The Pointy Birds' greatest hits on cassette – run of eight copies which we gave away free of charge. It was the least we could do. There was no sign of Ricky at this show. He had told me he liked 'Yeah Yeah Yeah' but it wasn't as good as our previous efforts. I hadn't really told him we were splitting up. And he seemed to be getting very busy with one thing and another – various crackpot schemes and projects. Maybe one day, one of them would come off for him.

We climbed on stage and started to play. The issue of not having a drummer resolved itself with Jeff the Chef on bongos.

Not that he could play the bongos or that we had asked him. But he decided to join us on stage, and no one had any strong feeling either way about it. The end was nigh. But something happened as we played. Each song took on a poignancy as they were lowered to the ground never to be performed again. We were playing our final respects. The eight-song set ended with 'Baby Can't You See', originally written with Pete for the comedy circuit as a Beegee's pastiche with falsetto vocal.

> Baby can't you see?
> There is no other.
> There will never be another.
> Because you are my lover.

As the song lowered to the ground, a jazz E ninth chord rang out on Josh's guitar which he embellished with a bit of tremolo. The Pointy Birds then left the stage, and I felt a strange sense of loss and liberation.

We packed up our gear, said goodbyes and thanked people for coming, especially on a Monday night, and tried to avoid the eyes of the promoter who was still sending those daggers my way. Then the four of us made our way into Camden to grab something to eat and maybe a quick pint at Quinn's before last orders. Our destination was a little cafe on Pratt Street which served delicious homemade chips. The owner cooked them twice and then did other magical things, and the twenty-minute wait was part of the experience. We sat outside on plastic chairs around a wobbly plastic table and watched the traffic go past and made conversation, but not about the band.

The pubs emptied and taxis hovered. Drunk people staggered past, Camden's weird and wonderful glitterati – everyone looked like they were in a band or wanted to be in a band or liked going to see bands and that's why I liked it. I would soon be one of them. Twenty minutes later, the owner served four plates of perfectly seasoned piping-hot chips with just the right amount of crunch-to-potato ratio. Marcus held a chip aloft and said something I had heard him say many times over the years, which always made me laugh. It was not what he said, it was the way he said it, like he was positing a deeply serious philosophical question.

'The humble potato – surely it's the most underrated vegetable? Bland yet versatile.'

We couldn't disagree, and for the next five minutes, we sat in silence filling our bellies, knowing these were the best chips in the world. It felt like the ideal way to end things, and although something was over, it also felt like something was just beginning.

Epilogue

1994–Present

In 1994 a new band from Manchester featuring two gobby brothers burst on to the UK music scene. Oasis had the Four Ds in abundance, didn't care what anyone thought and pretty soon were *NME* cover stars. But I knew we could give them a run for their money. My brother Dave and I had hunkered down in Camden writing songs and out of The Pointy Birds' ashes came Big Slice. A tall Frenchman called Guillaume joined us on drums followed by Sean, the Rough Trade rep who was now a music promoter putting on gigs at The Dublin Castle and Camden Falcon. He liked our tunes, could make the guitar sound fantastic and book us gigs whenever we fancied so three became four. The fifth slice was Sean's mate Phil, the 'Albino Priest', with his psychedelic Moog keyboard, to add an extra layer of musical icing to an already heaving cake.

I envisaged the press coverage. Oasis were from up north featuring two brothers, and Big Slice featured two brothers from down south. A bit of healthy competition across the classic north-south divide. The new Beatles versus the Stones. We had written a new batch of songs that bridged the gap between U.S. alt-rock and U.K. indie-pop and rivalled anything the Gallagher brothers had released. All Big Slice had to do was rock the Camden toilet-venue circuit, get signed on the dotted line, and then the battle could commence.

And from 1994 to 1996, as Britpop exploded, Big Slice rocked Camden's most salubrious toilet venues and demoed two albums worth of material until our Moog player Phil's side-project Lo-Fidelity Allstars played a one-off gig at the Dublin Castle. We went along to give some moral support, and by the end of their thirty-minute set they had been offered a deal with Brighton label Skint. They needed a manager, and guitarist Sean stepped in. It wasn't long before the Lo-Fis were on the *NME* front cover as pioneers of a new 'big beat' scene leaving Big Slice no option but to call it a day.

It was hard not to take it personally. Record companies were out in force in Camden signing anything that moved; it was harder not to get a deal. All around us bands were proving the dream was possible. Suede's album became the fastest-selling debut in British history and went on to win the Mercury Prize, Tindersticks scooped *Melody Maker* 'Album of the Year'. Radiohead blew me away with their second album *The Bends* and became one of the highly respected bands of all time. And in the battle of Jarvis Coker versus Horace, there was only one winner. With 'Common People' Pulp wrote undoubtedly the greatest pop song ever. It was the ultimate in storytelling that slowly climbed the biggest of mountains. It was jam-packed with witty rhyming couplets and pure pop melodies betraying the darkest of underbellies and a euphoric two fingers up to snobbery and the class divide.

And in the battle of the bands across the north versus south divide, Big Slice didn't take on Oasis. That honour went to Blur in their race to the UK number-one spot. Oasis's 'Roll With It' versus Blur's 'Country House' as indie went mainstream. Blur won that battle, but Oasis went on to win the war. Their second album *(What's The Story) Morning Glory*, and in particular the single 'Wonderwall' turned them into the biggest band in the world, and Selectadisc became a tourist attraction for Oasis fans from all around the world as the shop featured on the album cover. It was a nice way to complete the circle.

As the nineties drew to a close, I got a bit of clarity over where we might have gone wrong. It was no coincidence that the two biggest bands of the decade had one-word names that summoned up an ultimate destination, Nirvana and Oasis. Ultimately, bands were brands, and a name had the potential to tap into the zeitgeist, connect to a longing or hope in broader society. Perhaps if we had called ourselves Bliss or Perfection or Euphoria, we would have been massive. We simply had the wrong name. A name like The Pointy Birds was way too silly.

Still, I had my dreams, and we could revisit those songs later. For now, I needed to park rockstar and focus on the next stage of the plan – writing, directing and starring in my own films and sitcoms. Yes, it was all ahead of me. Things were going to click into place. I just needed to get it down and out there. And I was on a tight schedule. I was kicking 30.

FAST FORWARD >>

As I type these words, I am still not entirely sure how this story ends. These words may be a full stop, a goodbye, or they may be a ticket to a new beginning. After all these years, I am still not able to let go. I am still on the journey, and the passion still burns, but stage two of the plan is proving a tricky hurdle to jump. TV and film is a seductive world, but full of corporate types with certainty in their eyes, who seem to bar entry. It is frustrating as I have put over 10,000 hours in stockpiling ideas and treatments and half-finished scripts. Maybe it is time for stage three and to launch my career as a successful author and humourist instead. I have several novels and memoirs in me. All of them adaptable for TV serialisation or the big screen with options for spin-offs. And a musical is in the works too, repurposing some of the old songs.

Of course, there is always Ricky. I have sent his agent the odd thing over the years but never heard back. I know Ricky is a busy man and likes to work on this own projects. But if I could get five minutes with him, for old time's sake, I could pitch a couple of my ideas as possible collaborations. I am more than happy to cut him in, split things 50/50, not that he needs the money, but it would fast-track me to his fanbase of millions which seems a fair deal.

And then the other day my old chum fate intervened.

I was driving up through South End Green on my way to collect the kids from school when Ricky ran out in front of me. I slammed on the breaks and swerved out of his way. He had been jogging on Hampstead Heath. I pulled over and wound down the window.

'All right, Ricky. It's Andy… or Horace. Remember me?'

Ricky stopped running and peered into the car.

'All right, Horace or Andy.'

Apart from on TV, I hadn't seen much of him in the intervening years. We had kept in touch for a while after The Pointy Birds as I had become a music promoter in Camden and booked some of the new bands he managed, and then in a brief role reversal I tried to get his book *Flanimals* published to no avail. Publishers told me my friend Ricky needed to work on his profile. Well, he certainly achieved that. But once he hit the big time with *The Office*, our communication fizzled out. We bumped into each other once on Oxford Street, but he had seemed in a rush to get away. He was probably busy and didn't have time to stop and chat.

But here we were now by Hampstead Heath. I had recently sent him a manuscript but not heard back. Should I mention that now? He asked if I was *still doing it.*

'So, you still doing it?'

It was a simple question, but I wasn't sure what he meant. Was I still singing in a band? Was I still promoting gigs? Was I still writing? I nodded that I was *still doing it* and wiggled my fingers in the air – the universal sign language for typing at a keyboard that felt more like Oliver Hardy fiddling with his tie.

Ricky nodded but didn't seem that interested and started to tell me about his latest project – the new David Brent film *Life On The Road.*

As he spoke, thoughts whizzed through my head. Yes, in the intervening years I had been very much *still doing it* – still on the journey, still trying to jump that final hurdle but still not quite managed to get anything out there. Real-life and the day job had got in the way. Yet Ricky had effortlessly produced successful project after successful project. How had he done it?

But my time was due. My passion for songs and stories was the reason I was still doing it. That desire to create something out of nothing that lasts forever, that unravels the human condition in a compelling, believable and funny way and brings joy and laughter to others has not diminished. If anything, it burns brighter than ever. And when you tuned into the right frequency, that alternate reality; when you entered the wardrobe, that shed in your head, and the ideas connected and the words flowed; there was no better feeling.

And this was my chance. Here I was on the roadside with Ricky. Our old band manager. I had five minutes to pitch one of my ideas. He was my ticket to the big time, my own personal Willy Wonka. My own private Wizard Of Oz. But which idea should I pitch? The screenplay about the stay-at-home dad stalking a local celebrity? Or the sitcom set in the grassroots of the music industry called *Golden Ears*? Or maybe we could cut out the middle man and reform The Pointy Birds?

Marcus was pretty busy working in political research these days bringing the current government to account, but he would be tempted, and we could fly Josh over from Sydney. Dave would definitely be up for it. We'd need to find a drummer though. God knows what happened to Adrian or Paul. Maybe Dave, the drummer of Blur, would be interested? It was my birthday soon. Maybe we could reform for that? Surely Ricky would be able to make things happen now? He was a believer, perhaps the only believer – still a believer? As he said in countless interviews, it was never too late, and some of those songs were timeless classics.

Yet something was holding me back. Was it a fear of failure or its weirdo distant cousin fear of success? I didn't want to put Ricky in an awkward position. Far better to just chat, reconnect and then maybe next time we could go for a pint and talk through some of my ideas properly.

Ricky finished telling me about his latest project, and we said our goodbyes. I drove off, feeling a thrill that at last things were happening; the door was going to go *click.* The Tarot card reader was right. It was a long and winding road, but with hard work and patience, I would get there.

Hopefully, I will arrive soon. I am kicking 46.

'Yeah Yeah Yeah, Yeah Yeah Yeah.
She says she's heard it all before,
But one day, the door is going to go click.
I've got a picture I want to paint.
I've got this movie I want to make.
I've got this music that I want to play.
I've got this book that I want to write.
I've got this sun; it always shines.
I've got this mountain that I want to climb.
I've got a clock it always tells the right time.
But I ain't got you,
Yeah Yeah Yeah, Yeah Yeah Yeah.
She says she's heard it all before,
But one day, the door is going to go click.'

Yeah Yeah Yeah' by The Pointy Birds

STOP ⏸

EJECT ⏏

Another Exclusive Song Giveaway

I hope you enjoyed the show. And if you did, please leave a glowing review – good or brilliant, I don't mind, at your bookshop of choice.

Before you go, I thought I'd give you one more Pointy Birds song as a leaving present. This one is called 'Yeah Yeah Yeah'. It really should have been called 'Heard It All Before' because that's a bit more grown-up and gets to the nub of what the song was all about. But I'll leave the title of this song alone. 'Yeah Yeah Yeah' is a bit more spunky and I've airbrushed enough history in the telling of this tale. Anyway, enjoy the tune. It's really good. And the lyrics are on the previous page so you can sing along…

Enter this web link into your browser:

https://andymacleod.ck.page/b83d102e33

Acknowledgements

Many thanks to Phil Connor and Rachel Stout at Reedsy for their editorial skills and general enthusiasm; Matt Law for making the cover artwork perfect and Nainesh Shah for patiently recording the audiobook. Also to Dave for providing focus over numerous coffees and the lightbulb moment with the title. And lastly Chris Hornsby, Tom Otis, Nick Pahl and Dan Travers for reading early drafts and not telling me to stop. This book is kind of your fault.

About the Author

Andy Macleod is a music promoter, a cold-water swimming enthusiast/bore, a Spurs fan and a dad. When no one is looking, he likes to write. *Anoint My Head: How I Failed to Make It as a Britpop Indie Rockstar* is his first book. It took him six years to write, but it was in gestation for nearly fifty. His second book is *Soho Days, Camden Nights: The Chronicles of a Failed Indie Rockstar.* He lives in London with his wife, two kids and cat. He would like a dog.

https://andymacleodauthor.com